THE
LEGENDARY HISTORY
OF BRITAIN ॐ

in Lope García de Salazar's
Libro de las bienandanzas e fortunas

EDITED
with an Introduction by
Harvey L. Sharrer

The Twenty-Third Publication in
The Haney Foundation Series

University of Pennsylvania Press
1979

For
S. G. ARMISTEAD

Copyright © 1979 by Harvey L. Sharrer

Printed in the United States of America

Library of Congress Cataloging in Publication Data
Main entry under title:

The Legendary history of Britain in Lope Garcia de
   Salazar's Libro de las bienandanzas e fortunas.

   (The Haney Foundation series ; 23)
   1. Great Britain—History—Medieval period, 1066–
1485. 2. Arthurian romances. 3. Garcia de Salazar,
Lope, 1399–1476. Las bienandanzas e fortunas.
I. Sharrer, Harvey L.
DA175.L43   942   78-53334
ISBN 0-8122-7749-X

Contents

iii

Preface

Few students of medieval literature have heard of the *Libro de las bienandanzas e fortunas,* an enormous fifteenth-century universal chronicle by Lope García de Salazar. Yet this work is an important repository of lost and variant versions of a large number of medieval texts and legends. The last six of the twenty-five books which form the *Bienandanzas e fortunas* have received considerable if uneven attention for their graphically detailed account of the history and lore of northern Spain, particularly Salazar's native Vizcaya. However, only a handful of Hispanists have bothered to examine the other nineteen books, which contain adaptations and summaries of a wide range of literary and historiographic texts as well as oral traditions. In Book XI, for example, Salazar tells the history of England, including the reign of King Arthur, which he extracts from the Post-Vulgate *Roman du Graal.* The Salazar adaptation is the only surviving text to preserve all three branches of this romance as a continuous narrative, yet the fragments remain virtually unknown to Arthurian scholars, including *Roman du Graal* specialists.

Although the materials concerning the legendary history of Britain are scattered throughout the *Bienandanzas,* I bring them together in this edition because of their common origin and intrinsic unity. I hope thus to make them better known not only to Hispanists but to others interested in Hispanic manifestations of the Matter of Britain. The edition represents an extensive revision of my doctoral dissertation, submitted to the University of California at Los Angeles in 1970. An earlier revision was lost in the theft of my briefcase in Rio de Janeiro in 1973.

I am greatly indebted to Professor S. G. Armistead who suggested Salazar's Arthurian fragments as my dissertation topic and to whom, over the years, I have been able to turn for advice on every problem. My gratitude extends to Professor Edward Dudley who subsequently directed the dissertation and gave unsparingly of his assistance and wise counsel, as well as to the Del Amo Foundation for enabling me to examine the Salazar manuscripts at first hand, and to the helpful library staff at the Real Academia de la Historia. In preparing the first revision of the dissertation I profited greatly from the suggestions and criticisms kindly offered by Professors Arthur L. Askins and A. D. Deyermond, even though we were not always in complete agreement. My thanks to them, and to other friends and colleagues who have given generously of their time and knowledge to aid me with specific questions and difficulties in revising the edition yet a second time. Any shortcomings the work may have are, of course, my responsibility alone. Finally, I am most grateful to The Haney Foundation of the University of Pennsylvania whose generosity has made possible the publication of this edition.

Santa Barbara, California
March 1978

Abbreviations

BAE	Biblioteca de Autores Españoles
BHi	*Bulletin Hispanique*
BHS	*Bulletin of Hispanic Studies*
BRAH	*Boletín de la Real Academia de la Historia* (Madrid)
CFMA	Les Classiques Français du Moyen Age
HR	*Hispanic Review*
JHP	*Journal of Hispanic Philology*
MLR	*Modern Language Review*
NBAE	Nueva Biblioteca de Autores Españoles
NRFH	*Nueva Revista de Filología Hispánica*
PMLA	*Publications of the Modern Language Association of America*
RFE	*Revista de Filología Española*
RHi	*Revue Hispanique*
RPh	*Romance Philology*
SATF	Société des Anciens Textes Français
TLF	Textes Littéraires Français
UCPMP	University of California Publications in Modern Philology
UNCSRLL	University of North Carolina Studies in the Romance Languages and Literatures
ZRPh	*Zeitschrift für Romanische Philologie*

INTRODUCTION ∽

THE AUTHOR

We can learn a number of things about Lope García de Salazar from a reading of his two known works, the *Crónica de Vizcaya* and the *Libro de las bienandanzas e fortunas*.[1] He was born in the year 1399, and by the age of sixteen he was already participating in the family feuds that plagued his native province of Vizcaya and Castile and Navarre.[2] In the narration of one such dispute we learn of young Salazar's skill as a crossbowman: "ferio...con vn rallon por la caueça a Lope Ochoa de Mendieta, de parte a parte, con vna buena vallesta e cayo luego muerto."[3] Violence of this type was to dominate his life.

In 1451 Salazar challenged the authority of John II of Castile by preventing a new *corregidor*, or chief magistrate, from taking the oath of office at Guernica.[4] Five years later Henry IV, faced with an anarchical situation, exiled "todos los mejores destas tierras de Vizcaya," García de Salazar among them. But en route to his assigned place of exile, the Andalusian town of Jimena, Salazar was suddenly taken with a tertian disease, and he felt compelled to return to the more healthful "ayres de su tierra" even before royal permission to do so was given.[5] Later, after amnesty had been granted, Salazar and his sons turned once again to the violent internal struggles of northern Castile.[6]

3

Like his great-great grandfather, who is reputed to have had 120 bastard children in addition to many legitimate ones, Lope García de Salazar became the father of a large number of children. Before his marriage to Juana de Butrón in 1425, he had already fathered three illegitimate sons. Juana was to give him nine more children, and he tells us that after her death he had additional "fijos e fijas bastardos e naturales."[7] Not all of his sons were to survive the bloody battles in which they participated. In 1462 his son Lope was killed while fighting for Henry IV in Aragon.[8] Six years later, against Salazar's wishes, the other sons took part in hostilities between the Zaldíbar and Durango families. Salazar seems to have been particularly proud of Gonzalo, who was killed, calling him "el mas valiente omne de su cuerpo e esforçado que se fallaua entre los omnes."[9] Despite these losses, Salazar still took pride in the size of his family, stating at one point that there remained ".lxxxv. nietos e nietas e fijos e fijas legitimos e vastardos."[10]

But this pride was not to extend to his sons Pedro and Juan "el Moro." Salazar tells us that they, with the help of certain unnamed relatives, robbed him and laid siege to his house in San Martín.[11] It was during his subsequent imprisonment that he compiled the *Bienandanzas e fortunas.*[12] At the end of each of the twenty-five books that form this work, Salazar reminds the reader of his imprisonment by repeating the phrase "Aqui se acaua el ... libro que Lope Garcia de Salazar fizo en esta ystoria de las bienandanzas e fortunas, estando preso en la su casa de Sant Martin."

To such biographical details culled from Salazar's works can be added some external evidence concerning his final years. A royal summons dated 9 November 1476 reveals that he had been imprisoned for some five years prior to his death.[13] In 1926 a litigation document dated 1503 was brought to light giving vivid testimony to the cruel treatment Salazar received at the hands of his sons Juan and Pedro.[14] The document discloses that Juan had been repeatedly caught in the bedchambers of his father's mistresses.[15] After Juan was denied access to the family home, one witness reports that he and his brother Pedro assaulted their father, threw him into a cellar, and robbed him of all his possessions. Then, refusing to grant Juan the *mayorazgo*, or exclusive right of inheritance, Salazar found himself imprisoned in the tower of his *casa-fuerte* at San Martín. His determination to free himself is revealed through the narration of several escape attempts. The scribe of the 1503 document tells us that on one such occasion a witness saw García de Salazar "venyendo ensangrentado e cortado en los pies e en las manos e este testigo le pregunto que como benia asi e que dicho Lope Garcia le dixo que se abia descolgado con vnas sogas e maniculos o la dicha torre por la ventana della e que se avia fecho porque mas quysiere moryr uyendo de ally que no estar como dicho Juan de Salazar su hijo le tenia por so carcel dicha torre."[16]

Regarding the cause of Salazar's death, several witnesses testify that he was given poisonous herbs; but suspicious of what he was eating, Salazar gave some to an illegitimate daughter who was serving him. The effects of the poison are graphically recalled: "daba voces y se daba golpes en el cuerpo y decia que le dolian las tripas... despues que Lope vio muerta a su hija dijo a Juan de Salazar de Baracaldo e su hijo Iohan agora tenereis como quereis que yo me fueste muerto e que Iohan le rrespondio Lope Garcia no vos tengo culpa en ello que sy algo vos an dado esu huespeda de Avellaneda.... Y vio que Lope Garcia tenia el estomago muy ynchado e deciendo que le dolia e daba golpes a su cuerpo con los braços como no se podia tener en ningun modo ni estar ssosegado."[17] García de Salazar's remains have been discovered in a chapel near San Martín de Muñatones in the Valley of Somorrostro (Vizcaya).[18]

Like other men of action in the late Middle Ages, Salazar devoted part of his advanced years to literary activities, producing the *Crónica de Vizcaya* in 1454 and the *Libro de las bienandanzas e fortunas* between 1471 and 1476. Salazar had a keen interest in history. He opens the *Crónica de Vizcaya* by pointing out the tradition of recording the deeds of great men for the benefit of future generations: "Pensaron los antiguos dexar en escrito los echos de los grandes Señores y grandes omes, porque dellos quedasen rrembranza para aquellos que despues dellos viniesen, porque la alabanza de las sus bondades no quedase en olbido y perdida para siempre y porque de aquestas rrembranzas tales se siguen a los omes muchos e grandes aprovechos, especialmente tomar en ellos muy buenos avisamientos, para animar los corazones para hacer toda bondad."[19] For like reasons Salazar traces in the *Crónica de Vizcaya* the ancestry of important families of Vizcaya and Castile, and later, in the *Bienandanzas e fortunas*, follows the progress of man, beginning with the Creation. In the *Bienandanzas* prologue he states that he has written the work for the specific purpose of instructing his heirs: "por que aquellos que de mi suçediesen en la mi casa de Sant Martin que acostunbrasen de leer en este libro porque por el se fallaran de buena generaçion e mereçedores de fazer todo bien."[20] Moreover, he wants to preserve knowledge gathered from a large number of texts, texts which may not be available to others.[21]

At an earlier point in the *Bienandanzas* prologue he refers to the formation of his library as the result of a lifelong quest for knowledge of the past: "ouiendo mucho a uoluntad de saber e de oyr de los tales fechos desde mi mocedad fasta aqui, me trabaje de auer libros e estorias del mundo faziendo los buscar por las prouincias e casas de los reyes e principes cristianos de allende la mar e de aquende por mis despensas con mercaderes e mareantes e por mi mesmo a esta parte."[22] But written authority was not Salazar's only source of information, as he reveals in the preface to his *Crónica de Vizcaya*: "acordé de poner en escrito todo aquello que de los dichos rreyes y linajes susodichos yo fallare por todas las corónicas de Spaña, y otrosi por dichos é oydas de algunos omes ancianos que bieron é oyeron y fueron quedando en memoria de unos en otros...."[23] A similar statement appears in the *Bienandanzas:* "por las [recollections] que yo falle por memoria e por vista e nunca fueran escritas, escreuilas aqui por que non quedasen oluidadas por sienpre."[24]

Although Salazar took his material from disparate sources, occasionally copying the original virtually word for word, he sought to be objective in his own approach to history. After outlining the contents of the *Bienandanzas,* he explains: "non añadi nin amengue en cosa alguna de las cosas susodichas por parçilidad ni por otra manera de quanto Dios me dio a entender, por que con verdad reprehendido me deba ser."[25] And, in a statement that he may have borrowed from the early fourteenth-century writer Don Juan Manuel, Salazar asks his reader not to be too hasty in judging him for any shortcomings the book may have, especially if the copy is not the original written in the hand of the author: "De las menguas que en este libro se fallaren o de palabras mal puestas, non sea dada la culpa a mi fasta saber si es en el herror de los trasladores, segund suelen acaesçer, e si por este libro, que es escrito de mi mano e enmendado en muchos logares...fallaran las dichas [menguas] sea dada la culpa a la mi nigligençia e non a la mi voluntad, porque me entremeti a fablar en tantos e tan altos fechos avnque Dios sabe que lo fize por la dicha mi nesçesidad."[26] The autograph manuscript of Salazar's book suffered the same fate as the works of Don Juan Manuel. Only copies survive.

PREVIOUS EDITIONS AND STUDIES OF THE *LIBRO DE LAS BIENANDANZAS E FORTUNAS*

No reliable edition of the *Libro de las bienandanzas e fortunas* has been published. For many years, except for selected passages, the only edition available was Maximiliano Camarón's facsimile and transcription of Books XX–XXV, based on the earliest surviving manuscript copy, the 1492 Cristóbal de Mieres codex, Madrid, Real Academia de la Historia, MS. 9-10-2/2100: *Las bienandanzas e fortunas que escribió Lope García de Salazar estando preso en la torre de Sant Martín de Muñatones* (Madrid: Gabriel Sánchez, 1884). In 1955 Angel Rodríguez Herrero published a new transcription of Books XX–XXV, preceded by an introductory study and photographic reproductions of the corresponding folios in the Mieres codex: *Las bienandanzas e fortunas* (Bilbao: Diputación de Vizcaya, 1955). Twelve years later, following the same format and incorporating the same introductory study, Rodríguez Herrero produced an edition of the complete MS: *Las bienandanzas e fortunas*, 4 vols. (Bilbao: Diputación de Vizcaya, 1967). In this first edition of the whole text (less one folio page) Rodríguez Herrero also includes photographs and a transcription of folios 2^r–4^v of the sixteenth-century copy, Madrid, Biblioteca Nacional, MS. 1634, thereby providing the reader with prefatory material lacking in the Mieres codex. Rodríguez Herrero's edition was not meant to be scholarly. In an "Introducción" to the four-volume set, the Marqués de Arriluce de Ybarra explains that the editor wished to avoid polemic arguments and that "sólo de vez en vez utiliza la apostilla profesoral que señala senderos a los historiadores y a los eruditos actuales." Unfortunately, Rodríguez Herrero gives no indication of having examined the codices at first hand. He not only fails to cite the shelf-marks of the edited manuscripts, but he disregards the original foliation of the texts by arbitrarily assigning a separate number to each folio page and beginning the numbering anew with each volume. The edition is marred further by numerous errors in transcription, the duplication in the photographic section of folio 323^v (Vol. 3, "folios" 165–66), and the total omission of folio page 307^r (Vol. 3, between "folios" 132 and 133).

Although the *Libro de las bienandanzas e fortunas* is not a completely unknown work, the inaccessibility of the text has hindered scholarly study of the work. Most of the literature concerning the *Bienandanzas* is descriptive in nature, restricting itself largely to the life and times of the author as depicted in the last six books, the portion edited by Camarón in 1884.

Bibliographic information on the works of Salazar is first provided by Nicolás Antonio in the *Bibliotheca hispana vetus* (Madrid, 1788), 2, Nos. 793–95. General information on some of the extant manuscript copies of the *Bienandanzas* is given by A. Allende Salazar, in his *Biblioteca del bascófilo* (Madrid, 1887), No. 1199; and Agapito Rey and Antonio García Solalinde include references to many of the surviving MSS of the *Bienandanzas* in their *Ensayo de una bibliografía de las leyendas troyanas en la literatura española* (Bloomington, Ind., 1942), p. 48. The sixteenth-century MS. 1634 of the Biblioteca Nacional is described more fully by R. Paz y Remolar and J. López de Toro, in *Inventario general de manuscritos de la Biblioteca Nacional* (Madrid, 1953–), 5: 38–39; and a description of the late eighteenth-century copy, Valladolid, Biblioteca Universitaria de Santa Cruz, MS. 131 (*olim* 133), appears in Saturnino Rivera Manescau and Paulino Ortega Lamadrid, "Catálogo de manuscritos de la Biblioteca Universitaria de Valladolid," *Anales de la Universidad de Valladolid* 2 (1929): 406. A new description of MS. 131 and of MS. 7 (*olim* 209), the latter containing a copy made ca. 1780 of the first and last chapters of the *Bienandanzas* together with a portion of the prologue, is now included in María de las Nieves Alonso-Cortés, *Catálogo de manuscritos de la Biblioteca de Santa Cruz* (Valladolid, 1976), pp. 13–14, 107–8.

As a primary source for the history of northern Spain the *Bienandanzas* received recognition in the seventeenth century from Gabriel de Henao, who cites the Salazar text throughout his *Averigvaciones de las antigvedades de Cantabria...*, 2 vols. (Salamanca, 1689–91). Interest in the *Bienandanzas* was revived in the late eighteenth century by Rafael de Floranes. The Valladolid MS. 131 contains a biographical introduction written ostensibly in Floranes' hand. This introduction has received three separate editions. Benito Maestre, without mentioning the name of Floranes, adapted the introduction for his own purposes in "Biografía española: Lope García de Salazar," *Semanario Pintoresco Español* (Madrid), 1847, pp. 201–5. Three years later the Diputación de Guipúzcoa added the Floranes introduction as an appendix to an edition of Lope [Martínez] de Isasti's *Compendio historial de la...Provincia de Guipúzcoa en el año de 1625* (San Sebastián, 1850). Segundo de Ipizúa published the introduction (retitled "Noticia del escritor Lope García de Salazar") in his edition of various Floranes writings, *La supresión del obispado de Alaba y sus derivaciones en la historia del país vasco* (Madrid, 1919–20), 2: 165–85. Floranes quotes extensively from the last six books of the *Bienandanzas* in another study edited by Ipizúa, "De las memorias que tiene la Provincia de Guipúzcoa...," in *La supresión*, 2: 186–253.

Much of the information gathered by Floranes is repeated a century later by Antonio de Trueba in his preface to the Camarón edition ("Bosquejo biográfico de Lope García de Salazar"). In a review of the Camarón edition, Vicente de la Fuente expresses a negative attitude toward the unedited portion of the *Bienandanzas*: "No creo que se deba llorar mucho la no publicación de los veinte primeros libros, pues por el contenido de la Crónica general y las historias posteriores desde mediados del siglo XIII hasta fines del siglo XV, en que escribía el prisionero en su torre de San Martín, año 1492 [*sic*], podemos conjeturar lo que diría acerca de la creación del mundo, de nuestro padre Adán, el diluvio, venida de Túbal á España, los Geriones, cartagineses y fenicios, y aun con respecto á Vizcaya las noticias que aún sostenían en el siglo pasado el cándido Astarloa y otros" (*BRAH* 5 [1884]: 223). Fortunately, a few twentieth-century scholars have shown a different attitude toward the earlier books of the *Bienandanzas*.

The last six books are again used as source material by Carmelo de Echegaray in his study *Las provincias vascongadas a fines de la Edad Media* (San Sebastián, 1895). In a review of this work, Miguel de Unamuno sums up laconically what he believes to be Salazar's impassive narrative style: "cuenta verdaderos horrores con la mayor sencillez del mundo" (*Revista Crítica de Historia y Literatura Españolas, Portuguesas e Hispano-Americanas* 1 [1896]: 139). Salazar's genealogical descriptions in the last six books are misleadingly described as accurate by Luis de Salazar in *Origen de 300 apellidos castellanos y vascongados* (Bilbao, 1916), pp. 5–6.

Darío de Areitio's publication in 1926 of portions of a legal document testifying to García de Salazar's cruel death provided new biographical information: "De la prisión y muerte de Lope García de Salazar," *Revue Internationale des Etudes Basques* 17 (1926): 9–16. Four years later, Manuel de Lecuona attempted to reconstruct certain Basque expressions used by Salazar in the last six books, in "El texto vasco de Lope García de Salazar," *Revue Internationale des Etudes Basques* 21 (1930): 258–59. In the same year Salazar's descriptions of the internal struggles of northern Spain formed the basis of Juan Carlos Guerra's study *Oñacinos y gamboínos: Rol de banderizos vascos, con la mención de las familias pobladoras de Bilbao en los siglos XIV y XV* (San Sebastián, 1930).

Ricardo Baroja, brother of the famous novelist Pío Baroja, was so inspired by the family feuds narrated in the last books of the *Bienandanzas* that he wrote a "especie de tragicomedia...en romance de distinto metro," which, when the paper had decomposed after a number of years, he rewrote as a historical novel entitled *Bienandanzas y fortunas*, for which he won the Premio Cervantes in 1935. The work was finally published in Barcelona in 1941 by Ediciones Pal-las Bartrés.

In 1939 Salazar's life and works became the subject of a thesis for the M.A. degree at Columbia University: Juan Manuel Bilbao, "Lope García de Salazar (1399–1481): Estudio sobre su vida y obra, como fuente para el conocimiento de la cultura tradicional." Bilbao later published the more original part of his thesis, that dealing with traditional themes and motifs in the *Crónica de Vizcaya* and the last six books of the *Bienandanzas*: "La cultura tradicional en la obra de Lope García de Salazar," *Eusko-Jakintza* 2 (1948): 229–64.

For his 1955 edition of Books XX–XXV, Rodríguez Herrero includes a study (pp. vii–xxxiii) in which he reviews the life of the author, transcribes a royal summons from the Registro General del Sello of the Archivo General de Simancas, comments upon Salazar as a historian, and describes the content of both the *Crónica de Vizcaya* and the last six books of the *Bienandanzas*. The study is reproduced in volume 1 of the 1967 edition. Based upon the 1955 edition, Julio Caro Baroja prepared a sociological analysis of the family feuds of northern Spain during the late Middle Ages: *Linajes y bandos: A propósito de la nueva edición de "Las bienandanzas e fortunas"* (Bilbao, 1956).

The discovery of García de Salazar's remains is the subject of a study by Javier Ibarra y Bergé and Esteban Calle Iturrino, *La tumba de Lope García de Salazar en San Martín de Muñatones* (Bilbao, 1956). The history of Vizcaya by Francisco Elías de Tejada, *El señorío de Vizcaya* (Madrid, 1963) contains commentary on the life of Salazar (pp. 61–62), his use of the Basque language (p. 63, n. 27), his narrative skill (pp. 62–66), and also his lack of originality (p. 69). But it remains for Andrés E. de Mañaricua y Nuere to put García de Salazar as a historian into proper perspective, in his important study *Historiografía de Vizcaya (Desde Lope García de Salazar a Labayru)* (Bilbao, 1971), pp. 39–65.

Critical interest in the literary aspects of the *Bienandanzas e fortunas* begins in the twentieth century with Ramón Menéndez Pidal. In his study "Roncesvalles: Un nuevo cantar de gesta español del siglo XIII" (*RFE* 4 [1917]: 105–204), Menéndez Pidal transcribes a Salazar interpolation of the Roncesvalles legend (pp. 200–204)[27] and points to analogous passages in the *Poema de Fernán González* and the *Poema de Alfonso XI* (pp. 156–57). In the *Catálogo de la Real Biblioteca*, 3rd ed. (Madrid, 1918), Menéndez Pidal cites the *Crónica de 1344* as one of Salazar's principal sources (p. 46). That Salazar may have supplemented his interpolations of epic material with details derived from oral tradition is also suggested by Menéndez Pidal in *Poesía juglaresca y juglares* (Madrid, 1924), p. 411 (cf. 1957 ed., p. 319). In *La leyenda de los Infantes de Lara*, 3rd ed., (Madrid, 1971) Menéndez Pidal transcribes Salazar's version of the Infantes de Lara legend (pp. 345–51) and comments upon the possible historiographic and traditional sources (pp. 23, n. 27, 62, 94, n. 3, 96, n. 2, 179, n. 2, 448).

That Salazar's sources for his interpolation of the Roncesvalles legend may be multiple is studied in depth by Jules Horrent in "Le Récit de la bataille de Roncevaux dans le *Libro de bienandanzas y fortunas* de Lope García de Salazar," *Revue Belge de Philologie et Histoire* 28 (1950): 967–92, and *Roncesvalles: Etudes sur le fragment de cantar de gesta conservé à l'Archivo de Navarra (Pampelune)* (Paris, 1951), pp. 216–17. The use of popular and traditional elements in Salazar's retelling of the Cid's youthful exploits is explored by S. G. Armistead in *A Lost Version of the "Cantar de gesta de las Mocedades de Rodrigo" Reflected in the Second Redaction of Rodríguez de Almela's "Compendio historial,"* UCPMP, 38 (Berkeley–Los Angeles, 1963), pp. 344–45. A. D. Deyermond, in calling it "startling" that epic poems were still circulating in oral form during the latter part of the fifteenth century, prefers to think that the oral traditions embodied in Salazar's treatment of the *Mocedades de Rodrigo* were contained in earlier manuscripts to which Salazar had access: *Epic Poetry and the Clergy: Studies on the "Mocedades de Rodrigo"* (London, 1968), p. 14. Undaunted by neo-individualist criticism, Armistead continues to probe into the possible epic and traditional origins of Salazar's rendering of the Mocedades in "Las *Mocedades de Rodrigo* según Lope García de Salazar," *Romania* 94 (1973): 303–20 (see the review by Alan Soons, *Olifant* 2 [1974–75]: 150–52).[28] Armistead also points out Salazar's paraphrase of quatrain 44 of Juan Ruiz's *Libro de buen amor* in the prologue to the *Bienandanzas*: "An Unnoticed Fifteenth-Century citation of the *Libro de buen amor*," HR 41 (1973): 88–91; and in Book V he observes Salazar's use of quatrains 71, 73*b*, and 105*ab*: "Two Further Citations of the *Libro de buen amor* in Lope García de Salazar's *Bienandanzas e fortunas*," *La Corónica* 5 (1976–77): 75–76.

That the earlier books in the *Bienandanzas e fortunas* represent a mine for lost and variant versions of medieval texts is demonstrated in a paper I delivered to the twenty-first anniversary conference of the Association of Hispanists of Great Britain and Ireland, Durham, England, April 1, 1976. A summary of this paper is printed in *La Corónica* 4 (1975–76): 99. Two of my discoveries have now been given more extensive study: Salazar's fragments of the pseudo-travel book the *Libro del Infante don Pedro de Portugal,* a work commonly dated as early sixteenth-century; and what would appear to be a previously unknown prose Alexander romance based, in part, on the Alexander story in the *Bocados de oro*. See my articles "Evidence of a Fifteenth-Century *Libro del Infante don Pedro de Portugal* and Its Relationship to the Alexander Cycle," *JHP* 1 (1976–77): 85–98; and (with Dorothy S. Severin), "Fifteenth-Century Spanish Fragments of a Lost Prose Alexander," *Medium Aevum,* in press.

Concerning Salazar's use of the Trojan and Arthurian romances, only partial studies have been published. Agapito Rey in his edition of Leomarte's *Sumas de historia troyana, RFE,* Anejo 15 (Madrid, 1932) finds that Salazar follows the Leomarte text but in shortened form (p. 27, n. 5, p. 31, n. 1). Rey and Solalinde describe the content and possible sources of Salazar's narration of Trojan history in *Ensayo de una bibliografía,* p. 48. The Arthurian fragments found in Book XI of the *Bienandanzas* are partially edited by Pedro Bohigas Balaguer in an appendix to *Los textos españoles y gallego-portugueses de la Demanda del Santo Grial, RFE,* Anejo 7 (Madrid, 1925), pp. 130–43. Due to then unfavorable conditions at the Biblioteca de la Real Academia de la Historia, Bohigas based only some of his selections upon the Cristóbal de Mieres codex (MS. 9-10-2/2100), transcribing the others from MS. 1634, the sixteenth-century copy in the Biblioteca Nacional. On Salazar's sources Bohigas points out the use of both Vulgate and Post-Vulgate (then called Pseudo-Boron cycle) Arthurian traditions. The present book, the fullest study of Salazar's use of the Matter of Britain, is a revision of my doctoral dissertation, "The Legendary History of Britain in Lope García de Salazar's *Libro de las bienandanzas e fortunas,*" University of California, Los Angeles, 1970. Textual and bibliographic information concerning the Post-Vulgate *Roman du Graal* fragments is provided in entry Ae2 of my *A Critical Bibliography of Hispanic Arthurian Material,* 1: Texts: *The Prose Romance Cycles,* Research Bibliographies and Checklists, 3 (London: Grant & Cutler, 1977), pp. 35–37. I also investigate Salazar's treatment of the death of King Arthur in "The Passing of King Arthur to the Island of Brasil in a Fifteenth–Century Spanish Version of the Post-Vulgate *Roman du Graal,*" *Romania* 92 (1971): 65–73.

THE RELATIONSHIP OF THE GARCÍA DE SALAZAR TEXT TO TROJAN AND ARTHURIAN PSEUDOHISTORY AND PROSE ROMANCE

The legendary history of Britain, the body of literature that centers around the mythical figures of Brutus and Arthur, owes its development in the Middle Ages largely to the creative imagination of the British author Geoffrey of Monmouth.[29] In his *Historia Regum Britanniae* (finished ca. 1136), Geoffrey combines Trojan with British themes, using as a starting point the story of Brutus, the eponymous founder of Britain from the ninth-century *Historia Brittonum*, attributed to Nennius. Brutus, great-grandson of the Trojan Aeneas, having killed his father Silvius in a hunting accident, is expelled by the Romans, goes to Greece, where he leads a successful rebellion of Trojan descendants against the king, Pandrasus, and wanders about the Mediterranean with his followers until he receives the prophecy of Diana that he and his people are to inhabit an island that lies to the west beyond the realms of Gaul. Moving forward in time, Geoffrey's pseudohistorical narrative reaches the greatest British hero, Arthur, son of Uther Pendragon and Ygerna. In Nennius Geoffrey found the tale of Uther's enemy Vortigern and his collapsing tower, as well as the story of the fatherless child Ambrosius, whom Geoffrey adapted to Welsh legends about Myrddin to create the new figure of the prophet Merlin. According to Geoffrey, Arthur is victorious over his Saxon enemies, subjugates Scotland, Ireland, Denmark, and Norway, and later conquers all of Gaul, after slaying its tribune, Frollo. To cause Arthur's ultimate fall, Geoffrey introduces the treacherous figure of Mordred.

It is conjectured by one Hispanist that Geoffrey's *Historia* was introduced into Spain between the years 1170 and 1219.[30] The story of Brutus and the founding of Britain is first translated into Spanish in the thirteenth century as part of Alfonso el Sabio's *General estoria* and is later found in the fourteenth-century *Sumas de historia troyana*, a pseudo-historical romance ascribed to a certain Leomarte.[31] A much different version of the Brutus legend is contained in a fifteenth-century Spanish text by Díez de Games, the *Victorial* or *Crónica de don Pero Niño*.[32] García de Salazar begins his history of Britain (Bk. XI, chs. 1–10) by extracting the Brutus story from a now lost version of Leomarte's *Sumas*, one which shows readings in common with the two manuscripts known to have survived. My comparison of the *Bienandanzas* version with these manuscripts confirms Agapito Rey's statement that Salazar condenses the Leomarte text.[33] In general, he reduces descriptive detail and explanatory matter to the essential information, but he also continues the narrative beyond that of other known versions of the Brutus story with commentary on the ecclesiastical, economic, judicial, and warfaring customs of England, material for which I have found no written source. A reference to Luçes Pagano (= Lucius), first Christian ruler of Britain, serves to bridge the chronological gap between the Brutus legend and the Arthurian material that follows.

In 1155, the year of Geoffrey of Monmouth's death, a free paraphrase of the *Historia Regum Britanniae* was completed by the Norman poet Wace. This work, called the *Roman du Brut*, adds several new elements to Arthurian tradition, namely the founding of the Round Table and commentary on the survival of King Arthur.[34] The Matter of Britain was soon converted from its chronistic garb into what is commonly called romantic fiction by the French poet Chrétien de Troyes, who, around 1160, began a literary career that was to produce a series of long verse romances dealing with prominent knights of King Arthur's court.[35] Chrétien's poetic world was filled with the lais of the Breton bards, the love stories of Tristan and Iseut and Lancelot and Guenevere, the story of Perceval and the Grail, etc.[36] But to the more fantastic elements of the Matter of Britain Chrétien introduced subtle reasoning, the psychological development of characters, and the romantic treatment of love, additions which were no doubt influenced by his early training in classical literature, especially the works of *Ovid.*

In the thirteenth century writers of Arthurian romance tended to turn their attention from courtly love to the adventures and marvels associated with Arthur's kingdom, expanding and elucidating the material into a more coherent, unified corpus. The idea of a unified scheme of romances seems to have occurred first to Robert de Boron, a Burgundian knight whose literary activity spanned the years 1191–1212. Modern scholars believe Boron planned a trilogy of verse romances linking the Holy Grail legend with the story of King Arthur. The first part of the trilogy, the *Joseph d'Arimathie,* and some five hundred lines of the second part, the *Merlin,* have survived in a late thirteenth-century manuscript.[37] In Chrétien de Troyes' last romance, the *Perceval* or *Le Conte du Graal,*[38] the story of Perceval, one of Arthur's knights, is linked with the legend of the Grail, but Chrétien offers no explanation of the origin of the Grail. Boron, however, combines certain New Testament apocrypha from the *Gesta Pilatti,* the *Vindicta Salvatoris,* and the *Cura Sanitatis Tiberii* with the literary tradition of the Grail. Also, he identifies the Grail with the Chalice of the Last Supper, which is said to have come into the possession of Joseph of Arimathea, who collected in it some of the blood that flowed from the wounds of Jesus after his crucifixion. Following the Resurrection Joseph was thrown into a dungeon, where Christ appeared before him in a blaze of light telling him that the Grail was to be cared for by only three men, beginning with Joseph. After many years in prison, Joseph was released by Vespasian, the Roman emperor, who had gone to Jerusalem to avenge the death of Christ after being miraculously cured of leprosy. At this point, Boron adds to the apocryphal legends the figure of Joseph's sister Enygeus and her husband Bron, who, together with Joseph and a small band of followers, go to live in foreign lands, where Joseph sets up the Grail Table in memory of the Last Supper. The vessel is eventually entrusted to the care of Bron, who moves westward with his wife and twelve sons to preach the Christian faith and to await the birth of a grandson, who will fill a vacant seat at the Grail Table and become the vessel's third guardian.

The second part of Boron's trilogy, the *Merlin,* is a remodelled version of Geoffrey of Monmouth's *Historia Regum Britanniae* and *Vita Merlini.*[39] By linking the *Merlin* to the *Joseph d'Arimathie* through a series of references, Boron ties the Grail adventures of apostolic times to those of King Arthur's Britain. The fragmentary *Merlin* begins with an infernal plot against the work of the Messiah to be achieved through Merlin, son of an incubus and a virgin. Merlin possesses the ability to know the past and foretell the future, and within the narrative Merlin retells the story of Joseph of Arimathea and has King Uther establish the Round Table with its Perilous Seat after the model of Joseph's Grail Table.

Boron's initial attempt to combine the various Arthurian and Grail narratives into a coherent sequence led to the compilation of a new group of prose romances, the so-called Vulgate Cycle (dated between 1215 and 1230), consisting of five branches, in which the Grail story is combined with Lancelot's love for Queen Guenevere. This is the cycle edited by H. O. Sommer.[40] The first branch, the *Estoire del Saint Graal,*[41] is an elaboration of Robert de Boron's *Joseph d'Arimathie.* Joseph, together with his wife and son Josephés, take the Holy Grail to Britain, where they set out to convert the heathens. The anonymous compiler carries the narrative forward to the time of King Pelles, maternal grandfather of Lancelot. The second branch, the *Estoire de Merlin,*[42] is a prose rendering of Boron's *Merlin,* followed by a psuedohistorical continuation, in which the first three and a half years of Arthur's reign are marked by a rebellion of barons, a Saxon invasion, and the entombment of Merlin by Niviene, the woman he loves. The third branch, the *Lancelot,*[43] is the story of Lancelot from his birth, his love for Guenevere, and the preparations for the Grail quest. In the fourth branch, the *Queste del Saint Graal,*[44] Galahad replaces his father, Lancelot, as the world's greatest knight, and the adventures of the Grail reach their climax. In the fifth branch, the *Mort Artu,*[45] Arthur finally learns of Guenevere's adultery with Lancelot, the discovery of which creates dissension among the knights of the Round Table and Arthur's eventual downfall at the hands of his ill-begotten son, Mordred.

A new version of the Vulgate Cycle, in which the characters of the Tristan story play a prominent role, was composed between 1230 and 1240. This work used to be referred to as the "Pseudo-Robert de Boron Cycle," since the name of Boron is invoked in many of the surviving manuscripts. Dr. Fanni Bogdanow has re-named the cycle the Post-Vulgate *Roman du Graal*.[46] In an attempt to reconstruct this cyclical romance through the surviving French texts and Spanish and Portuguese adaptations, Dr. Bogdanow has demonstrated that the *remaniement* is not a "clumsy imitation"[47] of the Vulgate Cycle but rather a "closely-knit and coherent whole."[48]

It is not precisely clear at what point in time Arthurian romantic fiction first entered Spain and Portugal.[49] However, knowledge of the Arthurian legends is revealed by late twelfth and thirteenth-century peninsular poets who mention in their lyrics such figures as Tristan, Lancelot, Perceval, and Ivain. The earliest known date for a translation of a French Arthurian romance is 1313.[50] It is thought by modern scholars that in this year a certain Juan or João Vivas translated the Post-Vulgate *Roman du Graal*. The language of the Vivas text has been the subject of much debate. Castilian, Por-tuguese, Leonese, or a mixed language have all been proposed. However, it is generally believed that all subsequent versions are ultimately derived from the 1313 translation since the Vivas name is invoked in several of the texts.[51]

The following Portuguese and Castilian versions of the Post-Vul-gate *Roman du Graal* survive:

I. The *Joseph d'Arimathie* or *Estoire del Saint Graal*.

1. Lisbon. Torre do Tombo. MS. 643. Edited by Henry Hare Carter, *The Portuguese Book of Joseph of Arimathea*, UNCSRLL, 71 (Chapel Hill, 1967).

2. Salamanca. Biblioteca Universitaria. MS. 1877 (*olim* Ma-drid, Biblioteca de Palacio, MS. II-794; *olim* 2-G-5), fols. 252^r–282^r. Edited by Karl Pietsch, *Spanish Grail Fragments: El Libro de Josep Abarimatia, La Estoria de Merlin, Lançarote* (Chicago, 1924–25), 1: 3–54.

II. *Suite du Merlin* (the *Merlin* and its continuation).

3. Salamanca. Biblioteca Universitaria. MS. 1877, fols. 282^v–296^r. Edited by Pietsch, *Fragments*, 1: 57–81.

4. *Baladro del sabio Merlin con sus profecias* (Burgos: Juan de Burgos, 1498). Edited by Pedro Bohigas, *El Baladro del*

Sabio Merlin según el texto de la edición de Burgos de 1498, 3 vols. (Barcelona, 1957–62).

5. *La demanda del sancto Grial con los marauillosos fechos de Lançarote y de Galaz su hijo* [*El primero libro: El baladro del famosissimo profeta y nigromante Merlin con sus profecias*] (Seville, 1535). Edited by Adolfo bonilla y San Martín, *El Baladro del Sabio Merlín, primera parte de la Demanda del Sancto Grial,* in *Libros de caballerías,* 1: *Ciclo artúrico–Ciclo carolingio,* NBAE, 6 (Madrid, 1907), pp. 3–162.

III. *Queste del Saint Graal* and *Mort Artu.*

6. Vienna. Oesterreichische Nationalbibliothek. MS. 2594. Edited by Augusto Magne, S.J., *A Demanda do Santo Graal: Reprodução fac-similar e transcrição crítica do códice 2594 da Biblioteca Nacional de Viena,* 2 vols. (Rio de Janeiro, 1955–70).

7. Salamanca. Biblioteca Universitaria. MS. 1877, fols. 298^v–300^v. Edited by Pietsch, *Fragments,* 1: 85–89.

8. *La demanda del sancto Grial con los marauillosos fechos de Lançarote y de Galaz su fijo* [*El segundo y postrero libro*] (Toledo: Juan de Villaquirán, 1515).

9. *La demanda del sancto Grial con los marauillosos fechos de Lançarote y de Galaz su hijo* [*El segundo y postrero libro*] (Seville, 1535). Edited by Bonilla, *Libros de caballerías,* pp. 163–338.

The above list omits the text at hand, the fragments interpolated by Lope García de Salazar within his history of Britain (Bk. XI, chs. 11–26). Except for the portions edited in 1925 by Pedro Bohigas (*Los textos,* pp. 130–43), these fragments have been overlooked by William J. Entwistle, María Rosa Lida de Malkiel, Fanni Bogdanow, and other critics of Spanish–Portuguese Arthurianism.

Salazar seems to have had before him a version of the three branches of the Post-Vulgate *Roman du Graal.* A comparison of the Salazar fragments with the surviving texts of the *Roman du Graal* reveals a number of close verbal correspondences but scanty evidence toward determining the possible language of the original Hispanic translation from the French. Also, the fragments show certain distinctive features not found in other known versions of the Post-Vulgate text.

The Arthurian story proper in the *Bienandanzas* begins with a brief summary of the *Josep Abarimatia* or *Estoire del Saint Graal,* but Salazar may have changed a few details based upon his reading of a derivative version of the Old French poem of the late twelfth or early thirteenth century, *La Vengeance Nostre Seigneur,*[52] which was later adapted in a prose version and translated into the Hispanic languages.[53] Salazar's catalogue of the descendants of Joseph of Arimathea contains several proper names not found in other related texts. Salazar's summary of the second branch of the Post-Vulgate text, the *Merlin,* presents few significant departures from other known versions. However, in that portion known as the *Merlin* continuation (the narrative of the period between Arthur's coronation and the Grail quest), Salazar incorporates several details taken ostensibly from a version of the Vulgate Cycle: the reference to Arthur's fight with a monster cat and his defeat of Duque Flores. From the *Merlin* branch Salazar also seems to have taken a piece of proverbial wisdom, given by Merlin to Arthur, and appended it almost gratuitously, in the manner of the *fabliaux* writers, to his summary of the tale of Ibycus, which he interpolates in Book V concerning Alexander the Great and the wisdom of the ancient Greeks.[54]

The most original feature of Salazar's version of the Post-Vulgate *Roman du Graal* is found at the end of the *Mort Artu* section. Here Salazar uses, as I have explained elsewhere,[55] a tale which may have come to him from English seamen visiting the northern ports of Castile. To bring the tale of King Arthur's downfall to a conclusion Salazar has Morgain la Fée take Arthur by boat to the Island of Brasil, which she enchants so that it cannot be found. The destination of the boat is not specified in the other Post-Vulgate texts, and Salazar fills the void by supplementing his primary source with his own version of Arthur's passing.[56] Avalon, the well-known final resting place from other texts[57] is replaced with the traditional folk belief in the vanishing island (here the Island of Brasil disappears if it sees you before you see it) and the story of the recent "discovery" by the English of an island named Brasil off the coast of Ireland, an island said to produce valuable brazilwood. Although Salazar insists that the Island of Brasil exists but is enchanted, he disagrees with those who believe Morgan and Arthur to be still alive and on the island. In presenting this new version of Arthur's passing, Salazar refashions oral, cartographic, and literary traditions in terms more meaningful to his contemporaries.

Another curious adaptation of Arthurian material by Salazar is found within his history of Flanders, in Bk. X, ch. 3. Here the knights of the Round Table are said to defeat one hundred pagan knights, descendants of the cruel, cannibalistic Flemings who survive on an island called Gajola (formerly Luenga Ynsola). And the Arthurian figure Galehaut is said to have conquered this island, which is also the location of the Torre del Lloro. Salazar claims that the story may be found in the *Demanda,* an obvious allusion to the *Demanda del Santo Grial.* However, the story is not found as such in the surviving *Demanda* texts. Rather, it reveals some elements in common with two different episodes: one in the Prose *Tristan* regarding an island ruled by Galehaut where Joseph of Arimathea had once converted the pagan inhabitants; and the other in the *Demanda* texts regarding pagans living at the Castillo Follón, who strongly resist conversion. Salazar transfers the setting to Flanders, but, without additional evidence, it is impossible to say whether he himself combined the similar but separate episodes or whether he was following a version of the *Demanda* now lost. We may have here yet another example of how the Post-Vulgate text incorporated elements from the Prose *Tristan,* a romance which modern scholars believe to have been composed between 1225 and 1235 but subsequently enlarged with new material, including much of the *Queste* portion of the Post-Vulgate *Roman du Graal.*[58]

Salazar's text contains few actual references to the *Tristan* legend. Apart from those in the Arthurian story proper in Book XI, Salazar includes within the genealogical and historical framework of the histories of France and Brittany (Bk. IX, ch. 8, and Bk. X, ch. 15, respectively) brief passages concerning the *enfances* of Tristan and his marriage to Iseut of the White Hands. These passages would appear to derive from a version, possibly in French rather than Spanish, of the Prose *Tristan.*[59]

In Book XVII, his history of the reign of the fourteenth-century Castilian king Peter I, Salazar adapts Pero López de Ayala's *Crónica del rey don Pedro.*[60] Within this adaptation, Salazar copies verbatim the letter sent by the Moor Benhatin concerning a prophecy of Merlin. In the twelfth century Geoffrey of Monmouth had dealt with a series of Merlin prophecies in his "Prophetiae Merlini," in the *Historia Regum Britanniae,* Bk. VII.[61] The fame of these prophecies spread throughout Europe, including the Iberian Peninsula, where they were adapted by various authors, among them Rodrigo Yáñez, in his *Poema de Alfonso Onceno,*[62] the anonymous compiler of *La Gran Crónica de Alfonso XI,*[63] and the adaptor of the *Baladro del Sabio Merlín* as it survives in the 1535 Seville imprint.[64] López de Ayala is known to have read romances of chivalry, and he was obviously influenced by the theme of the prophet Merlin.[65]

With the exception of the Merlin prophecy, the distinctive feature of Salazar's handling of his sources for the portion of the *Bien-*

andanzas included in this edition is his preoccupation with brevity. To cut short one topic and pass on to another, Salazar occasionally employs formulaic transitional expressions, such as that found at the end of Bk. XI, ch. 11: "se dexa aqui de contar para no alargar escritura."[66] In some passages the narrative is so condensed that it is almost unintelligible (e.g., the reference to Arthur's coat of arms in Bk. XI, ch. 19), but in others the author provides us with a considerable amount of detail. At times it is possible to discern in Salazar a deliberate effort to gather together details which were scattered in different passages in his source. To consolidate his material, Salazar will change the position of the passage as well as the nature of the detail. In his version of the *Merlin* the sequence of events is altered on several occasions. He begins this branch with the story of Merlin's conception, whereas the other *Merlin* texts follow the Robert de Boron poem with a passage on the infernal plot to destroy mankind. Salazar defers this passage to later and puts it in the mouth of Merlin himself.

That Salazar was not totally successful in his compression of material is revealed, for example, in his use of the figure of Grifet for both the son of Antor and Arthur's cupbearer, Lucan. In the *Mort Artu* Lucan is accidentally killed by Arthur. In the text as copied by Cristóbal de Mieres, we find Lucan's name totally absent and Grifet serving as both Arthur's major-domo and cupbearer. At one point Grifet as Lucan is killed only to emerge a few lines later as Grifet (Bk. XI, ch. 25). Moreover, by including the detail that the town of Can was named after Arthur's major-domo, Salazar is forced to leave a blank when Lucan's name is to be invoked. Such blunders were due, undoubtedly, to hurried condensation.

In reducing his story Salazar also sacrifices much in the way of characterization and motivation. The details of the story of the Holy Grail, for example, are sketchy and seem indicative of the author's failure to understand the deep significance of the Grail theme. However, in the figure of Arthur, Salazar does manage to preserve the concept of a hero facing a fateful destiny. The figure of Arthur becomes, in fact, even more central in Salazar's adaptation than in the *Roman du Graal*. Other surviving texts continue the narrative beyond Arthur's death with an epilogue concerning the deaths of Lancelot and Guenevere and Mark of Cornwall from the Tristan texts,[67] but the Salazar text has its own dramatic ending with the account of Arthur's passing to the Island of Brasil.

Characteristically, the compiler of historical lore relies upon his sources rather than individual insight. Such is the case in Salazar's use of Trojan and Arthurian texts as authoritative documents for his *Libro de las bienandanzas e fortunas*. Although the pseudohistory of Geoffrey of Monmouth had generally been abandoned in favor of fictional romance, Salazar reunited legendary Trojan and British themes within the framework of a chronicle, thus treating the Matter of Britain as fact rather than fiction.

PHYSICAL DESCRIPTION OF MS. 9-10-2/2100

The Real Academia de la Historia MS. 9-10-2/2100 (*olim* 12-10-6-17) is the earliest known copy of the twenty-five books of the *Bienandanzas e fortunas*.[68] The text as it survives today consists of 439 leaves of paper measuring 388 × 260 mm. The leaves are slightly mildewed and worm-eaten. Some of the many tears to be found have been mended with either paper or transparent tape. Books XX–XXV have received the most wear.

According to the explicit, a single copyist named Cristóbal de Mieres finished the manuscript on 16 April 1492, at the behest of Ochoa de Salazar, grandson of Lope García de Salazar.[69] The text is written in *letra redonda* or chancellery hand and is generally quite legible. The scribe ruled his total writing space but not individual lines. Normally he wrote 40 to 50 lines to a column with two columns per folio page. The text is rubricated, with the initial letter of each chapter, a capital in the form of a majuscule, alternately stroked in red and violet. Chapter titles are written in red. *Calderones* or section marks, which appear frequently, are also in red but occasionally in violet. Several different hands have made corrections and have left numerals, insignificant comments and drawings in the margins. Arabic numerals have been inserted for most chapters by a later hand within or to the edge of the majuscule.

In foliation both Roman and Arabic numerals have been employed, but they rarely coincide. Textual evidence shows that the Roman numerals are correct,[70] but because many of the Roman are either illegible or have been cut away, in the present edition I follow previous example and utilize the Arabic.[71] Among the Arabic, however, the following irregularities are to be noted: folios 1–5 and 399 are lacking; folio numbers 23, 129 and 351 have been omitted, although the text is complete at these points; for folio 195 read 196, for 299–450 read 199–350, and for 473 read 373.

The manuscript contains forty-five quires of ten leaves each, the quires signed in three alphabetical series as follows: (1) [a], v, c, d, e, f, g, h, j, l, m, n, o, p, q, r, [s], t; (2) a, b, c, d, e, f, g, h, j, l, m, n, o, p, q, r, s, t, v, x, y, z; (3) a, b, c, d, e. The first quire is unsigned; the seventeenth, marked *y* (crossed out by the scribe), should read *s*. The signatures, placed in the lower right corner of the recto and occasionally cut away in the trimming which preceded the binding of the volume, are applied to the first five leaves of each quire (e.g., p i, p ij, p iij, p iiij, p v). Eleven leaves are missing: in series (1) the first two of quire [a] (text is incomplete at this point), the tenth of quire *v*, the eighth of quire *c*, and the seventh of quire *o*; in series (2) the seventh through tenth of quire *s* (text incomplete); and in series (3) the last two leaves of quire *e*.

The volume is preserved in a nineteenth-century binding. Printed matter used to back the inside of the spine, which has become unsewed, contains the date 1814. The paper-covered pasteboards are badly worn, especially along the edges. Likewise, the brown leather corners and spine are in poor condition. "SALA-ZAR/HISTORIAS" is stamped on the spine. Two earlier shelf-marks are written on the inside of the front pasteboard: Est. 10. Gr. C.ª num? 17 and 12-10-6/17.

The manuscript was the property of Francisco de Borja de Salazar before its acquisition by the Real Academia de la Historia.[72] It is entered in A. Rodríguez Villa's unpublished "Indice general de manuscritos" (p. 130) available for consultation at the Academia library.

NOTE ON THE LANGUAGE OF MS. 9-10-2/2100

The language of MS. 9-10-2/2100 is characterized by a number of features common to texts written or copied in Castile during the fifteenth century. Some peculiarities which appear may be explained, in part, by García de Salazar's use of a wide variety of written sources of disparate provenance and date of composition, the intrusion of Navarro-Aragonese forms in the speech of the author's region of northern Castile, changes in language made by the 1492 copyist and later hands, and the general lack of fixed orthographic norms toward the end of the fifteenth century.

An exhaustive study of the language of MS. 9-10-2/2100 falls outside the limits of this edition. I discuss below merely some of the more salient characteristics of the edited fragments.

I. Phonology and Orthography

A. *Vowels*

Occasionally tonic vowels show a vacillation between high and middle position, as in *mesmo* (Bk. XI, ch. 9: 22), *asimismo* (Bk. XI, ch. 8: *15*), and *asimesmo* (Bk. X, ch. 3: *7*); *logar* (Bk. XI, ch. 18: *22*) and *lugar* (Bk. XVII, ch. 48: *198*). The vacillation occurs particularly with learned or semi-learned words, such as *profeçia* (Bk. XVII, ch. 47: *5*) and *profiçia* (Bk. XVII, ch. 48: *172*); *vision* (Bk. XI, ch. 8: *23*) and *vesion* (BK. XI, ch. 23: *16*).

A peculiar development of OSp. phonology is the vacillation of the quality of the tonic and atonic vowels *o/u* and *e/i* of both regular and irregular verbs. The following examples may be cited: *dixieron* (Bk. V, ch. 67: *13*), *degistes* (Bk. XI, ch. 14: *36*); *fezistes* (Bk. XI, ch. 14: *37*), *fizieron* (Bk. I, ch. 1: *3*), *fezieron* (Bk. XI, ch. 9: *21*), *fiziese* (Bk. XI, ch. 14: *25*), *feziese* (Bk. XI, ch. 13: *10*), *feziere* (Bk. XI, ch. 18: *37*); *murio* (Bk. XI, ch. 16: *21*), *morio* (Bk. XI, ch. 1: *9*), *morieron* (Bk. XI, ch. 25: *3*), *moriese* (Bk. XI, ch. 17: *38*).

The expected development *u* < Latin atonic *u* does not occur in *cochillos* (from *cŭltĕllo*) (Bk. XVII, ch. 48: *166*).[73]

B. *Consonants*

In the MS the use of the graphs *b* and *v* (*u*) does not appear to reflect a phonemic distinction. In fact, the calligraphy of *b* and *v* is often nearly identical. The confusion, which was common in northern Spain,[74] is seen in such forms as *Bretaña* (Bk. X, ch. 15: *3*) beside *Vretaña* (Bk. X, ch. 15: *3–4*); *basteçieronse* (Bk. XI, ch. 2: *19*) but *vasteçimiento* (Bk. XI, ch. 5: *13*); *dAluion* (Bk. XI, ch. 9: *25*) beside *Albion* (Bk. XI, ch. 8: *14*); *marauillados* (Bk. XI, ch. 13: *29*) beside *maravillados* (Bk. XI, ch. 13: *31*).

Occasionally there is also confusion between the graphs *ç* and *z*, as in *donçella* (Bk. XI, ch. 5: *29*) and *donzellas* (Bk. XI, ch. 6: *12*). However, most historical phonologists hold that *ç* was pronounced [ts] and the *z* as [dz].[75]

In Spanish the use of the graph *h* for initial etymological *f* became widespread only after the phonetic change to zero [Ø] had already become commonplace.[76] In the fragments edited initial *f* dominates, although there are several cases of initial *h*, as in *hazer* < *făcĕre* (Bk. XI, ch. 21: *8*), *hito* < *fĭctus* (Bk. XVII, ch. 48: *51*). Learned influence often led to hypercorrection, and several examples of a non-etymological *h* are to be found in the text: *hedad* (Bk. XI, ch. 16: *10*), *heran* (Bk. XI, ch. 19: *19*), *hi* (Bk. XVII, ch. 48: *186*).

The use of the graphs *g, j, x,* and *y* varies considerably in the edited text. The graph *j* is frequently the sign for /i/ (and I transcribe it as *i*); and so is *y* occasionally, particularly in word-initial position: *Ynguelatierra* (Bk. I, ch. 1: *1*), *reynos* (Bk. I, ch. 1: *1*), *ystoria* (Bk. IV, ch. 54: *4*), *Ytalia* (Bk. IV, ch. 54: *10*), *ynfamia* (Bk. V, ch. 67: *20*), *syguiendo* (Bk. XI, ch. 7: *18*), *yndustria* (Bk. XVII, ch. 48: *203*). In OSp. an orthographic distinction was made between the voiceless palatal fricative [š], represented by *x*, and its voiced counterpart [ž] or [dž], as represented by *g* + *e* or *i*, and *j* (*i*) + *a*, *o*, or *u*. The confusion in orthography between *x*, *g*, and *j* is most likely due to the unvoicing of [ž].[77] The edited fragments consistently employ *x* in the various tenses of the verb *dexar* and in the preterite, pluperfect, and imperfect subjunctive of *dezir*. However, there is one case of a second person singular *degistes* (Bk. XI, ch. 14: *36*). Other vacillations are as follows: *mejores* (Bk. XI, ch. 19: *26*), *mexores* (Bk. XI, ch. 3: *20*); *linage* (Bk. XI, ch. 8: *16*), *linaje* (Bk. XVII, ch. 48: *141*); *acoger* (Bk. XVII, ch. 48: *175*), *acojer* (Bk. XVII, ch. 48: *21*).

Consonant clusters represent a particular problem in the development of Spanish from Latin. Spanish avoided, for example, the initial cluster *sc-*, although the Salazar text retains this combination in the toponym *Scoçia* (Bk. XI, ch. 10: *2*) alongside the preferred form *Escoçia* (Bk. XI, ch. 10: *8*). The -*nb*- combination in *anbos* (Bk. XI, ch. 14: *39*) is found together with its reduction to *m* in *amos* (Bk. XI, ch. 26: *29*). The tripartite cluster -*nbr*- is found in *onbros* (Bk. XI, ch. 9: *15*), *nonbre* (Bk. XI, ch. 10: *6*), and *fanbrientos* (Bk. XI, ch. 22: *26*); but only one case of *onbres* (Bk. XI, ch. 14: *22*) in favor of *omne* and *ome*. The problem of consonant clusters involving a nasal is complicated by the scribe's frequent use of the tilde for abbreviation.

The secondary cluster -*bd*-, alien to Latin and MSp, shows some vacillation in the edited text: *çibudad* (Bk. I, ch. 1: *2*), *çibdades* (Bk. IV, ch. 54: *9*); *codiçia* (Bk. XVII, ch. 48: *110*), *cobdiçia* (Bk. XI, ch. 7: *22*). The group -*pt*- is simplified in the semi-learned form *coRuçion* (from *corruptio*) (Bk. XVII, ch. 48: *228*). The -*nd*- cluster is found in *grand*, and, by analogy, a paragogic *d* is extended to *algund* (Bk. XVII, ch. 48: *75*), *ningund* (Bk. XI, ch. 26: *27*), and *segund* (Bk. XVII, ch. 48: *206*).

The substitution of *r* for *l*, normally a characteristic of western Ibero-Romance, is found in the form *robre* (Bk. XI, ch. 23: *8*) in the same column with *roble* (Bk. XI, ch. 23: *21*). Its presence in Salazar's adaptation of the Post-Vulgate *Merlin* text may be indicative of this text's provenance. The form *Bribia*, common in Alphonsine texts, appears once (Bk. XI, ch. 11: *19*). The confusion of voiced labials and velars is found in the substitution of *g* for *b* in the popular form *aguelo* (Bk. XI, ch. 12: *18*).

II. Morphology and Syntax

A. *Nouns*

The gender of several nouns in the edited text differs from that of the same nouns in MSp.: *la mi fin* (Bk. XI, ch. 25: *55*), *esa tu color* (Bk. XVII, ch. 48: *162*), *la mar* (Bk. XI, ch. 7: *6*). Such feminine forms are fairly typical of fifteenth-century Spanish.

B. *Adjectives*

There is no established pattern for the apocopation of *grande* before a noun; the form *grand* predominates, but a few examples of *gran* (Bk. XI, ch. 24: *11*) and *grande* (Bk. XI, ch. 8: *21*) are also found. *Alguno* and *ninguno* adopt a non-etymological *d* in place of the final *o*. The form *segund* is also common, but the edited text contains one example of *segun* (Bk. XVII, ch. 48: *226, n. 144*). The ordinal numbers *primero* and *terçero* are used in their whole forms, although the apocopated form *primer* is found on one occasion (Bk. XVII, ch. 48: *58*).

The short form of the possessive adjective is often preceded by an article, demonstrative or limiting adjective, as in *las sus çerbizes* (Bk. XI, ch. 3: *6*), *este mi estudio* (Bk. XVII, ch. 48: *40*), *otros tus enemigos* (Bk. XVII, ch. 48: *108*).

C. *Pronouns*

The stressed pronoun *vós* may be singular or plural, whereas *vosotros* is plural. Likewise, the unstressed form *vos* may be used with singular or plural meaning. The unstressed pronouns are often postverbal in the edited fragments, but no regular pattern emerges.

The position of enclitic pronouns has sometimes served as a clue to the provenance of medieval Hispanic texts.[78] For example, western texts, particularly Portuguese, are characterized by a high degree of interpolation, a phenomenon rare in northern Castile.[79] Thus the scarcity of examples in our text, written by a Vizcayan, should come as no surprise. Although the Hispanic Post-Vulgate *Roman du Graal* texts may all stem from an original translation in a western language, possibly Galician-Portuguese, the Salazar adaptation of this romance, so highly condensed and retold in the adaptor's own words, offers only a few examples of interpolation: *por que me vos fiziesedes matar* (Bk. XI, ch. 15: *44–45*), *que la no puede fallar ningund nabio* (Bk. XI, ch. 26: *27*). And the second example is from Salazar's own addition to the story of Arthur's death, the account of the Island of Brasil.

In future constructions there is still a tendency to separate the infinitive from the future auxiliary with a pronoun, as in *contarle ha* (Bk. XI, ch. 14: *64*), *enforcarse ha* (Bk. XI, ch. 14: *65*), *secarsele han* (Bk. XVII, ch. 48: *20*), etc.

The Latin syntactical combination dative *illi* + acc. *illum* yields *gelo* in some cases (Bk. XI, ch. 11: *14*, ch. 14: *35*, ch. 15: *49*, etc.), but the *se lo* combination predominates.

The alternation of *lo* and *le* as the third person masculine singular direct object pronoun, particularly when the referent is a male being, became common in OSp. The Salazar fragments provide several examples of such alternation within the same passage:

> commo [Jantus] vio que por el algo *lo* quisiesen matar, rogandoles con Dios que *lo* tomasen e non *le* matasen (Bk. V, ch. 67: *2-3*);

> E tobiendo*lo* por loco, mataron*le* e soterraron*le* mucho secreto (Bk. V, ch. 67: *6-7*);

> no tardo mucho que la tormenta *les* echase en tierra de Damasco.... abraçose con el capitan dellos e echo*lo* en la mar (Bk. XI, ch. 7: *4-10*).

The pronoun *quien* is invariable as singular and plural: *aquellos a quien vosotros matastes* (Bk. XI, ch. 4: *24*); *no sopiendo ellos quien era Merlin* (Bk. XI, ch. 17: *35*).[80]

D. *Verbs*

The edited text contains a wide range of verbal expression. Every tense, voice, and mood are represented.

The many passages of dialogue permit study of the use of second person and imperative forms. A puzzling feature of the syntax of these dialogues is the seemingly arbitrary alternation of *tú* and *vós* in direct address to an individual, when one would expect a distinction based upon different station or social rank. The alternation even occurs within the same speech. That such a phenomenon may be a deliberate stylistic device, to produce, for example, a dramatic effect, has been suggested for OFr., but the alternation in OSp. has received little study.[81] In the Salazar fragments, however, no clear stylistic preoccupation is apparent, and a comparison of the various dialogues with their sources or collateral versions produces no consistent pattern. For example, in the Brutus of Troy story, the Leomarte *Sumas* MSS contain an alternation of *tú* and *vós* in the following speech by Brutus to Pandraso: "Rey Pandraso, bien *sabedes* commo en pos de tantas premias fuertes que so el *tu* brauo sennorio..." (*Sumas*, ed. Rey, p. 329). The Salazar text uses only *tú*: "Rey Prandaso, bien *sabes tu* como despues de tantas e fuertes premias que so el *tu* brabo señorio..." (Bk. XI, ch. 5: *4–6*). But in a speech by Asaraco to Brutus the alternation is found in the *Sumas* MSS and the Salazar adaptation: "que seria bien que fuese pedida la fija Ynojenis del rey Pandraso para *vos* por muger...con la qual *tu serias* bien casado" (*Sumas*, ed. Rey, p. 330); "que Prandaso diese a su fija Ynomenis a *vos* por muger...con la qual *tu serias* bien casado" (Salazar, Bk. XI, ch. 5: *28–30*).

The dialogues in the Arthurian fragments also contain the *tú/vós* alternation. In the *Merlin* section, for example, Merlin addresses the judge in both second person singular and plural: "llamad a *vuestra* madre e a la mia e quatro onbres buenos del pueblo e alli respondere yo a *tu* madre e despues fagase como *quisieres*" (Bk. XI, ch. 14: *21–23*). The same occurs in corresponding passages in the other Spanish *Merlin* texts: Pietsch, *Fragments* 1: 73; Bohigas, 1498 *Baladro* 1: 44; Bonilla, 1535 *Baladro*, p. 9 (Chs. 20–21). But the texts differ in Merlin's address to his mother: Salazar employs *vós*, as do the 1498 and 1535 *Baladro* imprints (Bohigas 1: 40; Bonilla, p. 8*a* [Ch. 26]; the Salamanca MS. 1877 alternates [Pietsch, *Fragments* 1: 71]; the French Vulgate *Merlin* and the Post-Vulgate *Suite du Merlin* both use *tu* (Sommer, *Vulgate*, 2: 13; Huth *Merlin* 1: 21). No clear pattern emerges from these and other examples which could be cited. In the lengthy exegesis of the Merlin prophecy in Book XVII, the Salazar text and the MS versions of the *Crónica del rey don Pedro* coincide in having the king addressed in the second person singular in verb form as well as pronoun.

1. *Present Indicative*

The first person singular form *so<sum* is represented several times (Bk. XI, ch. 6: *30*, ch. 15: *26*, ch. 25: *31*), but *soy* is also found (Bk. XI, ch. 5: *20*). One instance of an apocopated verb form is found in *diz* (Bk. XVII, ch. 48: *65*), used as an impersonal.[82]

2. Preterite Indicative

In OSp. the verbs *tener, aver, estar, saber, placer,* and *andar* all
had *o* in the stem of the preterite, and this *o* is consistently used
with the preterite form throughout the edited text. Second person
plural preterites retain the etymological *-es* ending. The text has
two examples of the dialectal first person singular preterite form
fue (Bk. XI, ch. 6: *28, 31*) of the verb *ser.*[83]

3. Pluperfect Indicative

The consolidation of the present or imperfect of OSp. *aver* and
from the Latin pluperfect indicative is employed. The periphrastic
pluperfect shows the auxiliary verbs *aver* and *tener* struggling for
dominance.

4. Future and Conditional Indicative

The consolidation of the present or imperfect of OSp *aver* and
the infinitive to form the future and conditional tenses is the general pattern in the edited text, except occasionally where object
pronouns are involved (see "Pronouns," above, p. 26).

The edited text shows some vacillation in syncopated future
forms: *vernan* (Bk. XI, ch. 23: *23*), *terne* (Bk. XVII, ch. 48: *227*),
tenera (Bk. XI, ch. 4: *15*), *salira* (Bk. XI, ch. 14: *65*), *morra* (Bk.
XVII, ch. 48: *186*), *morira* (Bk. XI, ch. 16: *19*, ch. 21: *14*).

5. Future Subjunctive

The OSp. future subjunctive (the *-re* tense) goes back to the future
perfect indicative of Latin. It is commonly used in the text to ex-
press hypothetical and potential situations in the future. The Latin
pluperfect subjunctive form occurs as the imperfect subjunctive
(the *-se* tense).

6. Imperative

OSp. second person singular *sey* (Bk. XI, ch. 16: *18*) is replaced in
MSp by the analogical form *sé.*

7. *Past Participle*

One example of the OSp. *seydo* > MSp. *sido* is found in the edited text (Bk. XI, ch. 2: *13*).

8. *Present Participle*

The outstanding morphological feature of the Salazar text is its frequent use of "strong" preterite stems in the formation of present participles (e.g., *sopiendo, oviendo, quisiendo, toviendo, yoguiendo*), when used with adverbial force in opposition to the main action. This phenomenon is common in Navarro-Aragonese, but it is also found in texts from other regions of the Peninsula and in Judeo-Spanish.[84]

E. *Prepositions*

1. *Accusative "a"*

A characteristic of MSp. syntax is the use of the preposition *a* before the personal direct object of a verb. This accusative *a* is also found in OSp. but is used less consistently. In the edited fragments the *a* is often omitted, particularly if the noun object is indefinite or non-specific: *era de tal natura que no podria enpreñar muger* (Bk. XI, ch. 14: *34*); *fizo juntar sus estrolagos* (Bk. XI, ch. 15: *14*); *porque no dexaba quien la mantoviese* (Bk. XI, ch. 19: *32*); *ha de matar muchos buenos caballeros* (Bk. XI, ch. 24: *28–29*); *traxieran alli vn caballero muerto que dezian que era el rey* (Bk. XI, ch. 26: *16–17*). Omission is sometimes due to ligature with a following *a: saco dellos Adan e a Eva e a los otros* (Bk. XI, ch. 14: *51-52*); *E dio Artur a criar a su muger* (Bk. XI, ch. 17: *34–35*); *fizo luego quemar aquella su fija* (Bk. XI, ch. 22: *35*). This type of omission also occurs whenever the preposition *a* is followed by an indirect object beginning with *a: que des Asarato .x. quintales de oro* (Bk. XI, ch. 6: *10*); *dio por erençia Asaraco a Escoçia* (Bk. XI, ch. 10: 8).

2. *Passive voice: "de" and "por"*

In OSp. the agent in passive voice constructions is usually preceded by *de* but occasionally by *por*. In the Salazar text *de* is found more frequently, but *por* is sometimes used: *fueron apocados dellos por armas e dellos conbertidos a ser christianos* (Bk. X, ch. 3: *17–18*); *con falsedad me fagas morir cruel muerte despedaçado e comido de canes* (Bk. XI, ch. 22: *21–22*); *E fue acabado aquella demanda de las aventuras del Santo Greal por el santo Galaz* (Bk. XI, ch. 24: *43–44*).

3. Verbs + Preposition

Normally the verbs *ir, venir,* and *enbiar* take the preposition *a* before an infinitive, as in MSp. However, the Salazar text reveals some inconsistency in this regard:

> que se fuesen con el a poblar a Troya (Bk. XI, ch. 2: *18*); porque mas quisieran yr poblar a Troya (Bk. XI, ch. 8: *24–25*); algunos que lo vieron fueronlo dezir a los fieles (Bk. XI, ch. 18: *23–24*);

> E por aquello venian todas las animalias del mundo que calor avian ponerse a la su sonbra (Bk. XI, ch. 23: *9–11*); E las animalias que con el calor e frio se venian a poner so el senefica que vernan buscar la mi sabiduria (Bk. XI, ch. 23: *22–23*);

> los troyanos enbiaron demandar al rey Pandraso (Bk. XI, ch. 5: 1-2); te enbiaron a requerir que no quisieses que ellos tan largamente durasen en sujeçion (Bk. XI, ch. 5: *6–8*).

The OSp. verb *arribar* vacillates in taking *a* or *en* before a noun object: *e sus parientes aRibaron en Ynguelatierra* (Bk. X, ch. 22: *10–11*); *tormenta forçosa les echo en tierra de Africa cuydando aRibar a Troya* (Bk. XI, ch. 7: *13–14*).

F. Lexicon

The edited fragments offer but few unusual lexical items, and several of these may be attributable to Navarro-Aragonese influence upon the Castilian spoken in Salazar's native Vizcaya. For standard Spanish *normanes* 'Normans' and *Normandía* 'Normandy', Salazar uses the forms *lormanes* (Bk. X, ch. 3: *7*) and *Lormandia* (Bk. XI, ch. 9: *18*), the latter recorded in a fourteenth-century Navarro-Aragonese document.[85] Salazar's use of *flamenques* 'Flemings' instead of standard Spanish *flamencos* finds parallel in Catalan, and the same form is found in a fourteenth-century Aragonese text for 'flamingo, palmiped'.[86] A similar form, *flamanques* 'Flemings', is found in the *Gran conquista de Ultramar*, an early fourteenth-century Castilian text based primarily on French sources.[87] Salazar's expression for a prostitute, *mundaria publica* (Bk. XI, ch. 13: *10*), is uncommon, but the plural form, *mundarias publicas*, appears in the "Ordenamientos de D. Fernando de Antequera a Sevilla, de 1411 y 1412," along with the like expressions *mujeres mundarias*, *mançebas publicas*, and *mançebia publica*,[88] and I have observed *mundaria* and *muger mondaria* used in the same sense in surviving copies of the fifteenth-century Spanish translation of Quintus Curtius' life of Alexander the Great.[89] The adjectival form *artuxes*, in the expression *gatos artuxes* 'Arthur's cats' (Bk. XI, ch. 19: *14*), is, to my knowledge, unrecorded elsewhere in OSp., but it undoubtedly derives from the proper name *Artús* 'Arthur'.

Predictably, the Salazar text contains a number of lexical items which predate their earliest citation in the most respected but far from comprehensive Spanish etymological dictionary, Joan Corominas' *Diccionario crítico etimológico de la lengua castellana* (1954; rpt. ed., Berne 1970), 4 vols., and *Breve diccionario etimológico de la lengua castellana*, 3rd ed. (Madrid, 1973). For example, in Salazar's adaptation of the Brutus of Troy story from Leomarte's *Sumas*, he modernizes the language with forms which Corominas cites as appearing in texts of the late fifteenth and sixteenth centuries:

capitana 'vessel, ship, galley, boat' (Bk. XI, ch. 7: *8*); Corominas: ca. 1493

comarcanos, -as 'neighboring, bordering' (Bk. XI, ch. 8: *17*, ch. 9: *24*); Corominas: sixteenth-century[90]

deRamamiento 'spilling' (Bk. XI, ch. 8: *17–18*); Corominas: 1505

forasteros 'strangers, outsiders' (Bk. XI, ch. 8: *17*); Corominas: 1495

forçosa 'strong, heavy' (Bk. XI, ch. 7: *13*); Corominas: 1505

repartieron 'they divided' (Bk. XI, ch. 10: *2*); Corominas: 1490

Likewise, the Arthurian fragments contain forms which Corominas cites from the late fifteenth and sixteenth centuries, and, in one case, even the early seventeenth:

cansançio 'tiredness, fatigue' (Bk. XI, ch. 20: *6*); Corominas: 1495

desamando 'ceasing to love, detesting' (Bk. XI, ch. 23: *30*); Corominas: 1495 *descabalgando* 'dismounting' (Bk. XI, ch. 20: *5*); Corominas: 1495

descreçer 'dwindle, diminish in size' (Bk. XI, ch. 23: *13*); Corominas: ca. 1580

desesperaçion 'despair, desperation' (Bk. XI, ch. 22: *10*); Corominas: 1495

grandor 'size' (Bk. XI, ch. 20: *14*); Corominas: 1481

padron 'commemorative stone, marker' (Bk. XI, ch. 18: *8*); Corominas: 1605.[91]

THE METHOD OF EDITING

In transcribing the fragments of MS. 9-10-2/2100, I follow the generally accepted practice of North-American Hispanists in assuming that specialized texts such as the one at hand will be read and consulted by individuals sufficiently conversant with medieval manuscripts and their orthographic inconsistencies to make unnecessary the regularization of the labials *b* and *v* (*u*), the deletion of the cedilla in *ç* + *e* or *i,* and the accentuation of the text according to modern norms. However, for easier reading, I do regularize the use of *i* and *j,* when used as the sign for *i;* and I render the Tironian sign ꝫ as *e*. Word medial -*R*- is preserved in its upper case form, and initial *R*- is transcribed as a single *r*. Only one example of lower case *rr*- is to be found in the edited portion of the MS: *rrey* (Bk. XI, ch. 22: *5*). No distinction has been made between the various graphic variants of *s;* thus word-initial and word-medial long *s* or ſ and word-final -β and - ℓ have all been rendered as *s*. Initial double *s* occurs only once in the edited portion of the MS: *Ssigue* (Bk. XVII, ch. 48: *117*).

As far as possible, I resolve abbreviations and suppressions in accordance with the orthography of the scribe. The most common sign of suppression is that of the tilde, which the scribe uses in nearly every line for any letter or combination of letters he chooses to omit, e.g., *presiones* (Bk. X, ch. 3: *26*), *obispo* (Bk. X, ch. 22: *10*), *reliquias* (Bk. XI, ch. 3: *3*), *tienpos* (Bk. XI, ch. 7: *27*), *alcaldes* (Bk. XI, ch. 13: *12*), *cartas* (Bk. XI, ch. 26: *31*). The forms *coño, nõ,* and *nĵ* have been resolved as *commo, non,* and *nin,* respectively. The tilde may also be non-functional and merely decorative, e.g., *reỹ* (Bk. X, ch. 3: *21*), *muỹ* (Bk. XI, ch. 3: *4*), *menēster* (Bk. XI, ch. 3: 29–30).[92] A horizontal line through the vertical stroke of *p* is the abbreviation for *per-* or *par-,* e.g., *parte* (Bk. XI, ch. 1: *14*), *pero* (Bk.

XI, ch. 1: *22*), *perder* (Bk. XI, ch. 1: *23*), *para* (Bk. XI, ch. 2: *5*), *perteneçe* (Bk. XI, ch. 5: *22*), *desperto* (Bk. XI, ch. 20: *10*), *partir* (Bk. XI, ch. 24: *20*), *Persibal* (Bk. XI, ch. 24: *46*). Other auxiliary signs have been resolved as follows:

x̄p : chri*stianos* (Bk. X, ch. 3: *9*), Chri*sto* (Bk. XI, ch. 11: *4*)

x̧ : chri*stianos* (Bk. XI, ch. 3: *12*)

º = *o* in reduced superscript: *titulo* (Bk. IX, ch. 8: *1*), *hermano* (Bk. X, ch. 15: *10*), -*miento* (Bk. XI, ch. 2: *6*), *ninguno* (Bk. XI, ch. 18: *8*), *testimonio* (Bk. XI, ch. 22: *25*), *Juan* (Bk. XI, ch. 30: *1*), *Alfonso* (Bk. XVII, ch. 48: *73*), *alguno* (Bk. XVII, ch. 48: *157*), *profiçias* (Bk. XVII, ch. 48: *207*) *enero* (Bk. XVII, ch. 48: *228*). The mark is also used with Roman numerals in temporal expressions: *.ccco.º años* (Bk. XI, ch. 19: *3*), *viij.º dias* (Bk. XI, ch. 23: *32*)

Ӿ : ver*dad* (Bk. XI, ch. 1: *21*), *aver* (Bk. XI, ch. 3: *9*), *vergueña* (Bk. XI, ch. 5: *19*), *ver* (Bk. XI, ch. 14: *13*), ver*dad* (Bk. XI, ch. 14: *26*), *Vertiguo* (Bk. XI, ch. 15: *7*), *avergoñado* (Bk. XI, ch. 18: *26*), ver*nan* (Bk. XI, ch. 23: *23*), ver*tud* (Bk. XI, ch. 25: *48*)

ẞ : *seria* (Bk. XI, ch. 5: *25*), *serbiçio* (Bk. XI, ch. 14: *61*), *ser* (Bk. XI, ch. 22: *16*), *servido* (Bk. XI, ch. 25: *41*), *serbidor* (Bk. XI, ch. 25: *59*)

9 : *Jantus* (Bk. V, ch. 67: *1*), *Gajusete* (Bk. XI, ch. 12: *9*), *En-cobus* (Bk. XI, ch. 14: *55*), *Ejeus* (Bk. XI, ch. 16: *14*)

In capitalization and punctuation I follow modern norms. Likewise, graphic word divisions are resolved according to present-day criteria. The proper names *Ihesu Christo* and *Elisa Dido* are rendered as two words, although they appear as one in the MS. The adverbial suffix -*mente*, separated in the MS, is transcribed with the adjective form as one word. Expressions such as *aunque, comoquier, malfechores*, and *adonde*, usually separated in the MS, are also rendered as one word. Enclitic pronouns are generally joined to the verbs on which they depend. Elided forms are transcribed exactly as they appear in the MS (e.g., *dErlanda, dellas, del, quel, antel*, etc.). Roman numerals are placed in lower case ·with a period mark before and after as usually practiced by the scribe; final *j* for *I* is maintained, but the reduced superscript *o* omitted.

The beginning of each manuscript column is indicated within the body of the text by diagonal bars. The book and chapter divisions found in the MS are preserved, their numbers indicated within brackets. The division into paragraphs is my own.

In editing the text various emendations have been made for improved reading. Material added without paleographical justification is placed in italics. Scribal errors, deletions, and emendations that are not self-evident are explained in the paleographical notes. Where sources or analogous versions help to clarify garbled passages, citations of these texts are included in the commentary which follows the transcription.

I include in the paleographical notes significant variants from Madrid, Biblioteca Nacional, MS. 1634 (represented by the siglum *N*), which, although based on the Cristóbal de Mieres codex (represented by *A*), corrects some of its more conspicuous errors. In the case of Merlin's prophecy in book XVII, where the MS has obvious haplography, garbling, and nonsensical readings, I have added a number of words and altered others based upon variant readings from the many collateral MSS of Pero López de Ayala's *Crónica del rey don Pedro* as recently edited by Dr. Constance Lee Wilkins.[93]

Since the edited fragments represent only parts of chapters and books of the *Bienandanzas e fortunas*, I include for purposes of clarity and continuity brief transitional statements concerning the general nature of the deleted material.

NOTES

[1]The The first seven *títulos* or chapters of the *Crónica de Vizcaya*, written in 1454, have been edited by Juan Carlos de Guerra, "Crónica de Siete casas de Vizcaya y Castilla escrita por Lope García de Salazar, año de 1454," *Revista de Historia y de Genealogía Española* 3 (1914): 24–30, 66–71, 130–34, 171–73, 218–22, 258–60. Guerra based his edition on a fifteenth-century MS copy requested by one Juan Rodríguez Calvo, in the archive of the Casa de Salazar in Portugalete. An incomplete seventeenth-century copy containing eleven *títulos* is found in Madrid, Biblioteca Nacional, MS. 2430 (*olim* J.-J.Y.), fols. 116ʳ–128ᵛ. Two other MSS have been falsely ascribed as the *Crónica de Vizcaya:* Madrid, Biblioteca Nacional, MS. 11639 (*olim* Z-71), actually a copy of a chronicle dated 1577 which used the Salazar text as one of its sources; Madrid, Biblioteca Nacional, MS. 3440 (*olim* K-170), fols. 119ʳ–191ᵛ, an incomplete seventeenth-century copy of Books XXI and XXII of the *Bienandanzas e fortunas*. Also attributed to Salazar is a now lost *Crónica de Vizcaya*, said to have been printed in the reign of Carlos V by the chronicler Antonio de Varaona (see Guerra, "Crónica de Siete casas," p. 25).

The *Libro de las bienandanzas e fortunas*, compiled between 1471 and 1476, survives in a number of MS copies (see below, n. 68) and has been edited by Angel

Rodríguez Herrero, *Las bienandanzas e fortunas,* 4 vols, (Bilbao, 1967). In citing specific passages from the *Bienandanzas,* I follow my own transcription but refer the reader to corresponding plates ("folios") in Rodríguez Herrero's photographic reproduction of the earliest surviving MSS: the 1492 copy made by Cristóbal de Mieres, Madrid, Real Academia de la Historia, MS. 9-10-2/2100 (*olim* 12-10-6/17), hereafter represented by the siglum *A*; and a sixteenth-century copy based on the Mieres codex but preserving prefatory material which it is now lacking, Madrid, Biblioteca Nacional, MS. 1634 (*olim* G-4), referred to as *N*.

[2]*A,* fol. 417b; Herrero, *Las bienandanzas,* 4: 133. For an analysis of these feuds, see J. C. de Guerra, *Oñacinos y gamboínos: Rol de banderizos vascos, con la mención de las familias pobladoras de Bilbao en los siglos XIV y XV* (San Sebastián, 1930); J. Caro Baroja, *Linajes y bandos: A propósito de la nueva edición de "Las bienandanzas e fortunas"* (Bilbao, 1956). J. Vicens Vives places the factional disputes in broad historical perspective in *Aproximación a la historia de España,* 3rd ed. (Barcelona, 1962), pp. 103-13. See also R. B. Tate in his prologue to Fernán Pérez de Guzmán, *Generaciones y semblanzas* (London, 1965), pp. vii-x; and L. Suárez Fernández, "Los trastámaras de Castilla y Aragón en el siglo XV (1407-74)," in *Historia de España,* ed. R. Menéndez Pidal (Madrid, 1935-), 15: 11-22.

[3]*A,* fol. 417d; Herrero, *Las bienandanzas,* 4: 134.

[4]*A,* fols. 421a-422a; Herrero, *Las bienandanzas,* 4: 141-43.

[5]*A,* fol. 424a-b; Herrero, *Las bienandanzas,* 4: 147.

[6]*A,* fol. 424a-c; Herrero, *Las bienandanzas,* 4: 147-48.

[7]*A,* fol. 375c-d; Herrero, *Las bienandanzas,* 4: 50. Additional details are found in the *Crónica de Vizcaya.* See MS. 2430, fols. 122^v-123^r, and a variant reading in Herrero, *Las bienandanzas,* 1: xvii-xviii.

[8]*A,* fol. 425b-c; Herrero, *Las bienandanzas,* 4: 149-50.

[9]*A,* fol. 398a; Herrero, *Las bienandanzas,* 4: 95.

[10] *A,* fol. 425c; Herrero, *Las bienandanzas,* 4: 150.

[11]*A,* fol. 399a; Herrero, *Las bienandanzas,* 4: 97.

[12]*N,* fol. 2^r; Herrero, *Las bienandanzas,* 1: 1.

[13]The summons, found in the Registro General del Sello, Archivo General de Simancas, is published by Herrero, *Las bienandanzas,* 1: xii-xvii.

[14]Selected passages from Valladolid, Archivo de la Real Cancillería, Pleitos de Vizcaya, *legajo* 672, have been published by D. de Areitio, "De la prisión y muerte de Lope García de Salazar," *Revue Internationale des Etudes Basques* 17 (1926): 9-16.

[15]In the *Bienandanzas* we learn of Juan de Salazar's violent reaction at the theft of one of his own mistresses: "En el año del Señor de .mccccl333j. años mataron a Juan, fijo de Sancho Louo... porquel leuo vna mançeua de Juan de Salazar, e dixose quel lo matara" (*A,* fol. 429c; Herrero, *Las bienandanzas,* 4: 158).

[16]Areitio, "De la prisión y muerte," p. 13.

[17]Areitio, "De la prisión y muerte," p. 15.

[18]See J. de Ibarra and E. Calle Iturrino, *La tumba de Lope García de Salazar en San Martín de Muñatones* (Bilbao, 1956), p. 34.

[19]Guerra, "Crónica de Siete casas," pp. 25-26. On the continuation of this tradition in fifteenth-century Castile, see María Rosa Lida de Malkiel, *La idea de la fama en la Edad Media castellana* (Mexico, 1952), pp. 230, 238 et passim.

[20]A, fol. 7c; Herrero, *Las bienandanzas,* 1: 10.

[21]A, fol. 7c; Herrero, *Las bienandanzas,* 1: 10.

[22]N, fol. 4ᵛ; Herrero, *Las bienandanzas,* 1: 6.

[23]Guerra, "Crónica de Siete casas," p. 26.

[24]A, fol. 7c; Herrero, *Las bienandanzas,* 1: 10.

[25]A, fol. 7c; Herrero, *Las bienandanzas,* 1: 10.

[26]A, fol. 7c; Herrero, *Las bienandanzas,* 1: 10. Cf. Don Juan Manuel, *El Conde Lucanor o Libro de los enxiemplos del Conde Lucanor et de Patronio,* ed. José Manuel Blecua, Clásicos Castalia, 9 (Madrid, 1969), pp. 47–48. There also exists the possibility that such statements on the causes of textual corruption may have become a topos in medieval prologues, deriving perhaps ultimately from verses by Martial. See Alan Deyermond, "Editors, Critics, and *El Conde Lucanor,*" *RPh* 31 (1978): 618, n. 1; and Sesto Prete, *Observations on the History of Textual Criticism in the Medieval and Renaissance Periods* (Collegeville, Minn., n.d.), p. 5. For a general study of the medieval Spanish prologue, see Alberto Porqueras Mayo, "Notas sobre la evolución histórica del prólogo en la literatura medieval castellana," *Revista de Literatura* 11 (1957): 186–94; and Margo Ynes Corona de Ley, "The Prologue in Castilian Literature between 1200 and 1400" (Diss., University of Illinois, Urbana, 1976).

[27]Menéndez Pidal overlooks a passage on Roncesvalles within Salazar's history of the kings of France, Bk. IX, ch. 14 (A, fol. 164c-d; Herrero, *Las bienandanzas,* 2: 90).

[28]While praising the rigorous scholarship of Deyermond and other scholars who, based upon a careful reading of the surviving poems and fragments, advocate an essentially individualist theory regarding the origin and diffusion of medieval Spanish epic poetry, Armistead chides some of these same scholars and their followers for ignoring or failing to take into account the abundant evidence of oral tradition in the chronicles, including the *Bienandanzas,* and in the *Romancero.* See his article, "The *Mocedades de Rodrigo* and Neo-individualist Theory," *HR* 46 (1978): 313–27.

[29]For general background concerning Geoffrey of Monmouth and his works, see J. J. Parry and R. A. Caldwell, "Geoffrey of Monmouth," in *Arthurian Literature in the Middle Ages,* ed. R. S. Loomis (Oxford, 1959; rpt. ed., 1961), pp. 72–93. The Loomis volume is hereafter referred to as *ALMA.*

[30]See W. J. Entwistle, "Geoffrey of Monmouth and Spanish Literature," *MLR* 17 (1922): 381–83, and *The Arthurian Legend in the Literatures of the Spanish Peninsula* (1925; rpt. ed., New York, 1975), p. 36. Entwistle's book was translated into Portuguese by António Alvaro Dória with a few modifications by the author, *A lenda arturiana nas literaturas da Península Ibérica* (Lisbon, 1942).

[31]The Alphonsine material may be found in *General estoria, Segunda parte,* ed. A. G. Solalinde, L. A. Kasten, and V. R. B. Oelschläger (Madrid, 1957–61), 2: 264–78 (Chs. 53–73). On the use of Geoffrey's *Historia* in the works of Alfonso el Sabio, see Lloyd Kasten, "The Utilization of the *Historia Regum Britanniae* by Alfonso X," in *Studies in Memory of Ramón Menéndez Pidal, HR* 38, No. 5 (1970): 97–114. Leomarte's *Sumas* has been edited by Agapito Rey, *RFE,* Anejo 15 (Madrid, 1932). The work was also intercalated with Ovid's *Heroides* in an incunabulum printed at Burgos in 1490. See T. Beardsley, *Hispano-Classical Translations*

(Philadelphia, 1970), pp. 3, 22; and Anthony Cárdenas et al., *Bibliography of Old Spanish Texts,* 2nd ed. (Madison, Wis., 1977), No. 1216.

[32]*El Victorial: Crónica de don Pero Niño, Conde de Buelna por su alférez Gutierre Díez de Games,* ed. J. de Mata Carriazo (Madrid, 1940), pp. 142-77.

[33]*Sumas,* ed. Rey, p. 31, n. 1.

[34]For a general discussion of the *Brut,* see C. Foulon, "Wace," in *ALMA,* pp. 94-103.

[35]The life and works of Chrétien are discussed by J. Frappier, "Chrétien de Troyes," in *ALMA,* pp. 157-91.

[36]See E. Hoepffner, "The Breton Lais," in *ALMA,* pp. 112-21; H. Newstead, "The Origin and Growth of the Tristan Legend," in *ALMA,* pp. 122-33.

[37]*Le Roman de l'Estoire dou Graal,* ed. W. A. Nitze, CFMA, 57 (Paris, 1927). See P. Le Gentil, "The Work of Robert de Boron and the *Didot Perceval,*" in *ALMA,* pp. 251-62.

[38]Edited by A. Hilka as *Des Percevalroman (Li Contes del Graal),* Halle, 1932; and by W. Roach as *Le Roman de Perceval ou Le Conte du Graal,* 2nd ed., TLF, 71 (Geneva-Paris, 1959).

[39]The modern editions of the *Vita Merlini* are by J. J. Parry, University of Illinois Studies in Language and Literature, Vol. 10, No. 3 (Urbana, Ill., 1925); and by Basil Clarke, *The Life of Merlin* (Cardiff, 1973).

[40]*Vulgate Version of the Arthurian Romances,* 8 vols. (1908-16; rpt. ed., New York, 1969). Some of the branches of the Vulgate Cycle have been edited separately (see notes 41-45, below). For a general study of the cycle, see J. Frappier, "The Vulgate Cycle," in *ALMA,* pp. 295-318.

[41]Besides Sommer's edition, the *Estoire del Saint Graal* has been edited by E. Hucher, who used Le Mans MS. 354: *Le Saint Graal ou le Joseph d'Arimathie...,* 3 vols. (Le Mans, 1874-78); and by F. J. Furnivall, based on British Library, MS. Royal 14 E. iii: *Seynt Graal, or the Sank Ryal...,* 2 vols. (London, 1861-63).

[42]Alexandre Micha has announced his preparation of a new edition of the Vulgate *Merlin.*

[43]Sommer's edition is now superseded, except for the first part of the *Lancelot* proper, by Alexandre Micha's edition: *Lancelot: Roman en prose du XIIIe siècle,* 2 vols., TLF, 247, 249 (Paris-Geneva, 1978). The beginning of the *Lancelot* was edited by students of E. Wechssler, in *Marburger Beiträge zur romanischen Philologie* (1911-17). Dr. Elspeth Kennedy has completed a new edition of the first part (Oxford: Clarendon, forthcoming). The so-called "Charrette" portion has been edited by G. Hutchings, *Le Roman en prose de Lancelot du Lac: Le Conte de la Charrette* (1938; rpt. ed., Geneva, 1974).

[44]Besides Sommer's edition, the *Queste* has been edited by F. J. Furnivall (London, 1864), and by A. Pauphilet, CFMA, 33 (Paris, 1923; rpt. ed., 1967).

[45]The *Mort Artu* has been edited separately by J. D. Bruce, *Mort Artu: An Old French Prose Romance of the XIIIth Century...* (Halle, 1910); and by J. Frappier, *La Mort le Roi Artu: Roman du XIIIe siècle,* TLF, 58 (Geneva-Paris, 1956).

[46]"The Suite du Merlin and the Post-Vulgate *Roman du Graal,*" in *ALMA,* pp. 331-32; and *The Romance of the Grail* (Manchester-New York, 1966), pp. 10-11.

[47]See remarks by J. D. Bruce, *Evolution of the Arthurian Romance from the Beginnings down to the Year 1300,* 2nd ed. (1928; rpt. ed., Gloucester, Mass.,

1958), 1: 458–79; and by Frappier, "The Vulgate Cycle," in *ALMA*, p. 318.

[48]*The Romance of the Grail*, pp. 5–22.

[49]For a synthesis of the development of Hispanic Arthurian literature, see M. R. Lida de Malkiel, "Arthurian Literature in Spain and Portugal," in *ALMA*, pp. 406–18, which has been reissued in its original Spanish version in *Estudios de literatura española y comparada* (Buenos Aires, 1966), pp. 134–48. See also my entry on the *Ciclo Bretão* in Portugal, in *Grande dicionário da literatura portuguesa e de teoria literária* (Lisbon: Iniciativas Editoriais, in press), and my *A Critical Bibliography of Hispanic Arthurian Material, 1*: Texts: *The Prose Romance Cycles*, Research Bibliographies and Checklists, 3 (London: Grant & Cutler, 1977).

[50]Henry Hare Carter prefers the year 1314. See his introduction to *The Portuguese Book of Joseph of Arimathea*, UNCSRLL, 71 (Chapel Hill, 1967), pp. 38–40.

[51]Concerning the extremely complex question of priority of translation, see M. Rodrigues Lapa, *A Demanda do Santo Graal: Prioridade do texto português* (Lisbon, 1930); P. Bohigas, *Los textos españoles y gallego-portugueses de la Demanda del Santo Grial*, RFE, Anejo 7 (Madrid, 1925), pp. 56, 81–94; Bohigas' review of the Lapa book, *RFE* 20 (1933): 180–85, and his edition of the *Baladro del Sabio Merlín* (Barcelona, 1957–62), 3: 189–93; Entwistle, *The Arthurian Legend*, pp. 7–27; C. E. Pickford, "La Priorité de la version portugaise de la *Demanda do Santo Graal*," *BHi* 63 (1961): 211–16; R. J. Steiner, "*Domaa/Demanda* and the Priority of the Portuguese *Demanda*," *Modern Philology* 64 (1966): 64–67; and the studies by F. Bogdanow, "The Relationship of the Portuguese *Josep Abarimatia* to the Extant French MSS of the *Estoire del Saint Graal*," *ZRPh* 76 (1960): 343–74, *The Romance of the Grail*, Chs. 2 and 7, "An Attempt to Classify the Extant Texts of the Spanish *Demanda del Sancto Grial*," in *Studies in Honor of Tatiana Fotitch* (Washington, D.C., 1972), pp. 213–26, "Old Portuguese *seer em car teudo* and the Priority of the Portuguese *Demanda do Santo Graal*," *RPh* 28 (1974): 48–51, and "The Relationship of the Portuguese and Spanish *Demandas* to the Extant French Manuscripts of the Post-Vulgate *Queste del Saint Graal*," *BHS* 52 (1975): 13–32. The weight of the evidence points to a western origin, possibly Galician-Portuguese. Curiously, the Spanish version of the Vulgate *Lancelot* proper, as it survives in a sixteenth-century MS copy, Madrid, Biblioteca Nacional 9611 (*olim* Aa-103), also reveals strong linguistic evidence of an occidental origin, as I pointed out in a paper presented to the V? Congreso de la Asociación de Hispanistas, Bordeaux, France, September 1974.

[52]Early versions of the poem are edited by W. Suchier, "Ueber das altfranzösische Gedicht von der Zerstörung Jerusalems *(La Venjance nostre seigneur),*" *ZRPh* 24 (1900): 161–98; Loyal A. T. Gryting, *The Oldest Version of the Twelfth-Century Poem "La Venjance Nostre Seigneur,"* University of Michigan Contributions in Modern Philology, 19 (Ann Arbor, 1952); and Melitta S. Gahlbeck Buzzard, "*Cest li romanz de la vanjance que Vaspasiens et Tytus ses fiz firent de la mort Jhesucrist*, édition manuscrit 5201, Bibliothèque de l'Arsenal, Paris" (Diss., University of Colorado, 1970).

[53]Three early Hispanic printings of the prose romance contain material relating Joseph of Arimathea to the Arthurian legend: *La estoria de Vaspasiano emperador de Roma* (Toledo: Juan Vázquez, ca. 1492); *Estoria de muy nobre Uespesiano em-*

perador de Roma (Lisbon: Valentim da Morávia, 1496); *La ystoria del noble Uespesiano emperador de Roma* (Seville: Pedro Brun, 1499). The Toledo incunabulum has been edited by David Hook, "A Critical Edition of *La estoria del noble Vaspasiano enperador de Rroma* with a Literary and Historical Study including an Account of the Transmission of the Text" (Thesis, Oxford University, 1977); the Lisbon by F. M. Esteves Pereira, *Historia de Vespasiano, Imperador de Roma* (Lisbon, 1905); and the Seville by R. Foulché-Delbosc, *"Ystoria del noble Vespesiano," RHi* 21 (1909): 567–634.

[54]The tale of Ibycus is from the *Libro de los buenos proverbios,* one of several thirteenth-century Spanish translations of Arabic gnomic tracts. Two modern editions exist: Hermann Knust, *Mittheilungen aus dem Eskurial,* Bibliothek des litterarischen Vereins in Stuttgart, 141 (Tübingen, 1879), pp. 1–65; Harlan Sturm, *The "Libro de los buenos proverbios": A Critical Edition,* Studies in Romance Languages, 5 (Lexington, Ky., 1970).

[55]"The Passing of King Arthur to the Island of Brasil in a Fifteenth-Century Spanish Version of the Post-Vulgate *Roman du Graal,*" *Romania* 92 (1971): 65–73.

[56]Cf. Bonilla, 1535 *Demanda,* p. 330a (Ch. 334); Magne, Ptg. *Demanda,* 2: §680. The Vulgate *Mort Artu* provides a similar description of Arthur's passing (J. Frappier ed., §1193).

[57]Arthur is borne to Avalon in two Hispanic universal chronicles: the thirteenth-century Navarrese *Libro de las generaciones* and the fourteenth-century Portuguese *Livro das linhagens* or *Nobiliário* of Don Pedro, Conde de Barcelos, both edited by Diego Catalán and María Soledad de Andrés, in *Edición crítica del texto español de la Crónica de 1344 que ordenó el Conde de Barcelos don Pedro Alfonso* (Madrid, 1971–), 1: 283. The geographic vagueness of water crossings in traditional Arthurian literature is pointed out by G. Ashe, *Land to the West* (New York, 1962), p. 311. On the vanishing island motif, see H. R. Patch, *The Other World* (Cambridge, Mass., 1950), p. 27 ff.; A. C. L. Brown, *The Origin of the Grail Legend* (1943; rpt. ed., New York, 1966), pp. 14–90; G. Schoepperle, "Arthur in Avalon and the Banshee," in *Vassar Medieval Studies* (New Haven, 1932), pp. 3–25.

[58]Bogdanow, *The Romance of the Grail,* pp. 8–10.

[59]The *Tristan en prose* has been partially edited by R. D. Curtis, *Le Roman de Tristan en prose,* 1 (Munich, 1963), 2 (Leiden, 1976); and another MS version by F. C. Johnson, *La Grant Ystoire de Monsignor Tristan "Li Brut"* (Edinburgh–London, 1942). See also the comprehensive analysis of the romance by E. Löseth, *Le Roman en prose de Tristan* (1891; rpt. ed., New York, 1970). The surviving Spanish Prose *Tristan* texts are as follows: Madrid, Biblioteca Nacional, MS. 20262 (No. 19), a late fourteenth-century fragment edited by Adolfo Bonilla y San Martín, "Fragmento de un *Tristán* castellano del siglo XIV," in *Anales de literatura española* (Madrid, 1904), pp. 25–28; Vatican MS. 6428, a late fourteenth or early fifteenth-century version in Castilian and Aragonese, edited by George Tyler Northup, *El cuento de Tristán de Leonís* (Chicago, 1928); Madrid Biblioteca Nacional, MS. 22021, fols. 8^v–12^v, unedited late fifteenth- or early sixteenth-century Castilian fragments; *Libro del esforçado cavallero don Tristán de Leonís y de sus grandes fechos en armas (Valladolid, 1501),* ed. Adolfo Bonilla y San Martín, Sociedad de Bibliófilos Madrileños, 6 (Madrid, 1912); *Libro del es-*

forçado cavallero don Tristán de Leonís y de sus grandes hechos en armas [Seville, 1528], ed. Adolfo Bonilla y San Martín, in *Libros de caballerías*, 1: *Ciclo artúrico–Ciclo carolingio*, NBAE, 6 (Madrid, 1907), pp. 339–457; *Coronica neuvamente emendada y añadida del buen cavallero don Tristán de Leonís y del rey don Tristán de Leonís, el joven su hijo* (Seville: Domenico de Robertis, 1534). Fragments also exist in Galician-Portuguese and Catalan: Madrid, Archivo Histórico Nacional, *legajo* 1762 (no. 8$\frac{1}{-}$), a late fourteenth-century Galician-Portuguese version containing material lacking in other Peninsular Tristan texts, edited by José L. Pensado Tomé, *Fragmento de un "Livro de Tristan" galaico-portugués*, Cuadernos de Estudios Gallegos, Anejo 14 (Santiago de Compostela, 1962); a fourteenth-century Catalan MS fragment in the Arxiu d'Andorra, edited by R. Aramon i Serra, "El *Tristany* català d'Andorra," in *Mélanges offerts à Rita Jejeune* (Gembloux, 1969), 1: 323–37; and a late fourteenth-century Catalan fragment in the Arxiu Municipal of Cervera, edited by A. Duran i Sanpere, "Un fragment de Tristany de Leonis en català," in *Estudis Romànics (Llengua i Literatura)*, Biblioteca Filològica de l'Institut de la Llengua Catalana, 9 (Barcelona, 1917), 2: 284–316.

[60]For many years the only available edition has been that prepared in the eighteenth century by E. Llaguno y Amirola (Madrid, 1779–80), and reprinted in BAE, Vol. 66, pp. 393–614. Constance Lee Wilkins has recently prepared a new edition based on the Madrid, Real Academia de la Historia, MS. 9–26–1/4765 (*olim* A-14), with variant readings from most of the other extant MS versions: "An Edition of the *Corónica del rey don Pedro* by Pero López de Ayala based on manuscript A-14 of the Academia de la Historia," (Diss., Univ. of Wisconsin, 1974).

[61]On the *Prophetiae Merlini*, see Parry and Caldwell, "Geoffrey of Monmouth," in *ALMA*, pp. 75–79.

[62]*El Poema de Alfonso XI*, ed. Yo Ten Cate (Madrid, 1956), Sts. 1810–47.

[63]See D. Catalán, *Un cronista anónimo del siglo XIV* (La Laguna, Canarias, n.d.), pp. 89–91.

[64]Bonilla, 1535 *Baladro*, pp. 19a–22b, 155a–162b. Concerning these prophecies and early Catalan and Castilian MS versions, see Pedro Bohigas, "La 'visión de Alfonso X' y 'profecías de Merlín,'" *RFE* 25 (1941): 383–98.

[65]On Ayala's use of the prophecies, see M. Menéndez Pelayo, *Orígenes de la novela*, Edición Nacional (Santander, 1943), 1: 280–81; Entwistle, "Geoffrey of Monmouth," p. 39, and *The Arthurian Legend*, pp. 54–55; R. B. Tate, "López de Ayala, Humanist Historian?," *HR* 25 (1957): 164; Joaquín Gimeno Casalduero, "La profecía medieval en la literatura castellana y su relación con las corrientes proféticas europeas," *NRFH* 20 (1971): 64–89, and *La imagen del monarca en la Castilla del siglo XV* (Madrid, 1972), pp. 130–31.

[66]Concerning this topos of medieval rhetoric, see E. R. Curtius, *European Literature and the Latin Middle Ages*, trans. Willard R. Trask (1953; rpt. ed., New York, 1963), pp. 487–94.

[67]See Bogdanow, *The Romance of the Grail*, Appendix 2, pp. 261–70.

[68]A number of later copies survive, all apparently derived from the Cristóbal de Mieres codex. Four were made in the sixteenth century: Madrid, Biblioteca Nacional, MS. 1634 (*olim* G-4), and MS. 625 (*olim* G-3); Biblioteca de El Escorial, MS. &.II.12, fols. 13^r–292^r; Salamanca, Biblioteca Universitaria, MS. 2024 (*olim*

Madrid, Biblioteca Real de Palacio, 25; *olim* 2-B-2). One copy survives from the seventeenth century: Madrid, Biblioteca Nacional, MS. 3440 (*olim* K-170), fols. 119[r]-191[v]; and three from the eighteenth: Madrid, Biblioteca Nacional, MSS. 10339-40; Valladolid, Biblioteca Universitaria de Santa Cruz, MS. 7 (*olim* 209), fols. 11[r]-152[v], and MS. 131 (*olim* 133). Of these eight MSS, only MS. 1634 is complete. Another early MS copy has recently come to light: a copy of the last books made by Gonzalo Fernández de Oviedo, in the private Madrid library of D. José María de Areilza, Conde de Montrico (see "Mi biblioteca," *Los Domingos de ABC,* 24 December 1972, pp. 10–11). A version of the *Bienandanzas* (a MS copy?) in the Seville, Biblioteca Colombina, is cited by Gonzalo Moya, *Don Pedro el Cruel: Biología política y tradición literaria en la figura de Pedro I de Castilla* (Madrid, 1974), pp. 83–84.

[69]"Aqui se acauan los .xxv. libros que fizo Lope Garçia de Salazar estando preso en la su casa de Sant Martin e escreuiole e acauole Cristoual de Mieres en el año del Señor de mill y quatroçientos y nouenta y dos en el mes de abril a dias andados del dicho mes diez y seys. A Dios sean dadas muchas graçias por sienpre sin fin. Amen. DEO GRATIAS. E fue este dicho libro mandado escriuir e tresladar por el señor Ochoa de Salazar, proboste de Portogulete, fijo mayor de Lope de Salazar e nieto del dicho Lope Garçia e tresladose del registo que dexo el dicho Lope Garçia no le podiendo acauar en su vida segund por el oreginal pareçe o fue quitado parte del" (*A*, fol. 448d; Herrero, *Las bienandanzas,* 4: 196).

[70]Normally, at the conclusion of each book the scribe states the number of folios completed. At the end of Book I, for example, he gives the number ".xix.," which corresponds to the Roman numeral applied to that folio.

[71]See portions of the MS edited by Menéndez Pidal, "Roncesvalles," pp. 200–204; Bohigas, *Los textos,* pp. 130–33; and Armistead, *A Lost Version,* pp. 315–16, "Las *Mocedades de Rodrigo . . .*," pp. 307–11.

[72]See Antonio Trueba's unpaginated introduction to *Las bienandanzas e fortunas,* ed. M. Camarón (Madrid, 1884).

[73]On the development of this form, see R. Menéndez Pidal, *Manual de gramática histórica española,* 11th ed. (Madrid, 1962), §§14.2d, 20.2.

[74]See Rafael Lapesa, *Historia de la lengua española,* 4th ed. (Madrid, 1959), p. 147; on the articulation of *b* and *v,* see Amado Alonso, *De la pronunciación medieval a la moderna en español,* 2nd ed. (Madrid, 1967), 1, Ch. 1.

[75]See Alonso, 1, Ch. 3; and Lapesa, pp. 190–91.

[76]Menéndez Pidal points out that in northern Old Castile initial *f* was an aspirate from very early times, *Orígenes del español,* 5th ed. (Madrid, 1964), § 41.2. See also Lapesa, pp. 27–28.

[77]For an early study of the development, see H. Gavel, *Essai sur l'évolution de la pronunciation du castillan* (Paris, 1920), pp. 457–71.

[78]See H. Ramsden, *Weak-Pronoun Position in the Early Romance Languages* (Manchester, 1963), Chs. 4, 5.

[79]Ramsden, p. 134.

[80]The plural form *quienes* developed in the sixteenth century. See Menéndez Pidal, *Manual,* § 101.

[81]Elspeth Kennedy, "The Use of *Tu* and *Vous* in the First Part of the Old French Prose *Lancelot,*" in *History and Structure of French: Essays in the Honour*

of Professor T. B. W. Reid (Oxford, 1972), pp. 135–49. Ian Michael points out the mixture of *tú* and *vós* in laisse 19 of the *Poema de mio Cid*. See his edition, Clásicos Castalia, 75 (Madrid, 1976), p. 108, n. 409. The use of the formal *vós* vis à vis the familiar *tú* in heated dialogue in the thirteenth-century debate-poem *Elena y María* is cited by Marta De Pierris, "El preludio del voseo en el español medieval," *RPh* 31 (1977): 241.

[82]See G. Cirot, "Sur quelques archaîsmes de la conjugation espagnole," *BHi* 13 (1911): 89; Menéndez Pidal, *Manual*, § 107.4b.

[83]See Menéndez Pidal, *Manual*, §120.5.

[84]See C. Crews, *RPh* 9 (1955–56): 236; M. Alvar, *El dialecto aragonés* (Madrid, 1953), pp. 225–26, and *El habla del campo de Jaca* (Salamanca, 1943), p. 109; F. Ynduráin, *Contribución al estudio del dialecto navarro-aragonés antiguo* (Zaragoza, 1945), p. 80. For examples in literary texts, see R. Menéndez Pidal, *Poema de Yúçef: Materiales para su estudio* (Granada, 1952), pp. 80–81; Don Juan Manuel, *El Conde Lucanor*, ed. E. Juliá (Madrid, 1933), p. 261, n. 1; N. Alonso Cortés, *Romances populares de Castilla* (Valladolid, 1906), p. 28; and *La demanda del sancto Grial*, ed. Bonilla, p. 284a. Examples from Judeo-Spanish may be found in M. Luria, *A Study of the Monastir Dialect of Judeo-Spanish* (New York, 1930), § 100a; W. Simon, "Charakteristik das juden-spanischen Dialeks von Saloniki," *ZRPh* 40 (1920): 681; J. Subak, "Zum Juden-spanischen," *ZRPh* 30 (1906): 129, 138. Salazar's *Crónica de Vizcaya* also reveals his use of *tubiendo, tobiendo,* and *obiendo* (see Guerra, "Crónica de siete casas," pp. 68, 219, 222, 260).

[85]The document is reproduced by M. Alvar, *Textos hispánicos dialectales: Antología histórica* (Madrid, 1960), 1: 334.

[86]See Joan Corominas, *Breve diccionario etiomológico de la lengua castellana,* 3rd ed. (Madrid, 1973), p. 275a.

[87]*Gran conquista de Ultramar,* ed. Pascual de Gayangos, BAE, 44 (1858; rpt. ed., Madrid, 1951), p. 161b.

[88]Emilio Sáez Sánchez, "El libro del juramento del Ayuntamiento de Toledo," *Anuario de Historia del Derecho Español* 16 (1945): 543, 612, 613.

[89]Madrid, Biblioteca Nacional, MS. 9220 (*olim* Bb-90), fols. 88b, 88c; and Biblioteca Nacional MS. 10140 (*olim* Ii-190), fol. 111[v]. The translation, attributed to Alonso Liñán, is also preserved in Biblioteca Nacional MS. 7565 (*olim* T-144).

[90]Corominas does cite the verb *comarcar* as appearing in the early fourteenth-century *Libro del cavallero Zifar* (see *Diccionario crítico,* 3: 260a).

[91]The form is also used in the 1498 *Baladro del Sabio Merlín,* ed. Bohigas, 1: 170.

[92]Words with superfluous tildes are indicated in the paloegraphical notes, except for the frequently occurring *reÿ, reÿno,* and *muÿ.*

[93]See above, n. 60.

TEXT ⤳

[Libro I]

In the opening chapter of the Libro de las bienandanzas e fortunas *Lope García de Salazar outlines the contents of his work, making several allusions to the Matter of Britain to be narrated in Book XI.*

[1]   /6b/ Otrosi fablare de los pueblos de los reynos de Ynguelatierra e dEscoçia e dErlanda e de la çibudad de Londres e de la venida que /6c/ en ella fizieron Josep Abarimatia e Joses su fijo e de los nobles rey Artur de Ynguelatierra e rey Carlos de Françia e de sus nobles fechos.

[Libros I–III]

Books I–III tell of the Creation, the Flood, Noah's partition of the world, and the histories of Babylon, Israel, and Troy.

[Libro IV]

Continuing with his history of Troy, in Chapter 54 of Book IV Salazar gives a brief account of the diaspora of the Trojans, referring the reader to other sections of the Bienandanzas e fortunas *for individual accounts of Trojan settlements in Europe and North Africa, such as that of Brutus, whose founding of England will be told in Book XI.*

[54]   /74c/ Titulo de los fechos que conteçieron a los troyanos despues que Diomedes los desanparo quando se fue a su regno.

45

De los troyanos que escaparon a vida muchos dellos fueron[1] levados
cabtiuos en Greçia segund se contiene en la ystoria de Bruto quando
poblo a Ynguelatierra. E los otros que en Troya quedaron quando   5
Diomedes los desanparo e se fue a su tierra, los quales non se podiendo
defender de los vezinos, se fueron todos con mugeres e fijos buscar[2]
tierras donde poblasen segund que sus fechos se contaran adelante en las
pueblas de las çibdades de Beneçia, e de Milan, e de Paris, e de Londres,
e de las pueblas de Lonbardia, e de Ytalia, e de Cartago de Africa, e de   10
Roma, e de Ytalia, e de Alemaña, e de Françia, e de Ynguelatierra, e
dEscoçia, e de otras probinçias muchas se contiene.

[Libro V]

*Book V tells the story of Alexander the Great and includes material
from three thirteenth-century gnomic tracts of Arabic origin:* Poridat
de las poridades, Bocados de oro, *and* Libro de los buenos proverbios. *From the latter García de Salazar extracts the exemplary
tale of the Greek poet Ibycus, whose death at the hands of thieves is
witnessed by cranes, and adds several sententiae, one of which is
attributed to King Arthur's sage Merlin, taken apparently from the*
Merlin *branch of the Post-Vulgate* Roman du Graal.

[67] /94b/...Jantus /94c/ el poeta e versificador fue preso con
mucho algo de ladrones en vn monte. E commo vio que por el algo lo
quisiesen matar, rogandoles con Dios que lo tomasen e non le matasen,
e veyendo que non le montaba nada catando a cada parte si veria algund socorro, e vio vnas gruas que pasaban volando e dixoles: "Gruas,   5
seredes testigos de la mi muerte e derramamiento de mi sangre." E tobiendolo por loco, mataronle e soterraronle mucho secreto. E Dios que
non escaeçe los malos fechos guiso de tomar vengança dellos por
aquellas gruas en aquesta manera:

Titulo de commo las gruas los mesturaron   10

Seyendo ençelada esta muerte de Jantus estando estos ladrones en vna
festibidad con todo su pueblo guiso Dios que pasasen gruas sobre ellos.
E dixieron los vnos a los otros commo en secreto: "Catad alli las gruas
que son testigos de la muerte del loco de Jantus." E commo lo oyo vn
omne que fazia su neçesidad detras de vna[3] tapia dixolo al rey, e commo   15
estaba cobdiçioso de saber su muerte fueron luego muertos de cruel
muerte. E por tales cosas dixo el sabio Salamon en sus proberbios que de

---

[1]muchos dellos quer fueron *A*; muchos dellos fueron *N*.
[2]buscar se fueron *A*; buscar *N*.
[3]vn *A*.

los malos secretos las aves del çielo lieuan la voz; dando de las alas de-
nunçiaban[4] la cosa. E el sabio Merlin dixo al rey Artur por vna cosa que
queria fazer en secreto de mucho su probecho pero de grand ynfamia si   20
sabido le fuese: "Rey, non te trabajes de eso, que la cosa fecha mill estados so la tierra ha de ser sabida."

[Libros VI–VIII]

*Books VI–VIII contain the histories of Carthage and Rome, includ-
ing the Roman conquests of Spain, Gaul, and England.*

[Libro IX]

*In Book IX García de Salazar traces briefly the genealogical history
of Lombardy and Milan, then more extensively that of France, from
the founding of the city of Paris to the reign of Louis XI. Within the
early history of France Salazar includes an allusion to the* enfances
of Tristan, *derived presumably from a version of the Prose* Tristan.

[8] /160d/ Titulo de commo reyno en Françia Faramont, fijo de
Marcho Monueres e de los sus nobles fechos.

Muerto este Marcho Monueres reyno Faramont su fijo, que fue el
primero rey que de Françia ovo nonbre ca de en antes de Gaula se
llamaban, en el año del Señor de .ccccxx. años, que fue mucho buen   5
caballero e mucho ardit e para mucho e por eso lo tomaron los françeses
por rey e le dieron el gobierno de todo el reyno. Este Faramont creyo al
buen caballero Tristan de Leonis. Reyno .x. años. E su fija Vellida se
mato por amores del, commo mas largamente se contiene en su ystoria.

[Libro X]

*Book X treats the history of various dukedoms and counties, among
them Dauphiné, Flanders, and Burgundy, as well as the cities of
Venice and Milan. The history of Flanders is used by Salazar as the
framework for a series of fictional tales illustrating the cruelty and
perversity of the Flemings. In Chapter 3, for example, we find the
evangelization of the pagan and cannibalistic people of Flanders
linked to the tales of King Arthur and the Knights of the Round
Table. The Arthurian references may have been taken from the* Demanda del Sancto Grial, *the Spanish version of the* Queste *branch
of the Post-Vulgate* Roman du Graal, *to which Salazar alludes at the
end of the chapter.*

---

[4]denunçian *N.*

[3] /173b/ Titulo del fundamento e comienço e señorio del condado de Flandes e de las estrañas[5] e marauillosas cosas que en el
acaeçieron en los antigos tienpos e duran dellas[6] fasta agora.

El condado de Flandes antiguamente eran paganos e mucho cruel
gente e como aquellas[7] que eran del linage de los almonicas que venie-   5
ron de tierra de Caldea, commo dicho es en el titulo de los romanos. E
comarcaban con los lormanes, que eran asimesmo desta naçion e mucho
crueles gentes sin ley e mas sin piedad que otros paganos. E al tienpo
que en Ynguelatierra e en Françia se tornaron christianos, estos flamenques profiaron mucho en su eregia, atanto que de todas aquellas   10
tierras que son desde Françia e Alemaña e a todas aquellas partidas ellos
fueron los postrimeros christianos. Atanta era la su crueldad que gue-
rrando[8] a los christianos comian a todos los que dellos mataban en las
/173c/ vatallas e guerras, que vno mayor ni menor no dexaban a vida
que comer podian. E comianlos commo dicho es. E dezian que no avia   15
tal comer como carne de enemigo. E con la mucha guerra que les fazian
los christianos fueron apocados dellos por armas e dellos conbertidos a
ser christianos. E destos quedaron .c. caballeros solos en la ysla de Gajola, que se llamaba Luenga Ynsola, que eran mucho valientes e yguales
en el señorio de la dicha ynsola e de las comarcas que della señoreaban.   20
E estos, seyendo en el tienpo quel rey Artur de Ynguelatierra mantenia
la Tabla Redonda, fueron muertos vno a vno conbatiendose con los caballeros de aquella Tabla andando a las aventuras. E avn se dize que
desta ysla fue conquistador e señor Galiote, el grand señor, e avn que
alli era la Torre del Lloro donde estos caballeros gentiles daban las   25
crueles presiones a los dichos caballeros de la dicha Tabla Redonda, segund se contiene en la dicha Demanda.

In Chapter 15 of Book X Salazar opens a genealogical history of the
rulers of Brittany with an allusion to the story of Tristan and Iseut
of the White Hands, taken most likely from a version of the Prose
Tristan.

[15] /177b/ ... Titulo de commo en los tienpos antigos del rey
Artur e de los otros reyes de Ynguelatierra e de Françia el ducado
de Bretaña que es agora fue llamada el reyno de la Pequeña[9] Vretaña e de la causa porque fue tornado en duques como lo es agora e
la causa dello.   5

[5]los estraños *A*; las estrañas *N*.
[6]dellos *A*.
[7]aquellos *N*.
[8]gueReando *N*.
[9]pequena *A*.

El ducado de Bretaña en los tienpos pasados llamaban el reyno de la
Pequeña[10] Bretaña e ovo en ella reyes antiguamente. Del primero que
se falla memoria fue Hoel, rey de la Pequeña Bretaña, padre de Yseo[11]
de las Blancas Manos, que caso con Tristan de Leonis, e del buen caballero Cardoyn, que fue conpañero de Tristan e hermano de la Tabla   10
Redonda....

*Chapter 22, the last chapter of Book X, gives a brief account of the
rising of the Genoese against the Duke of Milan (= Francesco
Sforza) and his captain, Niccolò Piccinino. Salazar then concludes
Book X and introduces Book XI, in which he tells the history of Britain, from its founding by Brutus of Troy to the reign of Edward IV.
Chapters 1–10 deal with the Brutus story from a derivative version
of Geoffrey of Monmouth's* Historia Regum Britanniae *as contained
in the fourteenth-century* Sumas de historia troyana, *attributed to
one Leomarte, followed by indications of legal, ecclesiastic, and
warfaring customs in Britain. Chapters 11–26 consist of the tales of
Joseph of Arimathea and the Holy Grail, based on the three
branches of the Post-Vulgate* Roman du Graal. *The narrative concludes with the bizarre account of the passing of Arthur to the mythical North Atlantic island Brasil, a tale which brings together the
legend of Arthur's survival with contemporary tales of exploration,
late medieval cartography, and the brazilwood trade.*

[22] /179d/ ... Aqui se acaba el libro dezimo que Lope Garçia de Salazar fizo en esta[12] su ystoria de los .xxv. libros que fizo estando preso en
la su casa de San Martin. E comiençase el honzeno libro en que fabla
como fueron poblados e fundados los reynos de Ynguelatierra, e dEscoçia, e dErlanda, e de las çibdades de Londres, e de las otras çibdades e   5
pueblas dellas, e de las gentes que las conquistaron e poblaron. E de
como salio Bruto con los troyanos que eran catibos en Greçia, e Asaraco, e Corineo, e el[13] obispo Eleno, fijo del rey Priamo, e poblaron e
reynaron en los dichos reynos e yslas. E de como Josep Avarimatia e su
fijo Josefaz, que fue el primer obispo christiano del mundo, e sus pa-   10
rientes aRibaron en Ynguelatierra con el Santo Grial e fezieron conber-
ter[14] a muchos christianos e reynaron algunos dellos en ellas. E del
noble rey Artur e du sus fechos e del sabio Merlin....

[10]pequena *A.*
[11]ysco *A.*
[12]ensta *A.*
[13]corineo el *A.*
[14]coberter *A;* convirtir *N.*

[Libro XI]

[1]   Contado[15] ha la ystoria como Eneas, escapado de la postrimera destruyçion de Troya, vino en Cartago de Africa *e* caso[16] con la reyna Elisa Dido, *e* como[17] la dexo por que no fuese sabida su maldad, e de commo el avia vendido la dicha çibdad, e commo /180a/ ella se mato por ser burlada del, e como aRibo en Ytalia e caso alli e ovo fijos, quel e   5 ellos reynaron alli por muchos altos fechos de armas quel alli fizo, por donde alcanço reynar alli el e sus fijos Julio, e Escanio, e Silvias Postino, que alcançaron todos tres sendos reynos, como mas largamente se ha contado en la dicha su ystoria. E morio este Eneas conplido de sus dias en mucha honrra e noble estado, reynando Julio su fijo en Toscana e   10 fuendo su muger preñada e fallando los estrolagos que lo quella tenia en el vientre avia de matar a su madre e a su padre, segund Dios es, e moriendo ella del parto del despues del naçido.

E seyendo ya este Bruto mançebo de .xix. años e andando con su padre Julio a correr monte, atraveso vn venado, que yba Julio su padre   15 enpos del ençima de su caballo a todo correr. E no lo veyendo este Bruto tiro con vna flecha de arco al dicho venado e dio a Julio su padre que venia corriendo por el cuerpo de parte a parte, donde morio a poco rato. El pueblo de sus tios e suyo ovieron grand pesar por su muerte, comoquier quel padre mandase que no le fuese acaloñada su muerte,   20 pues que era ynoçente della. Pero los pueblos dixieron que era verdad, pero que omne que a su padre avia muerto, que no quisiese Dios que sobre ellos reynase, ca el su pecado los podria fazer perder a todos, que en ninguna manera lo tomarian.

[2]   Titulo de como Bruto salio de Ytalia e aRibo en Greçia, e de las cosas que le avenieron en Greçia, e de como de alli se partio e poblo en Ynguelatierra.

Viendo esto Escanio e Silui*as*,[18] tios de Bruto, quel no /180b/ podia reynar alli contra voluntad del pueblo, cataron manera para lo enbiar   5 de alli onrradamente. E dieronle dos naos, e gente, e todo guisamiento. Dio consigo en alta mar a fin de yr a poblar a Troya, que estaba desierta, donde era natural. El tienpo contrario echolos en Greçia en el reyno de Maçedonia, que reynaba el rey Pandraso, el qual lo reçibio muy bien. En aquel reyno avia .xd. catibos de los troyanos, sin fijos e sin   10 mugeres, que fueron traydos de la dicha destruyçion de Troya, entre los quales estaba el obispo Eleno, fijo del rey Priamo de Troya que *avia* seydo[19] catibo en la dicha destruyçion e lo avian traydo los griegos alli.

---

[15]Eontado *A*; Contado *N*.
[16]africa caso *A*; africa e caso *N*.
[17]elisa dido como *A*; elisa dido e como *N*.
[18]siluiuis *A*.
[19]que seydo *A*; que fue *N*.

Otrosi estaba[20] alli Asarato, que de parte de su madre era nieto de Archiles, fijo de su fijo, e de la madre era de los troyanos. Su padre quando　15
morio dexole tres castillos juntos con el reyno de Pandraso. Estos obispo
Eleno e Asarato trataron con aquellos catibos troyanos que Bruto to-
mase cargo dellos e que se fuesen con el a poblar a Troya. E recogieronse aquellos tres castillos de Asaraco. E basteçieronse todos con el
dicho Bruto, que era omne, avnque mançebo, esforçado e entendido. E　20
fizo catar todas las cosas neçesarias aquel fecho que començado avian.

[3]　Titulo de la carta que Bruto e los troyanos enbiaron al rey
Pandraso sobre la deliberaçion de su catiberio e de la dura respuesta.

"Al muy alto rey Pandraso: Bruto de las reliquias de los troyanos,
salud. Commo sea muy avorreçida e muy amargosa cosa aquello la antigua generaçion señorea tan larga *e* esquibamente sostener *yugo*[21] de su　5
sugeçion[22] /180c/ en las sus çerbizes. Por ende la clara e dina degenera-
çion dardania que so el tu duro e espantable señorio estobiese que
quieras dellos sufrida ser; e quieras darles tierra de libertad en tu reyno
e averlos de aqui adelante por tus buenos amigos. E do esto non te plazera de darles la salida para que[23] vayan a buscar tierra en que poblen.　10
Esto que sea por la tu liçençia del qual pedimiento que te fazen entienden tu estar deudor."

El rey Pandraso, reçebida esta carta, dixo con grand yra e saña contra
Bruto e los suyos duras e fuertes *palabras*.[24] E leuantando todo su reyno
fuelos a çercar. A la qual guerra Bruto e los suyos, como aquellos que　15
estaban bien basteçidos en aquellos castillos de aquella montaña, se
ovieron bien e sabiamente. Bruto salio muy esforçado e sabio guerrero,
por manera que por luenga guerra el rey Pandraso e los suyos fueron
vençidos e por muy grand arte presos e los sus fijos e hermanos e todos
los mexores de su reyno.　20

E asi presos e todo esto fecho, estando Bruto e los suyos muy gloriosos
por esta bienandança que avian avido sobre los griegos que estaban
ricos a marauilla, e partida aquella presa e asosegados, ayunto Bruto a
todas sus gentes para fablar con ellos en fecho de sus aferes, e dixoles
asi: "Amigos e buenos parientes, ya visto avedes la bienandança que　25
despues de tantos trabaxos Dios nos ha querido dar. Que le debemos dar
muchos loores e graçias, pero bien sabedes como estamos en Greçia
donde ha muchos nobles reyes e prinçipes poderosos. E avnque a este
tengamos preso e vençido no estamos bien seguros, porque es menester[25] que tomemos consejo para lo que queredes fazer. Si quere　30

[20]estaban A.
[21]jugo A; yugo N.
[22]suguçion A; sugecion N.
[23]para en que A.
[24]vatallas A.
[25]meñester A.

/180d/ des quedar en esta tierra con voluntad del rey Pandraso el fara
lo que le pedierdes, pues preso lo tenedes, o para vos partir desta tierra,
que todas las cosas que vos plazeran[26] soy presto, pues que esta carga de
vosotros tome. E agora que tenedes tienpo, fazed lo que vos plazera e
entendades *lo* que[27] vos cunple, que yo a todo sere contento." 35

[4] Titulo del acuerdo que Bruto e los troyanos ovieron sobre las
razones susodichas, e de lo que les aconsejo el obispo Eleno sobre ello.

Quistiones muy dibersas se levantaron entre ellos sobre esta razon, ca
los vnos aprobaban en lo vno e los otros en lo al. Pero al cabo acordaron
todos que por el obispo Eleno, fijo del rey Priamo, que era mucho sabio, 5
e por vn noble caballero que se llamaba Menbrudo, que era ançiano e
natibo de Troya, fuese determinado este fecho e como ellos lo mandasen
asi feziesen. E despues que ellos anbos ovieron acordado en vno, dixo el
obispo ante todo el pueblo: "Señores, muy cosa dura es e avorreçida a
toda criatura la guerra contina e muy peligrosa quanto mas a los omes 10
que son razonables criaturas, ca son las guerras en juyzio de la fortuna,
de la qual su natura es de nunca estar en vn prospuesto. E si vos a esfuerço desta bienandança que vos ella dio aqui queredes estar a toda
Greçia avedes de conquistar ante que segura vida en ella podades fazer.
La ventura que vos esto dio temome que no tenera con vosotros mayor 15
deudo que con vuestros anteçesores, que con muy grand logro les demando aquello que dado les avia. Puesto que a los mançebos parezca
bien la guerra, a los que la edad an conplida razon seria que con segurança /181a/ de paz gozasen la libertad que Dios les quiso dar. Otrosi
que con graçia del rey Pandraso, que preso tenedes, querades quedar en 20
la tierra por quanto vos otorgara todas las cosas que le pedierdes. Mas
¿como no pensades que Pandraso jamas vos querra bien? Quel bien os
quisiese e guardase lo que con vosotros posiese, ¿pensades que vos
querria bien, quel bien vos quisiese, aquellos a quien vosotros matastes
padre*s*[28] e fijos e hermanos? No vos guardarian cosa que vos prometiesen, 25
ca quando el matador paresçe razientanse las llagas. ¿Como podria ser
fecho de enemigo leal amigo, e si de omne que aya fecho calonia alguna
no puede ser leal amigo fallado? Porque si a todos vos ploguiese, que lo
que aviades de pedir al rey Prandaso para quedar en esta tierra que le sea
pedido para salir della. E Dios que conoçe este noble caudillo vos quiso 30
ayuntar e ayudar el vos dara adondequiera que vayades consejo."

[5] Titulo de las cosas que Bruto e los troyanos enbiaron demandar
al rey Pandraso *e* como[29] les fueron otorgadas e salieron de su tierra.

[26]plazera A.
[27]entendades que A.
[28]padrs A.
[29]pandraso como A; pandraso e como N.

A todos los troyanos plogo con este consejo e acordaron en el. E Bruto fizo venir al rey Prandaso alli delante todos e dixole asi: "Rey Prandaso, bien sabes tu como despues de tantas e fuertes premias que so 5 el tu brabo señorio los troyanos sentieron muy omildosamente te enbia- ron a requerir que no quisieses que ellos tan largamente durasen en *suje-* çion,[30] que de tu grado en tu tierra les quisieses dar fiança e otorgarles la antigua libertad en que sus anteçesores viuieron. E tu no queriendolo fazer, los /181b/ dioses vsando del su ofiçio faziendo justiçia posieronte 10 en el su poder. Ellos no vsando de tu crueça no te quisieron dar las penas que tu tienes mereçidas. Mas pidente que les otorgues de tu grado la salida de tu tierra e que les des naos e vasteçimiento con que della salgan en paz e que te soltaran e dexaran toda la tierra. Que si esto por tu voluntad no quisieres fazer por si lo entienden cobrar e avn do ellos 15 fueren a ti e a los tuyos leuaran en cadenas."

E Pandraso, pagado de la razon de Bruto, dixo asi: "Fazer deben los omes por saluar la vida todas las cosas, e avnque sean de aquellas que vergueña deban aver, quanto mas las que razonables fueren falladas. Por ende, pues los dioses asi lo quisieron, yo de mi buena voluntad soy pla- 20 zentero e otorgo todo lo que por ellos fuere demandado, ca ellos no podrian demandar tanto como en lo que contra mi perteneçe." E asi quedaron por estonçes pagados del rey. E tornaronlo a la presion fasta que les entregase lo que avian menester para su partida.

E mirado por los troyanos que seria lo que avian menester para su 25 conpaña, dixole Asarato a Bruto: "Yo avia pensado vna cosa conve- niente a mi pensar, que pues esta salida se ha de fazer en manera de paz, por que mas firme fuese, que Prandaso diese a su fija Ynomenis a vos por muger, la qual yo conosco por muy apuesta donçella e en condi- çiones la mas conplida del mundo, con la qual tu serias bien casado." E 30 mucho plogo desta razon a Bruto e a todos los suyos. E enbiaron al obispo Eleno a la demandar.

[6]   Titulo de como los troyanos enbiaron al obispo Eleno al rey Pandraso a le demandar a su fija e las otras cosas conplideras a su partida.

El obispo Eleno era tenido entre los griegos por honrrado e discreto despues que /181c/ fuera catibo en Troya, que le acataban mucha 5 onrra e avtoridad. Llegado antel rey Pandraso e ante los suyos que presos estaban le dixo esta razon: "Rey Prandaso, los troyanos dizen que les des .l. naos e vastiçimiento para vn año. Pidente todos los catibos troyanos que an quedado en todo tu reyno que ellos no podieron aver; que des Asarato por los tres castillos suyos .x. quintales de oro. Otrosi te 10 piden a tu fija Ynogenis para su cavdillo Bruto e a tu sobrina Noxia para

---

[30]soxuçion *A*; subjecion *N*.

Asarato, e con estas .xx. donzellas a tu escogiençia para que casen con
caballeros troyanos e que te soltaran e daran los dichos castillos, e donde
no, que moriras en su presion. E yo, porque en ti falle sienpre honrra,
queria te lo galardonar[31] e dotelo por consejo."   15

E acordado por Pandraso e por todos los de su reyno que con el
presos estaban, respondio e dixo asi: "Eleno, los menesterosos no dexan[32] de
cobrar de los omes sino aquello que no quieren. E por ende nosotros caydos
en vuestras manos queremos fazer todo aquello que pedis. E yo tengo por
bien enpleada a mi fija en tan alto e tan noble caballero como en Bruto, que   20
creo que en el mundo no ay otro mejor. ¿Quien fuera osado de tan alto fecho
començar e tan çierta çima le dar?; ¿omne desterrado e con poca gente por
esfuerço e seso sacar todos los catibos del poder de Greçia? E por ende
otorgo lo que pedistes."

E luego fueron fechas las vodas e traydas las naos con todo lo pedido. Mas   25
quando se ovieron de partir, la ynfanta Ynogenis dezia con grand dolor:
"¡Ay de mi, triste, como los dioses tobieron tantos males para mi guardados;
si fue yo engendrada de las dueñas amazonas que se deleytan en las pasadas
de las mares! E diran en todas las /181d/ tierras que ¿como se pudo poner
vna sinple donzella como yo a tantos males? En muy grand preçio so yo   30
puesta, pues fue yo fecha preçio e rabida de la mi tierra." E a las vezes se
amorteçia. E Bruto la conortaba muy dulçemente e a las otras tanbien. E
mandaba todavia a los mareantes que leuasen la via de Troya, adonde el e
todos los suyos codiçiaban de yr a poblar en la dicha tierra de Troya, por
que en el e en ellos se cobrase el nonbre troyano.   35

[7]   Titulo de como Bruto e los troyanos entraron en alta mar con
su flota e de las[33] cosas que les acaeçieron con las tormentas e
gentes.

E asi entrado Bruto e los troyanos en alta mar, no tardo[34] mucho que la
tormenta les[35] echase en tierra de Damasco. E despues de robada aquella,   5
entraron en la mar e toparon con muchos cosarios que sabian de su venida. Los quales seyendo mas poderosos avian conquistado e prendido
vna partida de su flota. E Bruto veyendo aquello aferro con la capitana de
los cosarios, e saltando dentro della abraçose con el capitan dellos e
echolo en la mar. E tan grande fue el esfuerço que los suyos tomaron en   10
aquello que a todos los cosarios mataron e prendieron e tomaron mucha
riqueza, comoquier que alli perdio Bruto muchos de los suyos.

E nabegando con todas aquellas naos e presos, tormenta forçosa les

---

[31] galardoñar A.
[32] dexanl A (l *crossed out*).
[33] les A.
[34] tardaron A.
[35] tormenta no les A.

echo en tierra de Africa cuydando aRibar a Troya. E alli fueron reçe-
bidos con mucha guerra. E oviendo vatalla con el señor de la tierra, lo 15
vençieron e prendieron con muchos de los suyos. E por redençion suya
les dieron todo el algo de la tierra.

E syguiendo su viaje aRibaron en Germania, que es en Alemania. E
fallaron alli a Corineo[36] de la grand /182a/ fuerça, que era de la gente
troyana que alli poblaron con Antenor. Por promesas que le Bruto fizo e 20
por deseo de tornar a poblar a Troya fuese con ellos. E nabegando por
cobdiçia de llegar a ella[37] con bientos contrarios ovieron de ser per-
didos. E aRibaron en la ysla de Locaçia, que agora se llama Chipre, que
era toda despoblada por cosarios e era toda montes. E fallaron alli vn
tenplo mucho marauilloso consagrado a la deesa Diana. E por consejo 25
de todos, el obispo Eleno fizo alli sus sacrefiçios por saber respuesta de
los dioses por que les venian aquellos tienpos contrarios, por que no
podian yr a la tierra de Troya.

[8] Titulo de las palabras quel obispo Eleno dixo, faziendo el
sacrefiçio en el su tenplo, e de la respuesta que Diana dello dio a
Bruto estando dormiendo.

Faziendo el obispo Eleno su sacrefiçio, dixo estas palabras: "Señora
Diana, que eres espanto de los montes e tormenta de las mares, deesa de 5
castidad, dinos por que no podemos yr a poblar a Troya, a la çibdad que
fue despoblada de nuestros anteçesores."

E acabado aquel sacrefiçio adormeçieronse todos en aquel tenplo. E
apareçio Diana a Bruto en dormiendo e dixole: "Bruto, no te trabaxes
de yr a poblar a Troya, ca sentençia fue dada en el çielo contra ella, que 10
fuese despoblada por sienpre. Pereçeredes todos si mas aquella via ydes.
Mas pasa los estrechos de la mar Oçiano a la parte de sententrion pasada oçidente. Fallaras vna ynsola despoblada de gente que antiguamente fue señoreada de vn gigante que /182b/ se llamaba Albion. E alli
esta aparexada a ti la silla adonde reynaras e asimismo muchos reyes de 15
tu linage e desas gentes que van contigo. Las quales a muchos reyes e
gentes comarcanas e forasteros fartaran de mucha angustia e deRamamiento de sangre con sus espadas e arcos e flechas. Tu creçeras en estado e honrra e en muchas gentes. E estonçes faras tenplo de castidad
por que yo sea en guarda de la tu generaçion e que se acaben los tus dias 20
en grande honrra en aquella tierra."

E Bruto desperto de aquel sueño e llamo al obispo Eleno e a todos los
otros de su conpañia. Contoles aquella vision que la deesa Diana le dixiera, con la qual fueron muchos alegres e muchos pesantes, porque mas

---

[36]corneo A.
[37]ellas A.

quisieran yr poblar a Troya donde eran naturales. Pero no osaron mas   25
profidiar contra la voluntad de los dioses. Tomaron la via a ellos ense-
ñada, e pasaron el estrecho de Marruecos, e trabesaron la mar dEspaña.
E tomaron tierra por refrescar en Equitania, que agora se llama Guiana.
Cuydando alli folgar, fallaron mucho trabaxo de guerra e de gentes.

[9]   Titulo de las guerras e vatallas e fechos que conteçieron[38] a
Bruto e a los troyanos con el rey Garafio de Guiana e con los catalanes e gaulos.

Sopiendo el rey Garafio, que estonçes reynaba en Guiana, la venida
de los troyanos, enbioles dezir con vn su pribado que le saliesen de la   5
tierra. Razonose tan mal con ellos que Corineo, que era muy valiente e
poco paçiente, diole con vn arco por ençima de la cabeça e echolo
/182c/ muerto. E viendo esto el rey Garafio enbio sus gentes a pelear con
ellos e fueron vençidos los suyos e muertos e presos muchos dellos.
Commo esto vio el rey Garafio envio demandar ayuda a los catalanes e a   10
los gaulos, que agora se llaman françeses. Venidos todos en su ayuda e
puesta su vatalla, los troyanos fueron vençedores e mataron e prendieron
muchos dellos. E los que escaparon recogieronse a sus fortalezas. En esta
vatalla cobro Corineo grand fama de la su fuerça, que fallaban en los
muertos el omne cortado por la çinta e otros por los onbros fendidos fasta   15
la çinta e otros pasadas las lanças por las armas e cuerpos de parte a parte.
Señorearon los de Bruto toda aquella tierra. E pasando[39] adelante ovieron
grand vatalla en Lormandia con los françeses. E vençieronlos e mataron
muchos dellos e dañaronles la tierra. E morio alli vn noble caballero,
primo de Bruto, que se llamaba Toreno. E ovieron por el grand pesar e   20
fezieronle rica sepoltura. E por honrra del poblaron alli vna villa e posie-
ronle nonbre del mesmo Torena, que se llama agora Torres en Torena.
Señorearon Bruto e los suyos toda aquella tierra fasta que fezieron treguas
con los comarcanos. E fecha esta tregua, paso Bruto con todos los suyos en
la ysla dAluion, que agora se llama Ynguelatierra. E fallaronla toda   25
/182d/ despoblada, saluo en Cornoalla, que fallaron vn gigante que se
llamava Magot, que era mucho valiente con pocas gentes. E ovieron
conbenençia que luchasen este Magot e Corineo e el que deRibase al otro
que oviese a Cornoalla. E deRibolo Corineo e lançolo a la mar, donde oy
dia llaman alli donde lo echo la Peña de Magot.   30

[10]   De como Bruto e los troyanos poblaron en Ynguelatierra e en
Scoçia e como la repartieron e en que tienpo e se poblo Londres.

En el tienpo que señoreaba Josue sobre el pueblo de Ysrrael, aRiba-

---

[38]conteçio *A*.
[39]pasado *A*; pasando *N*.

ron Bruto e los troyanos en la dicha ysla de Albion e poblaronla de villas
e de castillos. Reyno Bruto en Ynguelatierra sobre todos. E poblo la çib- 5
dad de Londres e fizola cabeça del reyno. Pusole nonbre la Grand Bretaña. Dio por eredamiento a Corineo a Cornoalla e pusole de su nonbre
Cornoalla. E dio por erençia Asaraco a Escoçia. Vn su fijo que la eredo
despues del, que llamaban Ysca, pusole de su nonbre Escoçia. E fizo
obispo mayor en este reyno sobre todos al obispo Eleno, fijo del rey 10
Priamo, que con ellos vino como dicho es, porque en el tienpo de los
gentiles los obispos eran los mas poderosos e ricos del reyno del rey en
fuera sacando los reyes.

Oy en dia la yglesia es poderosa en Ynguelatierra, que ereda la terçia
parte de las rentas del reyno. Paga la terçia parte de las guerras e de las 15
otras cosas conplideras del reyno. La comunidad paga la otra terçia
parte. Quando esto no vasta, echan talla a todas las cosas que venden.
Otrosi en todo el reyno de Ynguelatierra, asi en los /183a/ ducados e
señorios como en las çibdades, no se faze justiçia ninguna sino por el rey
solamente, ni la toca prinçipe ni caballero nin çibdadano como en los 20
otros reynos.

Deste Bruto e de sus gentes suçedieron e suçeden todos los yngleses e
escoçeses[40] e yrlandeses e las otras yslas comarcanas. De la costunbre de
Troya les quedaron la espada, el arco e las flechas. E sacaron dellos de suyo
la acha e las otras visarmas segund que las han oy dia. E asi reynaron e 25
suçedieron de vnos en otros fasta el tienpo que reynaba en la dicha çibdad
de Londres, seyendo cabeça de Ynguelatierra, el rey Luçes Pagano.

[11]   De como aRibaron en Ynguelatierra Josep Avarimatia e su fijo
el obispo Josefaz e sus parientes con el Santo Grial que eran
christianos.

Andados .l. años de la Pasion del Nuestro Señor Ihesu Christo, aRibaron en la ysla de Ynguelatierra Josep Avarimatia e su fijo Josefaz, que 5
fue el primero obispo christiano, con la sangre del Nuestro Señor, que se
llamaba el Santo Grial, *e* otros[41] sus parientes e grandes omes, que eran
christianos por graçia de Dios. E por muchos miraglos[42] que mostro por
aquel Santo Grial fueron conbertidos todos los de aquellas yslas o los
mas despues de muchas pedricaçiones e deRamamiento de sangre. E 10
reynaron algunos dellos en algunas çibdades e reynos e provinçias segund aqui se dira. Asi se falla que los primeros christianos del mundo
fueron en Ynguelatierra despues de los de Iherusalem.

/183b/ Este Josep deçendio al Nuestro Señor de la cruz que gelo dio
Pilatos en galardon de su soldada. E lo sepulto honrradamente. E alli 15

---

[40]escoçes *A.*
[41]grial otros *A.*
[42]miraglos *superposed upon* x̄pianos *A.*

tomo esta sangre del su costado en vn vaso que se llamo este Santo Grial.
E fue por ello preso .xl. años por los judios e confortado por el fasta que lo
sacaron Vaspasiano e su fijo Titus, enperadores de Roma, segund se contiene en la Bribia. E se dexa aqui de contar por no alargar escritura.

[12]   Estos son los que reynaron en Ynguelatierra de la conpañia
de Josep.

Sador, fijo de Erton, sobrino de Josep, fue rey de la çibdad de Leonis. E
del suçedio por derecha linea de rey en rey Eledus de Leonis, que fue
padre del buen caballero e fermoso Tristan de Leonis, que fue nonbrado   5
caballero.

De Perron, sobrino de Josep, suçedio de rey en rey por derecha linea
el rey Lot de Ortania, que caso con la hermana del rey Artur de Ynguelatierra e fizo en ella a Galuan e a Gajusete e a Gerres e a Garbayn e
a Morderet, que fueron nonbrados caballeros en la Tabla Redonda.   10

Galaz, fijo de Josep Avarimatia, fue rey de la çibdad de Lisoarta, que
por su nonbre la llamaron Galaz e asi *la*[43] llaman oy. E deste Galaz
suçedio el rey Vrian, que caso con Margayna, hermana del rey Artur,
que ovo fijo della, al buen caballero Yban, que fue mucho nonbrado
caballero en la Tabla Redonda.   15

Josue, hermano de Sador, sobrino de Josep, reyno en la çibdad de
Corberique de Tierra Forana. Del suçedio de rey en rey el rey Pelaz,
que fue aguelo del santo caballero Galaz,[44] padre de su madre.

/183c/ El rey Naçian, que se llamaba antes que fuese christiano, fue
rey de Ganuz. Suçedio del de rey en rey el rey Lançarote, que ovo fijos,   20
el vno el rey Vores de Ganus, que fue padre de Leonel e de Vores,
primos de Lançarote del Lago, que fueron nonbrados caualleros en la
Tabla Redonda. El otro fijo de Lançarote fue el rey Yban de Benuyt,
padre del famoso caballero Lançarote del Lago.

[13]   Titulo en que cuenta del naçimiento del sabio Merlin e de
algunos fechos suyos porque perteneçe al naçimiento del rey Artur.

En el reyno de la ysla de Ynguelatierra, en vna tierra que se llama
Tierra Forana, dormio vn diablo que se llama Ynquevides con vna donzella que fazia santa vida. Ovo poder de la engañar porque con saña de   5
palabras desonestas que vna mala muger, su hermana, le dixo, oluidosele
de se santiguar en dormiendo. Como desperto, fallose corronpida e con-
fesolo a su confesor, porque ella no sopo si era diablo o omne. Salio
preñada. E porque en aquel tienpo era costunbre que muger que adul-
terio feziese, si no fuese mundaria publica, que la matasen por ello.   10

---

[43]le A.
[44]santo caballero caballero galaz A.

Como se sopo su preñez, fue luego tomada de la justiçia e puesta a
juyzio ante los alcaldes. Los quales mandaronla quemar porque no daba
padre ni razon de su preñez. E commoquier quella dezia lo que le
aconteçiera e concordaba su confesor con ella, pero no le valia nada. E
por que era preñada e non moriese la criatura ynoçente, dieronle vida 15
de la parir e criar dos años. Metieronla en vna torre çerrada con dos
mugeres que la guardasen e serbiesen.

Parido vn fijo todo velloso e criado de vn año, estando vn dia e apar-
tada de la conpañia, miro aquel su fijo. E veyendolo feo demasiada
/183d/ mente, dixole llorando: "O fijo, que por mala e fea criatura que tu 20
eres, tengo de morir de cruda muerte." Como la criatura lo oyo que
mamaba, alço la cabeça aRiba, e reyendose, dixole catandole a los ojos:
"Madre, non ayades miedo, que no moriredes por mi, ca no lo tenedes
mereçido, que yo vos saluare." Commo aquello oyese ella, espauoreçiose
de guisa que se le cayo de los braços en tierra veyendo fablar criatura de 25
vn año tan osadamente. E como las mugeres que estaban con ella lo
vieron, tomaron la criatura valdonandola, diziendo que lo quisiera matar.
Commo ella vino en su acuerdo e les conto todo lo que oyo, fueron
marauillad*as*[45] e quisieronle fazer fablar, diziendo mal de su madre. Mas
no les respondio cosa. E sonado todo esto por el pueblo, fueron mucho 30
maravillados dello e venianlo a ver. Mas no les quiso fablar.

[14] Titulo de como venido el tienpo de los dos años Merlin saluo a
su madre. E de las cosas que con el alcalde e con su madre le conto.

Conplido[46] el tienpo de los dos años para conplir la justiçia de la
madre de Merlin o le diese padre, como ella lo oyese, llorando se aco-
mendaba a Dios e a Santa Maria, como aquella que era sin culpa, pero no 5
le valia nada. Como Merlin aquello oyese, al alcalde, leuantando su cabeça, dixole: "Alcalde, el que no faze justiçia de si no la debe fazer de
otro. Por ende trae aqui tu madre e dete padre e mi madre dara a mi
padre." Commo el pueblo que estaba presente esto oyeron, fueron maravillados en oyr fablar criatura de dos años tan sabia e osadamente e sobre 10
todos el alcalde, que avia dado la sentençia. Dixole: "Digote, Merlin, que
tienes razon." E mando enbiar por su madre e ayuntar todo el pueblo
para ver aquel marauilloso fe /184a/ cho. E asi venidos, dixo a la madre
de Merlin, que tenia su fijo en los braços: "Cata aqui a mi madre e dara
padre a mi. E a ti conbiene que des padre a tu fijo, si no, oy seras que- 15
mada como estas juzgada. E vos mi madre, dadme padre antes que esta
otra lo de a su fijo." Respondiole la madre e dixole: "Fijo señor, se que yo
padre vos tengo dado a mi señor vuestro padre, que Dios aya como lo

[45]marauillados *A*; maravilladas *N*.
[46]Eonplido *A*; Conplido *N*.

saben todos." E dixo Merlin al alcalde: "Señor alcalde, no me pareçe que
sodes muy entendido en querer fazer las cosas tan publicamente, porque   20
vos podria venir daño por ello. Por ende llamad a vuestra madre e a la
mia e quatro onbres buenos del pueblo e alli respondere yo a tu madre e
despues fagase como quisieres. Esto no entendades que lo digo por saluar
a mi madre, ca ella salua e ynoçente esta." E marauilladas las gentes
dello, dixieron al alcalde que lo fiziese asi. El alcalde dixo: "Plazeme de   25
lo fazer, pero digote que si no dizes verdad, que tu madre sera que-
mada." Merlin le dixo reyendo: "No te cures deso, que yo te mostrare
ante estos omes buenos que tu llamas quien es tu padre a quien es el mio
despues antel pueblo." Con estas palabras se apartaron.

Dixo Merlin a la madre del alcalde: "Vos bien sabedes que quando   30
vuestro marido estaba enojado, fulano vuestro confesor vos demando
vuestro cuerpo. Vos le respondistes que lo fariades sino por miedo de
vos enpreñar, que vuestro marido no dormia con vos ya de doliente. El
vos respondio que era de tal natura que no podria enpreñar muger. Con
esto echastes vos con el fasta que vos sentis /184b/ tes preñada e gelo   35
degistes. E por lo encobrir, fizolo el a vuestro marido que dormiese con
vos, mostrandole grand pecado porque no lo fazia. E asi fezistes al buen
ome creyente que erades del preñada." E dixole otras muchas cosas seña-
ladas que avian pasado entre anbos continuando su mal proposito. En
tanto estrecho la puso que no pudo fablar cosa.   40

El alcalde le dixo: "Commoquiera que sea, vos mi madre sodes. E yo
no vos fare sino como a madre. Por ende dezid la verdad." E dixole:
"Fijo, que te dire que yo creo que este es el diablo o su fijo, del qual cosa
no se puede encobrir." Dixo el alcalde aquellos que con el estaban:
"Agora vos digo que este moço dezia verdad, que mejor savia el quien   45
era mi padre que yo. Do por quita a su madre del mi juyzio. Pero dime,
Merlin, aqui ante todo el pueblo quien es tu padre, por que sepa dar
razon de mi a todos ellos, por que sepan que no fago justiçia de tu
madre."

Dixoles Merlin: "Buenas gentes, sabed que sañudos fueron los diablos   50
quando Nuestro Señor quebranto los ynfiernos e saco dellos Adan e a
Eva e a los otros que le plogo. Dixieron[47] fagamos omne mortal por que
cobremos por el tantas almas como perdimos por aquel Ihesu Christo
que vino en carne e nos los tomo de nuestro poder. Dixoles vn diablo,
que se llama Encobus, quel avia poder de engendrar fijo. Como Nuestro   55
Señor entendio su maliçia, consentioles de lo fazer, pero no para lo que
ellos cuydaron. Fue yo luego engendrado de aquel Encobus en esta mi
madre. E diome Dios por aquel diablo a saber todas las cosas pasadas
commo los diablos lo saben. E diome por esta mi madre que es de santa
vida a saber todas las cosas que son de /184c/ por venir, por que yo   60

---

[47]dixero *A*; dixieron *N*.

guardase el su serbiçio." Estas e otras muchas cosas les dixo Merlin, que
todos fueron marauillados. Dixo al alcalde en poridad: "Sabe que tu
madre es yda como tu la[48] mandaste. Como llegare a su casa llamara al
clerigo que es tu padre e contarle ha todo este fecho. El con grand temor salira fuera de la villa e enforcarse ha por sus manos. Enbialo saber,   65
por que sepas si digo verdad en todo." E faziendolo asi, el alcalde fallolo
verdad en todo. Muchas cosas se dexan aqui por no alargar escritura.

[15]   De como reynaron algunos reyes en Ynguelatierra por donde
suçedio dellos el noble rey Artur e de sus nobles fechos.

Muchos reyes reynaron en Ynguelatierra e en las otras yslas comarcanas, de los[49] quales suçedio el rey Moynes. El qual dexo a su
muerte dos fijos legitimos pequeños, que llamaban al mayor Padragon e   5
al otro Vter. E dexolos en guarda e encomienda de vn su hermano vas-
tardo, que llamaban Vertiguo, para que gobernase el reyno fasta que
Padragon, que dexaba por rey, fue de edad para gobernar el dicho reyno.
Como el se vio apoderado en las tierras cuydo matar a los sobrinos. E
fueron con ellos dos caballeros a Gaula, que agora se llama Françia.   10
Reçelandose dellos que creçidos tornarian en el reyno, fizo muchos castillos en el reyno para se defender dellos si veniesen. Entre los quales fizo
el castillo de Dobra, que es en el estrecho de Calez.[50] E porque se le cayo
tres vezes, fizo juntar sus estrolagos, que eran .xij. sabios, para que le
dixiesen por que no se tenia aquella obra. E juntados en vno fallaron que   15
avian[51] de morir por vna criatura que era naçida sin padre. E por escusar
esto fueron al rey e dixieronle /184d/ que feziese matar vn moço que era
naçido sin padre e que con la sangre de aquel vntando la cal estaria la
obra. El rey, marauillado de omne ser engendrado sin simiente de varon,
pero con el afirmamiento dellos enbio muchos omes a lo buscar cada vnos   20
por sus partes. Llegados dos dellos adonde el andaba, trebexando con
otros moços e sopiendo el todo aquel fecho por que lo conoçiesen, dio con
vn palo a vno de aquellos sus conpañeros. El qual, dando vozes e llorando,
dixo: "¡O como *me* mato[52]este fijo de sin padre!" Commo lo oyeron
aquellos dos omes, fueronse azia ellos. Como Merlin los vio, dixoles: "Yo   25
so el que buscades." E contandoles lo por que venian e despediendose de
su madre, se fue con ellos al rey.
Llegados antel rey, dixole: "Rey, esto que tu quieres saber desta torre
por que cae, yo te lo dire por tal que si mentiere que mates a mi. Si ellos
mentieron que fagas matar a ellos." Contentos todos, dixoles Merlin: 30

[48]le A; la N.
[49]las A.
[50]e *superposed upon an* i A.
[51]avia A; avian N.
[52]como mato A; como me mato N (me *inserted above line*).

"Rey, tu te reçelas de tus sobrinos Padragon e Vter. E fazes esta torre
por los destorbar este paso. E sabe que estos estrolagos preguntaron por
su estrologia al diablo que era la causa porque esta torre caya. El qual,
negandoles la verdad, codiçiando mi muerte, porque me la buscan
todos, porque saben que no he de fazer cosa que a ellos venga en pesar,   35
dixieron a ellos que matandome e vntando la sangre mia con la cal repa-
raria esta obra. Rey, sabe que so esta obra yazen dos dragones en vna
pequeña fuente. E como se les carga la obra de suso, rebuelben la tierra
e cae asi la torre." E fizolos sacar por cabas, e salidos mataronse el vno
al otro.   40

Pasaron aqui muchas cosas que serian largas de contar, saluo que dixo
a los .xij. clerigos: "Vos no moriredes por mi ni lo quiero yo, ca /185a/
otro vos metio en ello que vos lo quiso fazer. E aquel fue Luçifer que
vos fizo creyentes que por mi aviades de morir, por que me vos fiziesedes matar; ca porquel me ha perdido e porque yo no fago las cosas   45
quel cuydaba que yo faria, me buscaba la muerte. Mas yo tengo buen
señor que me guardara del. Vos confesad este pecado e non husedes mas
desta ynigromançia, pues no podedes dezir sino lo quel diablo vos enseñare, que nunca vos dira verdad." Ellos asi gelo prometieron.

Como el rey asi lo viese sabio, preguntole de sus avenimientos. Al qual   50
en secreto, ante quatro pribados suyos, dixo que sopiese de çierto que los
sobrinos lo avian de matar en fuego porquel fuera causa de fazer morir a su
padre e avia de reynar en Ynguelatierra el vno enpos del otro.

[16]   Titulo de como Padragon e Vter su hermano seyendo creçidos
pasaron en Ynguelatierra e mataron a su tio e despues lo quemaron.

Creçidos[53] estos dos hermanos Padragon e Vter, pasaron en Ynguelatierra. E oviendo fuerte vatalla con el rey Vertiguer su tio, vençieronlo
e mataron muchos de los suyos. Acogiose Vertiguer a la tierra de Ejeus   5
su suegro, que era poderoso. Luego reyno Padragon. El qual, aviendo
mucho a voluntad la conpañia de Merlin, fizolo buscar por todo el
reyno, pero no era cosa que le fallar podiesen si el mesmo no quisiese,
ca el sabia[54] todo lo que del dezian. Trasfigurabase en qual forma de
ome queria e de tal hedad. E commo el sopo esto, vinose de suyo ante   10
los hermanos. E despues de muchas marauillas que ante ellos fizo e
fablo, fizoseles conoçer. E prometioles su serbiçio, porque sabia que dellos avia de venir el noble rey Artur. Dixoles como Vertiguer su tio e
Ejeus su suegro /185b/ venian sobre ellos con poderosa gente, e que
saliesen a pelear con ellos, consejoles como fiziesen. Dixoles como serian 15
vençedores, pero que sopiesen quel vno dellos con muchos de los suyos

---

[53]Ccreçidos *A*; Creçidos *N*.
[54]sabian *A*; sabia *N*.

moreria alli e el otro que reynara en el reyno luengamente seyendo
poderoso. E dixo en secreto a Vter, el ermano menor: "Sey esforçado
caballero, que tu hermano Padragon morira en esta vatalla e tu reynaras
despues del." 20

Oviendo fuerte vatalla, fueron vençedores los hermanos. Murio[55]
Padragon alli como lo dixo Merlin a Vter. E morio Egeus con muchos
de los suyos. E acogiose Vertiguer a vn castillo e quemolo alli Vter con
muchos de los suyos como Merlin le dixo. E muertos estos, reyno Vter
en Ynguelatierra e en todas las yslas sobre todos los reyes dellas luenga- 25
mente. E por honrra de su hermano, que no dexara fijos, por que no
quedase sin memoria, por consejo de Merlin llamose Vter Padragon en
toda su vida.

[17]   De como fue engendrado e naçido el noble rey Artur de
Ynguelatierra e de los fechos que en su criança acaeçieron.

Reynando este Vter Padragon, commo dicho es, enamorose de
Ybernia, muger del duque de Tintoyl, que era mucho fermosa. E non la
podiendo aver por cosa, mando en achaque al duque su marido çercarlo 5
en vn castillo suyo. E tobiendolo çercado con grand cuyta de amor, des-
cobriose a Merlin, diziendo que moriria si el no lo mostrase conplir su
voluntad. E Merlin veyendo su cuyta e sopiendo lo de venir, leuolo solo
con Olfin su pribado a vn castillo adonde estaba la duquesa, ca el rey no
la osara çercar por no descobrir que por aquello tenia çercado al duque. 10
E llegados de noche al castillo, llamo Merlin a la duquesa, diziendo por
Vter Padragon que era el duque Avferion, que venia de secreto fablar
con ella solo con dos pri /185c/ bados suyos, trasfigurados[56] todos tres
en la figura del duque e de sus criados por los encantamientos de Merlin.
Dormio el rey con la duquesa mucho a su sabor. Conçibio del aquella 15
noche al noble rey Artur de Ynguelatierra. Aquella noche mesma salio
el duque Avferion de su castillo cuydando matar al rey Vter Padragon
en su tienda. E mataronlo los del rey. Commo el rey saliese del castillo
de noche, Merlin le dixo como el duque era muerto e que avia engendrado fijo que seria noble sobre los de su linage, pero que gelo diese 20
para criar en galardon del su trabaxo, en manera que ninguno no lo
sopiese sino Vlfin, que era alli con ellos. E el rey mucho gozoso dello, e
mas por casar con la duquesa, otorgolo todo.

Despues caso con la duquesa, encobriendo todo aquel fecho, mos-
trando que le pesaba de la muerte del duque e que por emendar a la 25
duquesa, que avia dos fijos del pequeños, que por eso la tomaba por
muger. Al tienpo que ovo de parir vino alli Merlin desconoçido. E fuele

---

[55]murio *in different hand* A.
[56]tresfigurados A; trasfigurados N.

dado el niño en secreto por Vlfin por mandado del rey, a pesar de la
duquesa que no sabia nada del secreto sino que cuydaba quel duque lo
avia engendrado aquella noche. E Merlin lo dio a criar a vn caballero en   30
la montaña que llamaban Antor, mandandole por mucho preçio que
dixiese que era su fijo, ca sopiese que avia de llegar a grande estado e del
se le siguiria mucho bien. E el caballero quito la teta a vn su fijo de dos
meses e diolo a criar a vna labradora que le llamaban Grifet. E dio Artur a criar a su muger, no sopiendo ellos quien era Merlin sino que pa-   35
reçia vn omne de .c. años e flaco.

E fue este Vter Padragon noble rey. E morio de su dolençia. E antes
que moriese fizo la Tabla Redonda de .cl. caballeros conoçidos por
conse /185d/ jo de Merlin. E yoguiendo el rey sin fabla, entro Merlin a
el e dixole: "Rey, vete con Dios, que tu fijo Artur reynara algund   40
tienpo." Esto dixo el callando a la oreja del.

[18]   Del reynamiento del noble rey Artur de Ynguelatierra e de
la marabilla que Merlin en ello fizo de su conoçimiento.

E muerto este rey Vter Padragon, porque no pareçia dexar fijo que
reynase enpos del ovo grand division en el reyno qual reynaria. No sopiendo tomar consejo, buscaron a Merlin e demandole consejo a quien   5
tomarian por rey por que se gobernasen bien. El qual, tomando el
cargo, estando todos los mexores del reyno en la çibdad de Londres sin
lo saber ninguno, fizo por sus encantamientos venir vn padron de piedra
de marmol[57] con vna espada metida en el por el rio de Artamisa adentro
e parose en la plaça de la çibdad. Dezian vnas letras de oro que   10
en el estaban escritas: "El omne que esta espada sacare deste padron,
aquel tomen por su rey los yngleses, ca sera rey noble e aventurado a si
e a su reyno." E vista aquella marauilla, todos los del reyno que algo
valian, codiçiando de reynar, se probaron en aquella espada, veniendo
de todas partes. En tal manera que en .xx. dias continos e mas no fallo   15
omne que la sacar podiese. Atanto que no sabian que fazer.

En este comedio vino Artur, que era ya de .xvj. años, mucho fermoso
e valiente de su edad, por mandado de aquel que lo criaba a la çibdad,
no sopiendo de aquello por leuar çiertas cosas como otras vezes solia. E
pasando por la /186a/ plaça, estando las gentes a comer, vio aquella   20
espada metida en el padron. E no sopiendo que fazia, trabo della e sacola muy ligeramente e mirola e tornola en so logar, ca los moços ni
labradores no la probavan. E fuendo a su menester, algunos que lo vieron fueronlo dezir a los fieles que guardaban el padron. E traxieronlo
alli, presentes ya[58] muchas gentes. E mandaronle que la probase. E el   25

---

[57]piedra marmol A.
[58]ya *inserted above line and in different hand* A.

mucho avergoñado trabo della e sacola mucho aRefezmente. E tobiendolo alli, llamaron aquel caballero Antor, que el les dixo que era su padre. E veniendo, preguntaronle de su fecho. El qual les dixo que era su fijo como estaba castigado.

E asi fue coronado por rey este noble Artur por Merlin, que entendido 30 no se fazia, de todos los del reyno que estaban deseosos de rey con muchos nobles e estraños juegos e juglares, ca vestido de paños⁵⁹ reales era el mas apuesto omne de todos los del reyno e palaçiano en palabra e fechos de todas cosas. E asi coronado, dixole callando aquel caballero que lo crio: "Señor, pues Dios te fizo rey en galardon de la tu criança, toma a Giflet mi 35 fijo por tu copero e serbidor para su vida, pues es tu hermano de leche. No gela quites por villania que faga contra ninguno, ca si la feziere sera de parte de la villana que yo le di por ama que mamo su leche por darlo de su madre a ti." Lo qual el le otorgo de voluntad.

[19] Titulo de los fechos que acaeçieron a este noble rey Artur de Ynguelatierra despues que fue coronado por rey.

En el año de Nuestro Señor Ihesu Christo de .cccc. años reyno este noble rey Artur en la /186b/ Grand Bretaña, que agora se llama Ynguelatierra, segund susodicho es, que seyendo mançebo e no sopiendo 5 cosa de su linage se puso a probar en todas las aventuras del Santo Grial que fueron. Eran muchas desdel tienpo que Josep Avarimatia lo traxo en Ynguelatierra e lo dexo en el castillo de Corberique a su muerte, segund dicho es. En las quales el deseo marauillosamente en el fecho de las armas, probandose con nonbrados caballeros vno por otro. En otras 10 cosas espeçialmente mato vn gato demasiado de fuerte en vna montaña solo, que avia muerto muchos nobles caballeros e otras gentes que lo yban a buscar. E el tomo por sus armas asi como las han oy en dia los reyes de Ynguelatierra, que les llaman gatos artuxes del su nonbre. Otrosi mato al duque Flores, cuerpo por cuerpo, que vino sobre el con 15 el poderio de Roma por le quitar el su reyno.

Seyendo en su corte vino alli Elena, muger del rey Lot dOrtania, que era mucho fermosa con .iiij. fijos pequeños de .x. años avaxo. E enamorose del que era de grand veldad e el della, non sopiendo como heran hermanos de madre. Dormio con ella e enpreñola de secreto de vn fijo 20 que se llamo Morderet, del qual vino mucho daño en el reyno como se dira. Estando el su fecho asi, Merlin, que mucho lo seguia e guiava, sopiendo que no envargante el rey ser tan noble que el reyno no era contento del por ser fijo de Antor, fizo descobrir todo el fecho de su engendramiento e naçimiento por su madre e por Vlfin, e por Antor e 25 por su muger que lo criaron, presentes los mejores del reyno en vna

---

⁵⁹panos A.

maravillosa manera. De lo qual todos fu /186c/ eron alegres como la
razon la adevdaua.

E acabado esto caso con Ginebra, fija del rey Leodanga de Norgales,
que era a la sazon la mas noble del reyno. Diole con ella la Tabla Re-   30
donda con .c. caualleros, que la ovo del rey Vter Padragon su padre
porque no dexaba quien la mantoviese. Guarneçiola de los .cl. caballeros como le convenia, sino sola la silla peligrosa, que era encantada e
no consentia caballero fasta que vino el santo Galaz.

[20]   Del sueño que este rey Artur soño e de commo vio la Vestia
Ladradora e de como gelo declaro Merlin con su muerte.

Estando este rey Artur enseñoreado en todos los reynos de las yslas en
Gavla quel señoreaba e fuendo vn dia a correr monte alongose de los
suyos tras vn çierbo fasta que le canso el cavallo. E descabalgando   5
echose en vn prado e con el cansançio adormeçiose cabe vna fuente. E
soño vn fuerte sueño en que salia del su cuerpo vna sierpe rabiosa que
con su ponçoña quemaba toda la caballeria de Ynguelatierra. E peleava
con el e la mataba el con su lança. Quedava el ferido de muerte.

E desperto mucho espantado. E pensando mucho en aquel sueño, oyo   10
muchos ladridos de canes. E alço la cabeça aRiba pensando que serian
los suyos que se le[60] eran ydos tras el çierbo. E vio venir vna vestia
desfigurada desta manera: quel cuerpo avia commo oveja e de su
grandor, e el cuello de çierbo, la cabeça commo de raposo, e la boca
con pico como aguila, e las manos como grifo, e los pies e la cola como   15
leon e toda de largo pelo. E venia mas yrada /186d/ quel viento, ladrando dentro della e por su voca ladridos de .xxx. canes e mas quando
van tras venado. Como llego a la fuente lançose dentro en la fuente e
veuiendo çesaron los ladridos. E como salio del agua començaron a la-
drar segund primero. E fuese a todo correr por el monte adelante con   20
tales ladridos.

E asi mirando el rey por donde se yba, vio venir vn omne viejo, medio
çiego, que no podia venir. E tornado el rey a sus pensamientos dixole:
"Rey, no te marauilles desta vestia, ca es de las marauillas del Santo
Greal. Ni te espantes del sueño que soñaste, ca es cosa que atañe a tu   25
muerte e asi ha de ser, que no es cosa que se escusa." Como esto oyo el
rey fue mas espantado que primero porque le fablaua en el sueño que
otro no podia saber. E preguntole: "Di, viejo, ¿que sabes tu de mi sueño
e de lo que yo me maravillo?" Dixole: Rey, mas se de lo que tu cuydas."
E contole todo lo que soñara e lo de la Vestia Ladradora e commo avia   30
de morir commo viera en el sueño e que no se podia escusar.

[60]les A.

[21] De como Merlin debiso al rey Artur el fecho del su sueño.

Oydas el rey estas razones e seyendo turbado, desfigurose Merlin de
aquella figura e tomo la suya propia por se fazer conoçer al rey. Con lo
qual el rey oviendo sobejo plazer lo abraço e dixo: "Merlin, nunca tanto
te ove menester como agora por dos cosas: la vna porque fablas en mi   5
muerte; la otra por saber razon desta vestia. E ruegote que me /187a/
sueltes derechamente como lo soñe."

E Merlin le dixo: "Plazeme de lo hazer, pues tan cuytado te veo, avnque no te plazera, pero asi a de ser. Rey, la sierpe que tu soñaste que
salida de tu cuerpo, que quemava con su ponçoña toda la caballeria de   10
Ynguelatierra, es vn fijo que tu engendraste en grand pecado, que
seyendo tu conplido de dias, estando honrrado mas que otro rey que en
este reyno ovo reynado ni reynara de aqui adelante, se alçara contra ti
con el dicho reyno e peleara contigo e morira alli toda la noble caballeria deste reyno. Tu mataras a el e el te dexara ferido de muerte. Por   15
ende, conortate que sabias que avias de morir, quanto mas que sera onrrada tu muerte."

[22] Titulo de como Merlin deuiso al rey Artur el fecho de la
Vestia Ladradora.

"Rey, el fecho desta Vestia Ladradora es fecho en esta manera, porque es de los fechos del Santo Greal: En el tienpo que reynaba en este[61]
reyno vn rrey[62] que llamaban Ypomenes avia vn fijo mucho noble e de-   5
boto contra su dios. E avia vna fija que llamaban Ypodonia, que era
sabia e mucho fermosa e deuota otrosi. E commo el diablo se trabaxa
sienpre en fazer pecar los buenos, puso en voluntad aquella donzella de
se enamorar de aquel su hermano. E siguiolo atanto por que se echase
con ella que no lo podiendo con el acabar se puso en desesperaçion de   10
se matar por amor del o de lo fazer morir. Veyendola el diablo en tal
desesperaçion, vino a ella de noche en forma de omne mucho fermoso.
E dormio con ella e enpreñola. E como se vio preñada aconsexose con
el. E consexola que dixiese que forçandola su hermano la enpreñara.
Como ella se vio preñada, querellose al padre, diziendo de su hermano   15
ser /187b/ preñada e que le fiziese justiçia. E luego lo fizo prender e
mando a la fija que ella lo juzgase a lo que quisiese. La qual ençendida
con el diablo mando que lo diesen a comer a .xxx. canes quel padre tenia
en vn corral, los quales daban a comer los omes malfechores. E comoquier quel hermano se escusaba con la verdad no le valia nada. Fue   20
lançado a los canes. E dixo en echandolo: 'Ermana, con falsedad me

[61]enste *A*; en este *N*.
[62]drrey *A* (d *crossed out*).

fazes morir cruel muerte despedaçado e comido de canes. Ruego yo al
Señor quel mundo ha en poder que cosa desfigurada salga del tu cuerpo
de lo que tu eres preñada e ladrando como canes rabiosos ande por el
mundo faziendo lazdrar las gentes en testimonio de la mi muerte cruel e   25
ynoçente.' E como los canes estaban fanbrientos fue luego despedaçado
e comido casi vibo. E como el padre oyo aquellas palabras luego entendio el mal que ella avia fecho. E fizola prender fasta que mas sopiese.
Como vino el tienpo de parir pario aquella vestia que vos vistes. E salio
del palaçio yrada como vistes con aquellos ladridos de canes e andado   30
despues aca faziendo mal en las gentes, espeçialmente en los caballeros
andantes que la siguen. E a de durar fasta que venga el santo Galaz que
dara çima a todas las aventuras del Santo Greal, que la matara el buen
caballero Palomades el pagano con la lança del. E commo el padre vio
aquella vision fizo luego quemar aquella su fija."   35

[23]   Titulo de como Merlin deuiso la su muerte mesma al rey Artur, pues le dixo la suya.

"Agora, Rey, pues te he deuisado la tu muerte que sera honrrada,
quierote deuisar la mia que sera cruel e desonrrada. Sepas que Nuestro
Señor me dio a saber todas las cosas pasadas e por venir, saluo de la mi   5
muerte que no quiso que yo sopiese cosa. E vi vna noche dormiendo vna
vision en esta manera: En vn can /187c/ po[63] fermoso naçia vna rama
pequeña de vn arbol de robre. E creçia en tanto grado *que* daba[64]
grande sonbra e sabrosa de si mas que todos los arboles del mundo. E
por aquello venian todas las animalias del mundo que calor avian po-   10
nerse a la su sonbra e por el semejante con las friuras, e oyendo la fama
de su fermosura. E creçiale al pie vna sinple rama e delgada e fea e de
otra natura. E como ella começo a creçer começo el arbol a descreçer
azia la tierra, en tanto grado que ella creçiendo e el arbol descreçiendo
que todo lo fizo somir so la tierra, que no quedo cosa fuera sino la non-   15
bradia. E querria que vos, Rey, me soltasedes esta vesion."
    Dixole el rey: "Merlin, eso a vos conbiene dezir que sabedes las cosas,
que no a mi. E ruegovos que me lo digades."
    "Rey, pues saberlo quieres, sabed que aquel arbol que naçio en el
canpo senifica a mi e el canpo senifica el mundo[65] donde yo naçi. E la   20
fermosura del roble, que es la mas sabrosa sonbra de los arboles, senifica
el mi saber. E las animalias que con el calor e frio se venian a poner so
el senefica que vernan buscar la mi sabiduria, que so el mas sabio del
mundo. La rama sinple que naçera cabo el arbol sera vna donzella de

[63]can canpo A (*scribal repetition at beginning of new folio page*).
[64]grado daba A.
[65]aquel arbol que naçio senefica a mi e el arbol e el canpo senifica senifica el mundo A.

poco saber que se llegara a mi e aprendera de mi tanto, que asi como 25
aquella rama creçio sobre el arbol e lo somio so la tierra, asi enterrara a
mi vibo so la tierra e me fara morir de cruda muerte. No quedara de mi
sino la mi fama que durara fasta la fin."

E asi se conplio despues que vna donzella se allego a el. E ena-
morandose della le vezo tanto de /187d/ su sabieza que, desamandolo 30
por que no la burlase, le çerro dormiendo en el su regaço en vn monumento de piedra, adonde morio a cabo de .viij. dias con grandes dolores.
E esta fue la Donzella del Lago, que despues crio al buen caballero
Lançarote del Lago.

[24] Titulo de como fue començada la demanda del Santo Greal e
se acabo en el tienpo deste rey e de la su muerte e de su fijo Morderet.

En el tienpo del Nuestro Señor Ihesu Christo andados de la Pasion
.ccccliij. años, el dia de Pascua de Mayo se conplio la Tabla Redonda de
los .cl. caualleros porque vino el santo Galaz. E se asento en la silla 5
peligrosa diziendo: "En el nonbre de Dios, caballeros, caballero quiero
ser en la silla peligrosa."

Estando el rey Artur a comer con ellos a la Tabla con grand plazer,
antes que troxiesen las viandas çerraronse todas las ventanas e puertas
del palaçio en manera que no veyan cosa alguna. E perdieron todos la 10
fabla que no podieron fablar. E vieron entrar el Santo Greal con gran
claridad, con mucho noble olor.[66] E no veyendo quien lo traya andobo
aRededor de la Tabla Redonda .iij. vezes. E como salio fuera dexolos a
todos fartos de todos los comeres e veberes que cada vno deseaba en la
su voluntad. E abrieronse las puertas e finiestras todas e quedaron con 15
maravillosos olores e contentos porque a la salida les dixo vna voz: "Caballeros, este es el Santo Greal." E tornoles toda su fabla.

E fablando vnos con otros de aquella maravilla que visto avian de
aquel Santo Greal, leuantose Galban, sobrino del rey, e juro de otro dia
partir en demanda de aquel Santo Greal donde tanto bien /188a/ avia, 20
e de la seguir vn año e dia e mas fasta algo saber del. E luego lo juraron
Galaz, e Lançarote su padre, e Tristan de Leonis, e todos los otros .cl.
caualleros della. E desto peso mucho al rey e a la reyna porque avian de
quedar solos.

E otro dia por la mañana,[67] quisiendose partir, entro vna donzella con 25
vn espada çeñida. E dixo al rey: "Mi señora, la Donzella del Lago, te
manda dezir que a vn caballero destos no dexes yr en esta demanda que
han jurado, sino que sepas que ha de matar muchos buenos caballeros destos que en ella van." El rey que mucho le peso desto dixo:

---

[66]l *superposed upon an* n A.
[67]mañaña A.

"Donzella, si vos me mostrades quien es ese caballero que tanto mal ha   30
de fazer yo no lo dexare yr con los otros." "Señor," dixo ella, "no lo
conosco yo mas que vos. Pero fazedlos probar en esta espada e el que la
sacare tinta de sangre caliente, aquel sera el que vos digo yo."
    E luego la probaron el rey, e Galaz, e Lançarote, e Tristan, e todos
los que alli estaban. Venido Galuan que estaba con la reyna le dixo el   35
rey: "Sobrino, probad esta espada," diziendole lo que en ella avia.
Trabo della e sacola toda llena de sangre caliente. E pesandole dello al
rey, dixole: "Sobrino, no vayades vos en esta demanda." Dixole: "Señor,
por çierto no lo fare, ca esto es encantamento e no cosa de creer e que
sopiese oy morir no lo dexare." E cabalgando en su caballo fuese a todo   40
correr. E asi salio verdad quel mato de aquel camino malamente .xij.
caballeros de aquellos de la Tabla Redonda.
    E fue acabada aquella demanda de las aventuras del Santo Greal por
el santo Galaz las mas dellas e por otros /188b/ algunos. E aquellos
vieron sobir el Santo Greal al çielo quel ni otra aventura non quedo en   45
el dicho reyno. Galaz e Persibal, que lo acabaron e fueron virgines, fueron reyes de Sarras e morieron bien demandando la muerte a Dios. E los
que escaparon vibos, que no eran la meatad, tornaronse al rey Artur. El
qual con muchas doloridas palabras los reçibio. Por conortar su reyno e
mostrar su grand coraçon forneçio de nobles caballeros las sillas de la   50
Tabla Redonda que faltaban los muertos e encobrio todo lo malfecho de
Galban, que valia mucho.

[25]   De como el rey Artur paso en Gaula a la defender de los
romanos e se alço Morderet con el reyno cuydando tomar a la
reyna su muger e de la vatalla en que morieron anvos a dos.

Estando este noble rey Artur reposado e sosegado en su reyno, poderoso mucho e honrrado, sopo como el enperador de Roma enbiaba   5
muchas de sus gentes por le tomar el reyno de Gaula que estaua por el,
avnque no eran christianos. Dexo por gobernador del reyno de Ynguelatierra a Morderet, su fijo, avnquel por su sobrino lo tenia, ca los hermanos ya eran muertos. E dexo con el la reyna e mucha de su caballeria.
E paso el mesmo en Gaula con la mas gente que pudo. Ovo fuerte va-   10
talla con los romanos. E vençiendolos mato el por su mano al capitan
dellos e morieron otros muchos dellos.
    Acabado todo esto e estando el e los suyos ricos e honrrados de aquel
vençimiento e onor, venieronle nuevas como Morder*et*,[68] su fijo, se avia
alçado con el reyno de Ynguelatierra, /188c/ faziendo fama quel rey e   15
todos los suyos eran muertos en aquella vatalla e pues no dexaba fijo quel
deuia ser rey, pues era fijo de su hermana. E quisiendo tomar a la reyna

[68]morder *A*; morderet *N*.

Ginebra que era enamorado della, porquel fizo todo esto, alçosele en el
castillo de Londres e que la tenia alli çercada. E pesandole mucho desto
paso luego en Ynguelatierra, conoçiendo que se le llegaba su muerte   20
como Merlin le avia dicho. Pero ni por eso dexaba el de mostrar su grand
coraçon, diziendo entre si que Dios era fazedor de todas las cosas.

E asi allegado, ajuntaronse en el canpo de Saravarre. Ovieron fuerte
vatalla adonde morieron toda la flor de la caballeria de Ynguelatierra
que danbas las partes estaba. E como el rey Artur oviese grand dolor de 25
asi ver morir los suyos, entro por medio de la vatalla de aquel traydor
de Morderet que fazia marauillas de su persona en el fecho de las armas
e avia muerto por sus manos muchos nobles caballeros de la Tabla Redonda. E acabaua de matar a don Yban, su primo, al qual el rey amaba
mucho como fijo de su hermana. E dandole grandes vozes le dixo: 30
"Vente, traydor, que contigo so." E dexaronse yr el vno al otro braba-
mente. E el rey paso su lança sobre las armas de parte en parte por el
cuerpo a Morderet. E sacandogela fue vista vna marauilla, que paso el
rayo del sol por la ferida de parte en parte. E Morderet dio de la espada
al rey por la cabeça sobre el yelmo que lo llago a muerte. E alli cayo   35
muerto Morderet. E el rey desbarato a los suyos que pocos escaparon de
muertos. Corto el mesmo la cabeça del e fizola poner en vn arbol.

E vençida la vatalla e parti /188d/ do el rey del canpo, non sentiendo
la ferida yendosele mucha sangre della, cayose del caballo del desmayo.
Dio sobre *Lucan*,[69] su mayordomo, que lo cuydo sostener, tal golpe sa- 40
liosele el alma alli. E oviendo el rey pesar dello porque lo avia servido
desde que fue rey seyendo su mayordomo, mandolo[70] soterrar alli e poblar alli vna villa e llamarla de su nonbre, como se llama oy la villa de
Can por el nonbre deste don *Lucan*.[71] Veyendo el rey llegada su muerte,
fizose cabalgar en su caballo. E fuese azia la ribera de la mar solo con   45
Glifed su copero, que no quiso que otro fuese con el.

E llegados en vn valle dezeñio su espada, que se llamaba Escalibor,
que era de grand vertud. E dixole: "Glifed, toma esta espada que Merlin
me fizo aver. E echala en vn lago que fallaras en aquella floresta, que no
quiero que despues de mi otro la aya sino quien a mi la dio." E fuendose 50
con ella, codiçiandola que no se perdiese tan noble cosa, escondiola. E
tornando al rey le dixo el rey: "Glifed, ¿echastela?"[72] Dixole que si. E
dixole: "¿Viste alguna cosa en el lago quando la echaste?" Dixo que no.
E dixole el rey: "Glifed, sienpre me fueste leal e mandado e ovediente.
E ¿por que no lo eres agora a la mi fin? E torna alla e echala en el lago   55
que si la echares señal veras." Torno alla e no osando al fazer echola e

[69]glifet A.
[70]mayordomo e mandolo A.
[71]*blank A.*
[72]echestela A; echastela N.

vio salir vna mano del lago fasta el codo que la reçibio antes que cayese
en el lago e metiose dentro con ella. Como vino, dixo que la echara e lo
que viera. Dixole: "Mi buen serbidor, agora se yo que la echaste, ca esa
mano que la tomo me la ovo dado en este lago por arte de Merlin que   60
me fue leal amigo." Llegando a la ribera dixole: "Glifed, tornate e vete
/189a/ a do quieras, ca mi postrimera ora es llegada. La qual no quiero
que sea sabida mas que fue de la primera venida, ca en vida fue llamado
por el mundo rey de las marauillosas aventuras. E asi quiero que lo sea a
la mi fin. Tornate de aqui e no me fagas pesar mas sobre ello, ca mi   65
muerte no ha de ser sabida ni mi sepoltura fallada. E tu, Glifed, puedes
dezir que fueste el primero que me aconpaño e el postrimero que de mi
se partio."

[26]   Titulo de como Margayna leuo al rey Artur en la varca a la
ysla de Brasil e la[73] encanto que no puede ser fallada.

Gifed, quando mas no pudo, partiendose del rey sobiose en vn otero
alto que estava sobre la mar por ver que se fazia del rey. Vio venir vna
varca cobierta de paños de seda e llego a la ribera. Vio salir a Mor-   5
gayna, que era hermana del rey de madre, con dueñas e donzellas en
tierra. E tomaron al rey en la varca con sus armas e caballo. E fueronse
con el por la ribera adentro al terçero dia de la vatalla, ca el dia mesmo
a la tarde se avia partido el rey solo con Glifed, commo dicho es.
Quando Grifet perdio la dicha varca de vista, fuese la ribera adelante   10
por saber mas nuebas del rey, tobiendose por pecador en asi se partir
del. E otro dia por la mañana fallo en la ribera de la mar vna yglesia
pequeña, vna sepoltura nueva, letras que dezian en ella: "Aqui yaze el
rey Artur de Ynguelatierra." E pregunto a vn hermitaño que fallo alli
que si lo viera enterrar alli. E dixole quel dia ante viera salir de vna   15
barca a Morgayna con otras dueñas e donzellas e que traxieran alli vn ca-
/189b/ ballero muerto que dezian que era el rey e que lo sepultaran
alli. Giflet, por ser mas çierto deste fecho, alço la tunba de la sepoltura e
no fallo en ella cuerpo ninguno. E fallo el yelmo mesmo del rey sobre el
que fue ferido en la vatalla, que le viera meter en la varca, e no otra   20
cosa, pesandole dello por no fallar mas del rey. E dixo: "Pues esta es la
postrimera cosa que fallo del rey mi señor, aqui quiero feneçer mis dias
a serviçio de Dios e suyo." E pusose alli hermitaño.
E dizese por este rey Artur, e avn asi lo dizen los yngleses agora, que
lo leuo Margayna, su hermana, a la ysla de Brasil, que es a .xxv. leguas   25
del cabo de Longaneas, que es en Erlanda, e que encanto aquella ysla
que la no puede fallar ningund nabio, ca ella era mucho sabia de en-
cantamentos que le mostro Merlin, cuydandola aver por enamorada, e

[73]lo A.

que estan alli vibos amos. E dellos ser bibos no es cosa de creer, pero
desta ysla ser alli no ay duda e de ser encantada, ca todos los mareantes   30
la fallan en las cartas por donde se guian e marean las mares que fueron
fechas en el comienço del mundo mucho antes desto. E dizen los yngleses que aquella ysla puede ser fallada si el nabio puede ver la ysla
ante que la ysla al nabio, que vna nao de Bristol[74] la fallo vna alborada e
que no sopiendo que era ella, cargo alli mucha leña para el fuego que   35
era todo de brasil, que lo traxo a su dueño e conoçiendolo que enRe-
queçio mucho e que fue el e otros en busca della e que no la podieron
fallar. E algunas vezes la vieron nabios e con tormenta no podieron llegar a ella. E es toda redonda e pequeña e vaxa.

*Several references to King Arthur are to be found in the remaining
chapters of Book XI, which form a genealogical history of the English kings Richard I to Edward IV, extracted, it would appear, from
a chronicle of the kings of France.*

[27]   /189c/ Muchos reyes reynaron en Ynguelatierra, en Scoçia, e en
Erlanda despues deste rey Artur de que non faze memoria sinon por la
coronica de los reyes de França.

*Concerning the reign of Edward II (the Third according to Salazar),
it is said that after Arthur, Scotland and Ireland no longer obeyed
the English throne.*

[30]   /191d/ E muerto este rey don Juan, reyno su fijo Aduarte, terçero
deste nonbre, que ovo a Guiana como los otros, ovediçiendo por ella a
França, e oviendo guerra con Escoçia e con Erlanda, ca estos dos
reynos despues del rey Artur nunca ovedeçieron a Ynguelatierra.

*And Edward III (the Fourth according to Salazar) is compared to
Arthur and Charlemagne.*

[36]   /193b/ ... e morio vençedor e acabador de sus fechos en el mayor
estado e nonbradia que rey que reynado oviese en Ynguelatierra ni en
França, *eceptos*[75] el rey Artur de Ynguelatierra e el rey Carlos de
França. E por esto lo llaman los yngleses el Grand Duarte.

[Libros XII–XVI]

*Book XII treats the history of the Muslims and Turks as well as the
Crusades. Books XIII–XVI deal specifically with Spanish history,
from the beginnings to Alfonso III of Castile.*

[74]briscol A.
[75]aceptos A; ecebto N.

[Libro XVII]

Book XVII is a condensation of the Crónica del rey D. Pedro I *by Pero López de Ayala, composed in the late fourteenth century. From the* versión vulgar *of this chronicle Salazar reproduces, in full, a prophecy of Merlin which Peter the Cruel asks the Moorish sage Benharin (Avenamatin in the Salazar text) to interpret.*

[47]   /320c/...El rey don Pero avia grand ansia por yr socorrer a la çivdad de Toledo, que avia diez meses que estava çercada e estava mucho afincada por mengua de viandas e cataua por averlas mas gentes que podia aver. E esperava[76] gentes del rey de Granada e de algunas villas e çivdades que estavan por el, porquel avia fallado vna profeçia   5
de Merlin que endereçava toda su persona.[77] Enbiola aquel moro Avenamatin, filosofo del rey de Granada, que le avia enbiado la carta de los castigos de suso contenidos. El tenor de la qual es este que se sigue.

[48]   Titulo de la profeçia de Merlin quel rey don Pero enbio al filosofo Avenamatin e de lo que por ella le enbio dezir de su fecho.

"Ensalçado rey e señor que Dios onRe e guarde, amen. El tu siervo, Avenamatin, pequeño filosofo del rey de Granada e del su consejo, con todo recomendamiento e vmildad, poderoso e nonbrado rey entre los   5
reyes, no niego yo quel mi seruiçio no sea sienpre aparejado a la tu honrra e ensalçamiento e señorio real, en quanto el mi saber alcançe[78] e el mi poder sofrirlo pueda. Las *cosas* que lo[79] adevdan, quales e quantas son, pues tu eres ya sauidor con grand diligençia e acuçia[80] de gran /320d/ estudio.[81] Otrosi por manera de grand seso que en mi fallavas en tus   10
negoçios, que te fiziese sauidor en qual manera podrias palpar por verdadero saber vn *di*cho[82] de profeçia. El qual dizes que fue fallado en los libros de profeçias que dizes que Merlin fizo,[83] del qual las sus palabras, por los terminos que lo[84] yo reçeui, son est*as*[85] que se siguen."

Siguese la carta   15

"En las partes de oçidente, entre los montes e la mar, naçera vna ave negra, comedera e robadera. Todos los panares del mundo querra coger

[76]podia aver para las socorrer e esperava A.
[77]toda a su persona A.
[78]alcançare A.
[79]las que la A.
[80]acudiçia A.
[81]custudio A.
[82]fecho A.
[83]s *superposed upon a* z A.
[84]los A.
[85]estos A.

en si. Todo el oro del mundo entrara en su estomago. E despues gor-
marlo ha e tornara atras. E no pereçera luego por esta dolençia, ca dize
caersele an primero las peñolas e secarsele han las plumas al sol. E an-   20
dara de puerta en puerta e no la querra ninguno acojer. E ençerrarse a
en la selua e morira[86] ende dos vezes, vna al mundo e otra ante Dios.
Desta guisa acava."

Sigue la carta

"Rey alto, rogasteme, ca todo es en *tu* poder[87] rogar e mandar, que yo   25
pensaria quan graue era e podria ser, segund el menester en que estas e el
deseo grande en que estas, por ser çerteficado en el entendimiento desta
profeçia e en que manera podrias ende ser savidor, e que por la amistança
e deudo de seruidunbre que yo en la tu merçed he, traspasase yo en mi
toda la mayor carga que podiese tomar deste tu cuydado, por que por el   30
plazer de la mi espalanaçion[88] que en las mis palabras atiendes ovieses
buena fiuza[89] de sofrir lo avenidero, e todavia que la verdad no te fuese
negada por amorio que contigo oviese, maguer que en algunas cosas, o en
todo, podrias tomar mayor pesar de lo que entiendo."

Sigue la carta   35

"Rey alto e poderoso, saue que yo, con grand ovediençia del tu man-
damiento, con cuydoso estudio, seyendo partido de todos qualesquier
negoçios mundanales que dello me agrauiasen, esforçe la natura /321a/
mucho sobre ello. Escudriñe[90] por todas partes el mi saber por conplir
lo que me enviaste mandar, e lo que por este mi estudio o mi sauer pude   40
alcançar, e en acuerdo en que fue ayuntado con otros grandes savios, e
sin vandera e sin sospecha. E fallaron en esta misma materia, no por
manera de adiuinança en que algunos fechos se ponen, *en* la qual es
repoyda[91] en todo buen sauer, e saluo sienpre ante e despues en cada
logar, el solo e mejor de Dios e el su non semejante poderio,[92] al qual   45
toda cosa es ligera. E fue esta profeçia *in*terpretada[93] por la forma con-
tenida en cada *seso*[94] della. E *cree*[95] que ha de ser trayda a esecuçion en
la tu persona real, de lo qual Dios solo te guarde. En que manera ella es
e a de ser puedes saverlo por las esplanaçiones que se syguen."

[86]i *inserted by different hand A.*
[87]en poder *A.*
[88]espalañaçion *A.*
[89]fizusa *A.*
[90]estudieme *A.*
[91]se ponen las quales Repoydas *A.*
[92]semejante e poderio *A.*
[93]perpretada *A.*
[94]contenida la qual es en cada sello *A.*
[95]trae *A.*

"Rey alto ensalçado, save que esta profeçia endereça el hito contra el
rey que en ella era, que en fin del libro que enviaste dezir que seria rey
della, en la qual tierra agora no es visto ser rey dende otro alguno sino
tu, que por derecho *e* antiguedad[96] lo tienes. Quanto mas pues es manifiesto que tu eres el rey en que la profeçia dize que naçera entre los   55
montes e la mar, ca el tu naçimiento fue en la çivdad de Burgos, segund
entendi, que bien puede ser dicho que es en tal comarca. Asi entiendo
quel primer seso de los articulos de la profeçia, que fabla del primer
naçimiento, que se prueva quanto cunple."

"Siguese adelante que dize esta ave asi naçida que sera comedera *e*
robadera.[97] Rey, save que los reyes que comen de los averes, e algos, e
rentas que a el no son deuid*os*[98] son llamados estos tales comedores e
robadores. Pues si tu comes e gastas de las tus rentas propias al tu
señorio convenientes, tu solo saves. Mas la tu fama es contrari*a*,[99] ca diz   65
que tomas los algos e vienes de tus naturales doquier que los puedes
aver e de otros, e fazes tomar e robar, e que esto por el puro derecho. E
asi esplana quel /321b/ tu comer e robar es tal como lo que tiene la
segunda esplanaçion del segundo seso de la profeçia."

"Otrosi dize que todos los panares del mundo querra cojer en si. Rey,
saue, pensando *en* esta[100] esplanaçion solamente por la traer a buena
concordança creedera, que fa*l*le[101] que quando el rey don Alfonso, tu
padre, era vivo, e avn despues de su finamiento e despues aca que tu
reynaste algund tienpo, que todos[102] los del tu señorio viuian gran pla-   75
zer de la vida por las muchas buenas costunbres que vsava tu padre. E
este plazer les finco pendiente despues del finamiento en tienpo del tu
señorio. El qual plazer avian por tan deleytoso que bien[103] podrian dezir que dulçor de panares de miel ni de otro savor alguno no podria ser
a ello conparado. De los quales plazeres son tirados tienpo ha a todos los   80

[96]derecho antiguedad *A*.
[97]comedera robadera *A*.
[98]deuidas *A*.
[99]contrario *A*.
[100]pensando esta *A*; pensando en esta *N*.
[101]fable *A*.
[102]que todos en todos *A*.
[103]que que bien *A*.

tus suditos, porque tu eres el açidente dello por muchas amarguras, e quebrantos, e desafueros en que los has puesto e pones de cada dia, faziendo en ellos muchas cruezas de sangre, e de finamientos, e otros muchos agrauios, los quales lengua no puede pronunçiar. E asi tengo que desplana este terçero seso desta profeçia de los panares, pues el tu   85 açidente fue el robador dellos."

Sigue la carta

"Otrosi dize que todo el oro del mundo metera en si e en su estomago. Rey, save lo qual creo que eres bien sauidor, maguer pareçe que no curas dello, que tan manifiesta es la tu codiçia desordenada de que   90 vsas que todos los que han el tu conoçimiento por vso e por vista, e avn eso mesmo por oydas, o por otra qualquier conversaçion, tienen que eres el mas señalado rey codiçioso desordenado que en los *tienpos* pasados[104] ovo ay en Castilla ni en otros reynos. E tan grande es la tu codiçia e tan descobierta que muestra en acreçentar thesoros desordenados, que non tan solamente avonda lo ordenado, mas avn mas mal,   95 que *t*omas e *r*obas[105] algunos bienes de las yglesias e casas de oraçiones. Asi acreçientas todos estos thesoros que te non vençe conçiençia ni verguença. A tan grande[106] /321c/ es la *acu*çia[107] que pones en la codiçia que fazes nuebas obras e fuertes, asi de castillos commo de otras forta-   100 lezas e labores donde puedes asegurar estos tales tesoros, porque no puedes caver en ellos en todo el mundo, andando fuyendo de[108] vn logar a otro todavia con ellos, porquel partir dellos te es grave de lo probar. Por lo qual todos afirmando el testo de la profeçia en este caso. E bien creo que si en el tu estomago lo podieses meter, por te non partir de-   105 llo*s*[109] e traerlos contigo, que te ofreçerias a ello. E asaz se muestra asi verdad, porque bien saues quanto tienpo ha en como el tu enemigo, que se atitulo en el tu nonbre de rey, con otros tus enemigos la segunda vez entrados por las tierras e señorios dende e donde tu te llamas rey, afirmando el titulo que ha tomado real e por no te partir desta codiçia,   110 fazete olvidar verguença e vondad. E estas asentado en los postrimeros del tu señorio en esa frontera açerca contigo de tus thesoros, pues de ti no los entiendes partir ni otrosi leuar contigo, metidos en tu estomago do los querrias poner, si caso fuese e podiese ser, e donde oluidas la honrra e el estado que avias, el qual te va menguando cada dia. E asi   115 tengo que se esplana este quarto seso desta profeçia."

[104]los pasados *A*.
[105]comas e sobras *A*.
[106]grand *A*.
[107]codiçia *A*.
[108]fuyendo con ellos de *A*.
[109]dello *A*.

Ssigue la carta

"Otrosi lo al que desto se sigue *do* dize[110] que lo gormara, Rey, çierto es quel mucho codiçioso codiçia, e con escazeça desordenada, que es su hermana, allega thesoros en esta manera. Puedele conteçer como con-   120 teçio al omne gloton que pone en su estomago mas vianda que la natura pide que puede sofrir. Asi por el poner de la demasia quel estomago no puede sofrir, de gormar lo ordenado e lo desordenado, por lo qual no se puede escusar que no crezca por ello en el açidente, *el* qual[111] traye desmayo e flaqueza en todos los otros mienbros. E pues tu por esta   125 mesma manera allegas thesoros con codiçia desordenada, tengo que te abra aconteçer por esta mesma forma que per /321c/ deras[112] lo orde- nado por lo desordenado, e communalmente todo en vno que lo gor- maras por superfluydad[113] que es tu ocasion, e creçerte ha el açidente por ello. El qual verna en ti aquella dolençia que diz que pone Merlin   130 en este quinto *seso* desta[114] profeçia e que no seria fallado remedio para ello ninguno de sanidad. E asi tengo que es esplanado el quinto seso desta profiçia."

Siguese la carta

"E dize otrosi que se secaran las peñolas e se le caera la pluma. Rey,   135 saue que los filosofos naturales, entre los otros negoçios que dellos *man*- daron,[115] trataron buenamente en[116] tales materias o en semejantes seyendo *pue*sto[117] el caso e disputada[118] la quistion entre ellos. E la aso- luçion[119] es esta: que las peñolas[120] con que los reyes anobleçen a si mes- mos e anparan e defienden sus tierras e su estado, que son los mas   140 grandes en sangre e en linaje, que son sus naturales, porque estos *son* conparados[121] e llamados alas con que los reyes buelan a vnas tierras e a otras, e con quien fazen sus consejos, e con las peñolas que de*stas*[122] tales alas se crian en los cuerpos de los reyes e nobleçen mucho sus per- sonas e sus figuras, e que se refazen mucho apuestos por ello, e creçen   145 en su orgullo, e apremian en ello mucho sus contrarios. E con estas alas

[110]sigue dize *A*.
[111]en quel *A*.
[112]per perderas *A* (*scribal repetition at beginning of new folio page*).
[113]su perfuleydad *A*.
[114]quinto deste *A*; quinto desta *N*.
[115]mudaron *A*.
[116]buenamente ca en *A*.
[117]por esto *A*.
[118]dispustada *A*; disputada *N*.
[119]asoluiçion *A*.
[120]l *superposed upon an* s *A*.
[121]estos conparados *A*.
[122]despues *A*.

pueden fazer muy ligeros buelos los reyes quando los sus naturales son
pagados dellos. En lo qual deven mucho afirmar los reyes, por que entre
ellos, e los reyes, e los nobles en sangre no aya desmano a culpa[123] del
rey, pero todavia guardando el conoçimiento real del rey e la su alteza,   150
lo qual en ninguna guisa no deve ser quebrado. E quando asi en ellos se
guarda, es ver Dios terçero por guarda e por entre medianero, e es el
rey çierto de sus alas en el tienpo de sus menesteres. De lo qual desplaze
mucho a sus enemigos, e desto todo por ventura, muestra ser contra ti lo
contrario, por lo qual temo que la profeçia quiere çerrar de grado en ti   155
seguiendo /322a/ su esecuçion, que en ti no aya alas de buelo ni peñolas
con que afermoses tu persona. Asi que no pareçe en ti esfuerço alguno
por fazer voladura[124] sin lision[125] de tu cuerpo, sin grand daño del tu
estado, ca tus malquerientes pujan en la tu osadia. E puesto que alguna
muestra quieras fazer so color de buelo, deziendo que tienes plumas,   160
save que muy fuerte cosa e muy grave es de encobrir lo que es manifiesto, ca estas tus plumas con que en esa tu color piensas fazer no son
tales con que puedas fazer buelo ninguno, por muy pequeño que sea, sin
te estar aparejada la lision[126] antedicha mayormente por el grand menester en que estas, ca lo manifiesto de ti si *es que* las[127] plumas enteras 165
en los cochillos que solias aver en tus alas con que volar solias, que son
caydas, pues todos los tus naturales mas nobles e mas poderosos *que* a[128]
esto eran conparados, que fasta aqui tenias por peñolas de tu buelo, han
puesto en oluido el amorio que te solian aver e el señorio tuyo *que*
fasta[129] aqui ovedeçian trataronlo con el tu contrario. E la ocasion e el   170
açidente[130] por quien vino fuera de Dios tu eres el sauidor dello. E asi
tengo que en esto se dispone este sesto seso de la dicha profiçia."

Siguese la carta

"Otrosi avn dize mas que andara este rey de puerta en puerta e que
ninguno no lo querra acoger. Rey, saue que todo lo savemos, que tan   175
manifiesto es solamente esto contra ti que sinple saver de qualquier omne
puede fazer su esplanaçion, porque mal pecado tengo que los del tu
señorio no quieren acojerte yrado ni pagado en quanto ellos podiesen,
porque sienpre quesiste ser de los tuyos mas temido que loado, e
commoquier que en esa çivdad onde estas agora asentado te ovieses   180

---

[123]desmano e aculpa *A*.
[124]voladera *A*.
[125]ligion *A*.
[126]ligion *A*.
[127]si as en *A*.
[128]poderosos a *A*.
[129]tuyo fasta *A*.
[130]oçidente *A*.

apoderar. Pero Dios te libre del poder del diablo, que del no sean tentados
los que ay son por que fagan algun movimiento contra la tu persona, que
oy dezir que dizen de ti e he temor que se querran mover e fazer contra
/322b/ ti. E asi tengo que se desplana la razon deste setimo seso."

Siguese la carta   185

"Dize otrosi que se ençerrara en la selua e que morra hi dos vezes.
Rey, save que lo que a mi fue mas grave, e el mayor afan que en esto
tome si fue por apurar el seso deste vocablo que dize en la selua, e para
esto acarree su entrepetraçion[131] en esta guisa: Yo re*queri*[132] los libros
de las conquistas que pasaron fasta aqui entre las casas de Castilla, e de   190
Granada, e de Velamarin, e por los libros mas antigos de los fechos que
pasaron falle escrito que quando la tierra que llamavan Alcaraz, que en
el tu señorio era poblada de los nuestros moros, e fue perdida, e fue
cobrada de los christianos, que avia çerca della vn castillo que a ese
tienpo era llamado por nonbre Selua, el qual fallo por estos mesmos   195
libros que a esta sazon perdio luego este nonbre que avia de Selua e fue
llamado Montiel, que agora es asi llamado. E si tu eres aquel rey que la
profezia dize que ha de ser ençerrado, luego esta es la selua e el lugar de
ençerramiento segund por esta profeçia se pone. En el abra de conteçer
estas muertes. E lo al que la profeçia dize, Dios solo es dello sauidor, al   200
qual perteneçen los tales secretos, e porque en este logar canso el mi
saver e en este caso, que era de menester de sauer, no pude mas alcançar, ca lo pase a mayor otro logar, e no ovo[133] por yndustria, saluo por
quanto se dexo vençer[134] de alguna opinion,[135] que la mi ymaginança no
parte despues aques*te*[136] de si, tiene que bien asi commo en cada vno de   205
los otros mienbros esta profeçia faze contra ti en cada materia, segund
seguia por las profiçias, que bien asi yra[137] faziendo su curso por su conclusion de vno al otro, de grado en grado, contra esta ave negra que asi
dize que naçera, en la qual todas estas cosas han de ser conplidas. E
porquel postrimero seso en que faze conclusion del ençerramiento seria   210
antes adeuinança, que no *alcanç*amiento[138] de sauer, lo qual en todo
buen saver deve ser repetido e dexada su esplanaçion aquel en quien es
el poderio, que lo tal reseria en sus secretos, e tu ventura que la /322c/
querra Dios guisar e desviar, por que las cosas antedichas[139] no ayan

---

[131]entrepētraçion *A*.
[132]regi *A*.
[133]ove *A*.
[134]saluo por quanto se dexo por yndustria saluo por quanto se dexo vençer *A*.
[135]opiñion *A*.
[136]aquese *A*.
[137]yran *A*.
[138]asentamiento *A*.
[139]antes dichas *A*.

logar de fazer en ti la esecuçion que trae tan espantosa, en *lo* qual[140] yo 215
seria muy agradable, maguer que en mis juyzios fincase contrario, e no
verdadero, lo qual seria *agradable* e muy ligero[141] de lo sofrir, porque
mayor buena andança seria a mi en la tu merçed del bien e vida segura
que ovieses, que no del contrario que temo, ca en lo que te conplira,
mandame como a tuyo, e en esto me faras grand plazer. Mas no me 220
escrivas este vocablo rogar porque en el tu ruego me fazes pesar, e no
cae en razon. E si algo fue atreuido, no culpes la mi osadia, porque de la
parte del tu cu*i*doso[142] seso me atreui, e mandasteme por tu carta que la
verdad desto no *te* fuese[143] negada en aquello quel mi sauer alcançase.
Yo fable contigo segund lo entendi sobre ello, mas no por otra çerti- 225
dunbre que podiese afirmar. Pero *si en*[144] la tu corte ay omnes sauidores
e justos de quien las tales cosas no se encubren, me[145] terne a la mejor
coRuçion del su saver. Escrita en Granada a .xx. de enero."

[Libros XVIII–XIX]

In Book XVIII García de Salazar recounts the deeds of the Castil-
ian kings from Henry II to Henry IV. In Book XIX he tells the
history of the kings of the other realms of the Peninsula: Navarre,
from Iñigo Arista to John I; Aragon, from Ramiro I to John I; and
Portugal, from Afonso Henriques to Afonso V.

[Libros XX–XXV]

The last six books of the Bienandanzas e fortunas *treat the history*
and lore of Spain's northern provinces, especially the region of
Vizcaya. In Books XXI, XXII, and XXV the impact of the Tristan
and Grail romances at the social level in the north of Spain may
be observed in references to individuals living in the fourteenth
and fifteenth centuries whose given name was Tristán, Galaz
(English "Galahad"), or Persival. The references (in modernized
spelling) and their folio location within MS. 9-10-2/2100 are as
follows:

Tristán de Leguizamón, son of Martín Sánchez of Bilbao (Vizcaya)
and brother of Floristán and Galaz of Leguizamón (fols. 367a,
391a, 393d, 396a).

[140]en el qual A.
[141]seria grave e verdadero e muy ligero A.
[142]cudioso A.
[143]no fuese A.
[144]pero segun A.
[145]encubren e me A.

Tristán de Leguizamón el mozo, son of Tristán de Leguizamón (fols. 367a, 394c, 396a).

Tristán, son of Sancho Díaz de Leguizamón and grandson of Tristán de Leguizamón (fol. 367a).

Tristán de Valdés, son of Melén Sánchez de Valdés of Luarca (Asturias) and brother of Galaz and Perrot de Valdés (fol. 442c).

Galaz de Leguizamón, son of Martín Sánchez de Leguizamón and brother of Tristán and Floristán de Leguizamón (fols. 367a, 391a, 393d, 396a).

Galaz de Valdés, son of Melén Suárez de Valdés and brother of Tristán and Perrot de Valdés (fol. 442c).

Persival (*var.* Perseval) de Múgica, son of Fray Juan de Múgica of Vizcaya (fols. 394d, 395c, 396a).

TEXTUAL COMMENTARY

The commentary gives the results of my study of Salazar's sources. Included are word-for-word comparisons of the text with available manuscript and printed sources or collateral versions. Where no known source has been uncovered, I have attempted to present facts which may throw light on the author's originality and his use of oral, literary, and historiographic traditions.

To the left of each entry I indicate the chapter and line references to the present edition. The abbreviations used for frequently mentioned texts and critical works are as follows:

A	Madrid, Biblioteca de la Real Academia de la Historia, MS. 9-10-2/2100.
ALMA	*Arthurian Literature in the Middle Ages*, ed. Roger Sherman Loomis (Oxford, 1959; rpt. ed., 1961).
Bogdanow, *Romance*	Fanni Bogdanow, *The Romance of the Grail* (Manchester–New York, 1966).
Bohigas, 1498 *Baladro*	*El Baladro del Sabio Merlín según el texto de la edición de Burgos 1498,*

ed. Pedro Bohigas, 3 vols., Selecciones Bibliófilas, Segunda Serie, vols. 2, 14, 15 (Barcelona, 1957–62).

Bohigas, *Los textos*   P. Bohigas Balaguer, *Los textos españoles y gallego-portugueses de la Demanda del Santo Grial*, RFE, Anejo 7 (Madrid, 1925).

Bonilla, 1501 *Tristán*   *Libro del esforçado cauallero don Tristan de Leonis y de sus grandes fechos en armas (Valladolid, 1501)*, ed. Adolfo Bonilla y San Martín, Sociedad de Bibliófilos Madrileños, 6 (Madrid, 1912).

Bonilla, 1528 *Tristán*   *Libro del esforzado caballero don Tristan de Leonis y de sus grandes hechos en armas* [Seville, 1528], ed. Adolfo Bonilla y San Martín, in *Libros de caballerías*, 1: *Ciclo artúrico–Ciclo carolingio*, NBAE, 6 (Madrid, 1907), pp. 339–457.

Bonilla, 1535 *Baladro*   *El Baladro del Sabio Merlín con sus profecías* [Seville, 1535], ed. Adolfo Bonilla y San Martín, in *Libros de caballerías*, 1: *Ciclo artúrico–Ciclo carolingio*, NBAE, 6 (Madrid, 1907), pp. 3–162.

Bonilla, 1535 *Demanda*   *La Demanda del Sancto Grial con los maravillosos fechos de Lanzarote y de Galaz su hijo* [Seville, 1535], ed. Adolfo Bonilla y San Martín, in *Libros de caballerías*, 1: *Ciclo artúrico–Ciclo carolingio*, NBAE, 6 (Madrid, 1907), pp. 3–162.

Cast. 1515 *Demanda*   *La demanda del Sancto Grial con los maravillosos fechos de Lanzarote y de Galaz su fijo* (Toledo, 1515).

Entwistle, *Legend*   William J. Entwistle, *The Arthurian Legend in the Literatures of the Spanish Peninsula* (1925; rpt. ed., New York, 1975).

Frappier, *Mort Artu*   *La Mort le Roi Artu: Roman du XIII*ᵉ *siècle,* ed. Jean Frappier, TLF, 58 (Geneva–Paris, 1956).

Herrero, *Las bienandanzas*   *Las bienandanzas e fortunas,* ed. Angel Rodríguez Herrero, 4 vols. (Bilbao, 1967).

Huth *Merlin*   *Merlin: Roman en prose du XIII*ᵉ *siècle,* ed. Gaston Paris and Jacob Ulrich, 2 vols. (1886; rpt. ed., New York, 1965).

Löseth, *Le Roman*   E. Löseth, *Le Roman en prose de Tristan* (1891; rpt. ed., New York, 1970).

Magne, Ptg. *Demanda*   *A Demanda do Santo Graal: Reprodução fac-similar e transcrição crítica do códice 2594 da Biblioteca Nacional de Viena,* ed. Augusto Magne, S.J., 2 vols. (Rio de Janeiro, 1955–70).

Northup, *El cuento*   *El cuento de Tristán de Leonís,* ed. George Tyler Northup, Modern Philology Monographs (Chicago, 1928).

Pauphilet, *Queste*   *La Queste del Saint Graal: Roman du XIII*ᵉ *siècle,* ed. Albert Pauphilet, CFMA, 33 (1923; rpt. ed., Paris, 1967).

Pietsch, *Fragments*   *Spanish Grail Fragments,* ed. Karl Pietsch, 2 vols. (Chicago, 1924–25).

Ptg. *Josep*   *The Portuguese Book of Joseph of Arimathea,* ed. Henry Hare Carter, UNCSRLL, 71 (Chapel Hill, 1967).

Rey, *Sumas*   Leomarte, *Sumas de historia troyana,* ed. Agapito Rey, *RFE,* Anejo 15 (Madrid, 1932).

Sommer, *Vulgate*   *The Vulgate Version of the Arthurian Romances,* ed. H. Oskar Sommer, 8 vols. (1908–16; rpt. ed., New York, 1969).

Wilkins, *Corónica*   Constance Lee Wilkins, "An Edition

of the *Corónica del rey don Pedro* by Pero López de Ayala based on manuscript A-14 of the Academia de la Historia" (Diss., Univ. of Wisconsin, 1974).

For other abbreviations, see the list of abbreviations following the Preface.

Book V

67: 1 ff. Salazar summarizes the tale of Ibycus as found in the *Libro de los buenos proverbios*, the Spanish version of al-Harizi's thirteenth-century Hebrew translation of the ninth-century Nestorian Ḥunayn ibn Isḥāq's book of proverbs. The Spanish text is edited by Hermann Knust, in *Mittheilungen aus dem Eskurial*, Bibliothek des litterarischen Vereins in Stuttgart, 141 (Tübingen, 1879), pp. 1–65; and reedited by Harlan Sturm, *The "Libro de los buenos proverbios": A Critical Edition*, Studies in Romance Languages, 5 (Lexington, Ky., 1970). Only a few verbal correspondences are to be observed between the Salazar summary, which alters the sequence of elements, and that of the edited MSS (see Sturm ed., pp. 43–46; Knust ed., p. 2). I have not had an opportunity to examine the version of the Ibycus tale in Salamanca, Biblioteca Universitaria, MS. 1763 (*olim*, Madrid, Biblioteca Real de Palacio, 105; *olim* 2-B-5), an unedited fifteenth-century (?) copy of the *Buenos proverbios*. Concerning this MS and the influence of the Ḥunayn text in Spain, see John K. Walsh, "Versiones peninsulares del *Kitāb ādāb al-falāsifa* de Ḥunayn ibn Isḥāq: Hacia una reconstrucción del *Libro de los buenos proverbios*," *Al-Andalus* 41 (1976): 355–84.

67: 1. Ancos (*var.* Anchos) is the name given to Ibycus in the Spanish versions edited by Knust and Sturm.

67: 10. The rubric, somewhat out of place here, would seem to be the invention of Salazar.

67: 11–12. Cf. *Buenos proverbios:* "por esso aguiso Dios que el dia que se ayuntaron que passassen las gruas por que oviessen emiente aquellos ladrones de aquel fecho malo que fizieran" (Sturm ed., p. 46).

67: 13–14. Cf. *Buenos proverbios:* "Y vieron gruas que bolavan en el ayre y pararon mientes aquellos ladrones, y risieronse y dixieron unos a otros: —Estos son los testimonios y los demandadores de la sangre de Anchos el torpe (Sturm ed., p. 44).

67: 14–15. The scatological comment is lacking in the edited MSS of the *Buenos proverbios.* Cf. Bellido Adolfo's assassination of Sancho II of Castile when the latter is relieving himself outside the walls of the city of Zamora, as related by Salazar in Bk. XV (*A*, fol. 261a; Herrero, *Las bienandanzas*, 3: 70). For a brief study of the episode in other chronicles, see Alan Deyermond, "Medieval Spanish Epic Cycles: Observations on their Formation and Development," *Kentucky Romance Quarterly* 23 (1976): 289–90, and n. 32.

67: 17–19. Salazar takes this piece of proverbial wisdom from his earlier adaptation of the book of Ecclesiastes. Cf. "ca las aues del çielo lieban la voz e dien non [*sic*] de las alas denunçia la cosa" (*A*, fol. 31b; Herrero, *Las bienandanzas*, 1:55).

67: 19–22. The Arthurian reference is also lacking in the *Buenos proverbios*. Salazar may have found Merlin's piece of advice to Arthur in the Spanish adaptation of the *Merlin* branch of the Post-Vulgate *Roman du Graal*. In this text, Merlin appears to Arthur in disguise as an eighty-year old man, and Arthur tells him that a young boy (actually Merlin again in disguise) had come to him a short time before and revealed knowledge of matters known only to him. In response, Merlin tells Arthur, "No os marauilledes ende, ca no ay cosa tan encubierta que no sea descubierta, e si cosa fuesse hecha so tierra, la verdad ende es sabida, quanto mas sobre la tierra" (Bonilla, 1535 *Baladro*, p. 56a).

BOOK IX

8: 1-9. It is said that Faramont, son of Marcho Monueres, raised the good knight Tristan and that his daughter Vellida killed herself because of her love for Tristan. Salazar's source for this information, as the allusion to the *ystoria* of Tristan would indicate, is the Tristan story concerning the hero's childhood; but Salazar's historiographic source for the remainder of the chapter, and the early history of France as well, is still unknown. The figure of Pharamont is first mentioned in the *Liber historiae Francorum* (see *Monu-*

menta Germaniae historica: Scriptores rerum Merowingicarum [Hannover, 1885–1919], 2: 224). According to this eighth-century chronicle Faramundo was the son of Marchomiris, the young son of Priam of Troy. The edited medieval Peninsular histories of the French kings, the *Liber Regum*, the *Livro das linhagens*, and the *Crónica general de 1344*, do not include the Pharamont material (see *Crónica Geral de Espanha de 1344*, ed. L. F. Lindley Cintra [Lisbon, 1951–61], 1, pp. xxxv, xcvii, xcix, civ-cv); but the reign of Pharamont (less the Tristan material) is found in an unedited fifteenth-century text, Diego de Valera's *Genealogía de los reyes de Francia*: "los tres estados eligieron por rrey vn noble e muy virtuoso cauallero llamado Faramon hijo [*scribe crosses out* 'paryente muy çercano'] del duque Marcomedes ya dicho que era pagano o gentil. Y este fue el primero rrey que los galos o françeses ovieron. El qual començo a rreynar en el año de la encarnaçion de Nuestro Redentor de quatroçientos e veynte [*scribe crosses out* 'e ocho años'] e rreyno quarenta años e nunca fue christiano. Fue muy buen rrey e tuvo sus rreynos en gran paz e sosyego. En tienpo deste rrey en el año primero de su rreynado fue fallado por rreuelaçion de Dios el cuerpo de Santiesteuan, primero martir; en este año murio Sant Jeronimo en Belem e fue ally sepultado seyendo en hedad de nouenta e ocho años; y en su tienpo fue convertido la tierra de Yrlanda a la fe catolica e fueron christianos los persyanos segund lo pone el cardenal Martino en la coronica martiniana que de los rreys de França escruio" [*marginal note by later hand:* 'Nota. Antes de Faramon ovo veynte e quatro reyes. E Faramon fue rey vente e çinco. Nota esto y enmienda este passo'] (Madrid, Biblioteca Nacional, MS. 1341 [*olim* F-108], fol. 328ᵛ; a similar reading, less marginal notes, is found in another fifteenth-century copy, Vienna, Oesterreichische Nationalbibliothek, MS. 5612, fol. 77). Salazar would appear to have derived his information independently of Valera's *Genealogía* and the source cited therein.

Precisely when Pharamont and his daughter Belide were linked to the story of Tristan has yet to be thoroughly investigated. The Pharamont/Tristan narrative is extraneous to the early poetic versions of Tristan's youth, such as the poems of Eilhart von Oberge (*Tristrant*, ed. Danielle Buschinger [Göppingen, 1976], vv. 1-350b.) and Thomas (*Le Roman de Tristan...*, ed. J. Bédier [Paris, 1902], 1: 2–42). The episode is included in the early thirteenth-century Fr. Prose *Tristan* (for two different MS versions, see *La Grant Ystoire de Monsignor Tristan "Li Brut"*, ed. F. C. Johnson [Edinburgh–London, 1942], §§5–8; and *Le Roman de Tristan en prose,* ed. R. D. Curtis [Munich, 1963], 1, §§ 23–27). Critics of the *Tristan en prose* have tended to ignore the thorny problem of tracing the sources of the material the adaptor added. Vinaver, however, is of the opinion that some of the material was taken from "romans de chevalerie" *(Etudes sur le Tristan en prose* [Paris, 1925], p. 11); and, more recently, he has remarked that the inclusion of the Pharamont matter in the prose romance "is an indication of the author's constant readiness to emancipate himself from traditional patterns" *(ALMA,* p. 344). F. Bogdanow concurs with Vinaver: "When the prose writer remodelled the poetic versions of the *Tristan,* he combined them with new material, some of which he derived from the Vulgate. But the alterations and additions that he made, far from being haphazard, served above all, as Vinaver has shown, to rationalize and elucidate the various themes" *(Romance,* p. 19). Emmanuèle Baumgartner follows Vinaver's approach in a series of textual explanations, and suggests the Maid of Escalot episode in the Vulgate *Mort Artu* as the specific source for the Belide material *(Le "Tristan en prose": Essai d'interprétation d'un roman médiéval* [Geneva, 1975], pp. 112–13, 122, 139, 204–6). Alan Fedrick also points out that the episode of Belide's death foreshadows Tristan's ill-fated love for Iseut ("The Account of Tristan's Birth and Childhood in the French Prose *Tristan,*" *Romania* 89 [1968]: 354).

The story of Tristan's upbringing at Pharamont's court is known in several Spanish redactions of the Prose *Tristan:* the late fourteenth or early fifteenth-century Vatican MS. 6428, edited by G. T. Northup as *El cuento de Tristán de Leonís* (Chicago, 1928), pp. 79–84; the 1501 Valladolid imprint *Libro del esforçado cauallero don Tristan de Leonis,* ed. A. Bonilla (Madrid, 1912), pp. 14–27; and the Seville 1528 version, ed. A. Bonilla, NBAE, 6 (Madrid, 1907), pp. 344a–348a. The use of proper names in these Spanish texts reflects a source different from that followed by García de Salazar. In the printed *Tristán de Leonís,* for "Faramont" and "Vellida" of the *Bienandanzas* we find "Feremondo" and "Belisenda"; and in Vatican MS. 6428, "Framont de Gaulas" and "Barisen" *(var.* "Balisen"). The names given by Salazar would seem to reflect a Fr. source, but those of the older Sp. texts may ultimately stem from a Provençal, Catalan, Aragonese, or possibly even an Italian intermediary (see Entwistle, *Legend,* pp. 112–13, 115 ff.; Northup, *El cuento,* pp. 13 ff.; the reviews of Northup's edition by P. Bohigas Balaguer, *RFE* 16 [1929]: 284–85; and P. H. Coronedi, *Archivum Romanicum,* 16 [1932]: 172 ff.).

BOOK X

3: 1 ff. Although Salazar's immediate source for his history of Flanders is not known, the onomastic references in this chapter indicate a blending of literary and historiographic traditions. The matters alluded to are clearly related to events described in some versions of the Prose *Tristan* and Post-Vulgate *Queste del Saint Graal* and to material introduced into Spanish historiography by Alfonso X el Sabio.

3: 4-8. The story of how the *almonicas* of Chaldea migrated to Western Europe is told by Salazar not in his chapters on the Romans (Bks. VI–VIII) but as part of the pre-Roman history of Spain (Bk. XIII, ch. 9). The matter appears in Alfonso el Sabio's *Estoria de España* (see *Primera crónica general,* ed. R. Menéndez Pidal [Madrid, 1955], 1: 14*a*–15*b*). The *lormanes* or Normans are linked to the *almonicas* (cf. *almujuces* in the *Estoria de España*) in Arabic tradition (see R. Dozy, *Recherches sur l'histoire et la littérature de l'Espagne pendant le Moyen Age* [Leiden, 1881], 2: 253).

3: 12-16. I have not discovered Salazar's precise source for the cannibalistic Flemings, but the notion of cruel and anthropophagous heathens is common to a wide number of medieval texts. Salazar may have taken his material from a text that he uses elsewhere in the *Bienandanzas*: the *Libro del Infante don Pedro de Portugal,* a pseudo-travel book which has generally been regarded as a sixteenth-century product. Cf. the following passage: "& auemos gentes en algunas partes que no han sino vn ojo, y esso mesmo en otras partes que han quatro ojos delante y detras. Y esta gente de que alguno muere los parientes lo comen que dizen que la mejor carne del mundo es la del hombre" (Gómez de Santiesteban, *Libro del Infante don Pedro de Portugal,* ed. Francis M. Rogers [Lisbon, 1962], p. 51.) Concerning Salazar's use of this work, see my article "Evidence of a Fifteenth-Century *Libro del Infante don Pedro de Portugal* and Its Relationship to the Alexander Cycle," *JHP* 1 (1976–77): 85–98.

3: 18-27. Salazar curiously links the early history of Flanders to the time of King Arthur and the knights of the Round Table, a connection not found in any Arthurian texts I have consulted. At the end of the passage Salazar alludes to his source, the *Demanda,* which is the Hispanic version of the Post-Vulgate *Queste del Saint Graal* (on the relationship of the Cast. and Ptg. versions of the *Demanda* to the Fr. texts, see Bogdanow, *Romance,* pp. 88–120). He tells us that in the *Demanda* the "Torre del Lloro" (the "Chastel des Pleurs" of the Prose *Tristan*, cf. "Castillo del Ploto" in the Sp. *Tristán de Leonís*) was the place where the knights of the Round Table were subjected to the "crueles presiones" of the pagans. F. Bogdanow has shown that some episodes found in the Prose *Tristan* are also incorporated independently in the Cast. and Ptg. *Demanda* texts (Bogdanow, *Romance*, pp. 91–120). However, none of the *Demanda* texts include the "Torre del Lloro" incident, although several references are made to Galeote, "el señor de las luengas ynsolas" (cf. Cast. 1515 *Demanda*, Chs. 450, 453; Bonilla 1535 *Demanda*, pp. 335*a*, 336*b*; Magne, Ptg. *Demanda*, 2: §§ 697, 698; and the Fr. Prose *Tristan*, wherein Tristan and Iseut are shipwrecked on one of the "Isles Lointaines" ruled by Galehaut where the "Chastel des Pleurs" is located [Löseth, *Le Roman*, §§40–41]). There is, nevertheless, an episode in the Post-Vulgate *Queste*, including the *Demanda* texts (Cast. versions, Ch. 272; Magne, Ptg. *Demanda*, 2, § 497), which greatly resembles, both in content and in spirit, the brief account related by Salazar. Both the Cast. and Ptg. texts tell us that the pagan inhabitants of the "Castillo Follón" or "Castel Felom" resisted conversion to Christianity. The Ptg. texts provides the best reading:

Sabede que o castelo estava em ũa grã montanha e era tam forte que rem nom timia. Aquêle castelo fezera Galmanasar, uũ parente de Príamos, rei de Tróia. Aquêle Galmanasar era boõ cavaleiro de armas, e houve seus filhos boõs cavaleiros, que teverom a terra depós êle tam em paz, que nom houverom vezinho que os ousasse guerrear. Aquela terra teve sa linhagem de uũ heree em outro, atá que veerom cristaãos. E nunca rei Mordraim nem Nasciam, quando veerom aa Grã-Bretanha, nom lhis poderom nuzir, nem Joseph Abaramatia, nem Josefes seu filho nom nos poderom tornar cristaãos, nem Santo Agostĩo, que aquela saçom foi em Inglaterra; ante lhi fezerom i muito escarnho. Unde aveo que, porque achou i os mais felões homens que nunca achou, pôs nome ao castelo "felom", que nunca pois perdeu seu nome.

It is also at this castle that the knights of the Round Table receive the "crueles presiones" referred to by Salazar (Magne, Ptg. *Demanda*, 2, §§496–99; Cast. 1515 *Demanda*, Chs. 270–84; Bonilla, 1535 *Demanda*, pp. 265*a*–269*b*).

In the *Tristán de Leonís* Tristan and Iseut are shipwrecked on the "ysla del Gigante" (cf. *Bienandanzas* "ysla de Gajola," which later was named "Luenga Ynsola"). We are told in the *Tristán* that Joseph of Arimathea came to this island to "predicar le fee de Christo":

Sabed que el que fizo este castillo auia nombre Edon, & era gigante, & auia doze fijos, & esto era en el tienpo de Josep Abarimatia, & vino en esta ysla por predicar la fee de Christo, & conuertio gran parte de las gentes, ca bien las dos partes eran conuertidos a Iesucristo; & por esto fue el muy triste, & fizo prender a Josep Abarimatia & fizole cortar la cabeça a el & a onze de sus fijos, que eran conuertidos a la fe de Cristo; & no le quedo saluo vn fijo. E quando todos los vuo muerto, fizolos echar en la plaça, por dar enxemplo & castigo aquellos que heran conuertidos a la fe de Cristo, & fizo venir a todas sus gentes & dixoles: "si alguno de vosotros no quisiere vsar mi ley complida, esso mesmo hare que fize de mis fijos." E luego fizo tomar los huesos de sus fijos & de Josep Abarimatia, & fizo fazer el cimiento de aqueste castillo sobre los huesos de aquella gente que tomo entonces martyrio por Iesucristo; & esto fizo el por escarmentar la gente estraña que le fazian gran daño, e por esto, de entonces aca, es esta vsança & esta costunbre: que todo ombre estraño que aqui (a) aportare, que sea muerto o preso, & metido en tal prision, que jamas dende salga por ninguna auentura, si no ay entre ellos algun cauallero que se combata con el señor de la ysla por fuerça de armas. E si el cauallero lo venciere, que quede por señor de la ysla, & si el cauallero trae consigo alguna dueña, aquel que venciere el campo ha de tomar la mas fermosa, & la otra que le corte la cabeça (Bonilla, 1501 *Tristán*, pp. 86–87; cf. Bonilla, 1528 *Tristán*, pp. 366a–367a; and Löseth, *Le Roman*, §40).

And in the Spanish *Tristan* of Vatican MS. 6428 knights are said to be imprisoned on the Isla del Gigante (Northup, *El cuento*, p. 112). The *Bienandanzas* fragment contains elements common to both episodes cited. As Bogdanow has pointed out, the author of the Post-Vulgate *Queste* sought to prolong the evangelization of the pagans into the time of King Arthur, thereby establishing a degree of continuity between the early history of the Grail in the first branch of the cycle (the *Estoire del Saint Graal*) and his own version of the Grail quest (see *Romance*, pp. 168–69). A similar procedure is followed in the Prose *Tristan*, and the Salazar passage reflects the same technique, but in a considerably altered and abbreviated form.

15: 1-11. Salazar makes reference to certain personages in the Tristan legend: Hoel, king of Brittany and father of Yseo de las Blancas Manos, who married Tristán de Leonís. Mention is also made of Tristán's companion, Cardoyn, who is called an "hermano" of the Round Table. These sketchy details correspond to traditional elements of the Tristan legend (on the origin and development of the legend, see H. Newstead, *ALMA*, pp. 122-33;

the story is retold in the poems of Eilhart and Thomas, and again in the Prose *Tristan*). After being banished from King Mark's court, Tristan travelled to Brittany, where he gained the friendship of Hoel's son Kaherdin and was persuaded to marry his daughter, Iseut of the White Hands. Salazar's allusion to Cardoyn's being part of the Round Table corresponds to the Fr. Prose *Tristan,* wherein "Kahedin le blanc" is included in a list of the knights of the Round Table (see Löseth, *Le Roman,* §395a).

BOOK XI

1: 1 ff. The source for the Brutus material is Leomarte's *Sumas de historia troyana,* of which there are two extant MSS and an incunabulum: from the mid–fourteenth century, Madrid, Biblioteca Nacional, MS. 9256 (*olim* Bb-100); the fifteenth-century Biblioteca Nacional MS. 6419 (*olim* S-30); and a 1490 Burgos printing (see Anthony Cárdenas et al., *Bibliography of Old Spanish Texts,* 2nd ed. [Madison, Wis., 1977], Nos. 1214–16). Agapito Rey has edited MS. 9256 with variants from MS. 6419. The comments on Chs. 1–10 attempt to show how Salazar's version differs from the text edited by Rey. Where readings in MS. 9256 vary significantly from Rey's edition, I cite them within brackets.

1: 1-13. Salazar summarizes here material previously related in Bk. VI, chs. 4–11 (A, fols. 100a–101d; Herrero, *Las bienandanzas,* 1: 193–96). On the figure of Dido in the *Sumas,* see María Rosa Lida de Malkiel, *Dido en la literatura española: Su retrato y defensa* (London, 1974), pp. 8, 49, 61, 96.

1: 14-21. These lines correspond to Rey, *Sumas,* pp. 320–21: "que andando ya Bruto mançebo de veynte annos que andando a caça vn dia Julio, su padre, e estando amos en vna armada en el monte que vino el venado a la armada e que yendo Julio por le feryr que lanço Bruto, su fijo, vna saeta de vn arco por feryr al venado e atrauesando Julio diole la saeta por el cuerpo, de que murio. Pero ante que muriese, de que se sentio mortal, mando que no le fuese demandada aquella muerte nin le fuese retraydo." Also included here is the beginning of *Sumas,* "Titulo ccxvj" (p. 321): "El pueblo de Julio e de su hermano Escanio quando lo vieron ouieron muy grand pesar e fezieron por el muy grand llanto."

1: 21-24. Rey, *Sumas,* p. 321: "pero ellos no quisieron que sobre ellos reynase onbre que a su padre ouiese muerto e echaronlo del reyno." The Salazar version adds greater moral significance to the forced exile of Brutus.

2: 1-3. Rey, *Sumas*, p. 321: "Titulo ccxvj.—Commo partio Bruto del reyno e aporto en el puerto de Greçia." The telling of how Brutus settled in England is not told by Salazar until Chs. 9–10.

2: 4-6. Rey, *Sumas*, p. 321: "Mas su tio Escanio e Syluio Postuno de que aquello vieron aguisaron commo fuese a su onrra, pues de la tierra auia a salyr a buscar su ventura, e dieronle vn nauio e gente para el."

2: 7-10. Rey, *Sumas*, p. 321: "e lançose en la mar. E su voluntad era de yr en Troya, e lleuando para alla su viaje ouo tormenta en la mar e echolo en la tierra de Greçia en el regno de Maçedonia, e reynaua ally entonce el rey Pandraso." Salazar summarizes in one phrase Brutus' reception. Cf. Rey, *Sumas*, p. 321, lines 21–33.

2: 10-16. Rey, *Sumas*, "Titulo ccxvij" (p. 322): "auia en su regno bien diez mill cativos de los troyanos, e avn estos syn fijos e mugeres. Entre los quales estaua Eleno, fijo del rey Periamo. E estaua con estos otrosy Asaraco, nieto de Archiles, que de parte de su madre era muy çercano pariente de los troyanos. E su padre quando muriera auiale dexado tres castillos que eran en la frontera deste rey Pandraso."

2: 16-21. Cf. Rey, longer version of *Sumas*, pp. 322–23.

3: 1-2. MS. 6419: "De la carta que enbio Bruto al rey Pandraso" (Rey, *Sumas*, p. 323).

3: 3-12. Rey, *Sumas*, p. 323: "'Al muy noble esçelente rey Pandraso de Macedonia: Bruto, de las reliquias de los troyanos, salud. Commo sea muy aborreçible cosa e muy cargosa aquellos que la antigua e clara generaçion dio sennorear tan larga e esquiuamente sostener yugo de sugeçion en las sus çeruizes, por ende la clara e deuina generaçion dardana que so el tu duro e espantable sennorio es te dizen que sueltes los graues decretos de la sugeçion tanto tienpo dellos sofrida e quieras darles tierras de lybertad en el tu reyno e averlos [*MS. 9256*: verlos] de aqui adelante por tus fyeles amigos. E do esto non te plaze dales la salyda que vayan buscar tierra en que pueblen; e esto que sea con la tu liçençia. Del qual pedimento tu estas debdor.'" The Salazar text is slightly garbled.

3: 13-20. Cf. Rey, longer version of *Sumas*, pp. 325–27.

3: 21-35. Rey, *Sumas*, "Titulo ccxxiij" (pp. 327–28): "Con muy grande alegria estaua Bruto con tan grant bien andança commo sobre los griegos auia auido, e quedo el e los suyos tan ricos que fue vna grant marauilla. E pues que el despojo fue partido, que duro quatro dias, e todas las cosas asosegadas ayunto Bruto todos los mayores de su hueste e dixo asy: 'Amigos e buenos parientes que aqui estades, ya visto avedes la bien andança que en pos de tantos lazerios Dios vos ha querido dar, por que le deuemos dar muy grandes loores; e otrosy vos bien sabedes commo estamos en Greçia en que ha muchos nobles reyes e prynçipes, e avn que este tengamos vençido non estamos bien seguros, por que es menester que tomedes consejo lo que queredes fazer. E sy queredes quedar en esta tierra con voluntad del rey Pandraso, pues preso lo tenedes e otorgara quanto quisieredes, o quedar en ella para vos parar a todas las cosas que vos avernan, ca yo pues esta carga de vos otros tome con lo que vos otros escogierdes so contento. E agora que tienpo tenedes tomad lo que entendierdes [*MS. 9256:* entendieredes] que a vos otros mas cunple.'"

4: 1-2. Rey, *Sumas*, p. 328: "Titulo ccxxv. —Commo acordaron los de la hueste que todo lo que Eleno e Menbruto mandasen que por aquello estouiesen."

4: 3-31. This chapter corresponds to "Titulo ccxxv" in Rey, *Sumas*, pp. 328–29.

4: 3-8. Rey, *Sumas*, p. 328: "Quistiones muy dyuersas se leuantaron en la hueste sobre esta razon, ca los vnos aprouauan lo vno e los otros lo otro, tanto que ouiera de aver grand vuelta entre ellos. Mas al cabo acordaron que por dos omnes de muy grant seso que en la hueste eran fuese determinado este consejo, e que commo ellos mandasen que asy fuese fecho. E estos dos omnes fueron Eleno, fijo del rey Periamo de Troya, e Menprudo."

4: 8-9. Rey, *Sumas*, p. 328: "E pues que estos ouieron acordado Eleno dixo ante toda la hueste...." MS. 6419 uses the same phrase found in the Salazar text: "ante todo el pueblo."

4: 9-10. Rey, *Sumas*, p. 328: "Sennores, muy dura cosa es e aborreçedera a toda natura."

4: 12-14. Rey, *Sumas*, p. 328: "ca sy en esfuerço desta bien andança que vos ella dio aqui queredes quedar sabet que toda Greçia avedes a destruyr ante que segura vida podades fazer."

4: 15–16. Rey, *Sumas*, p. 328: "E la ventura que vos esto dio temome que non querra con vos otros mayor debdo de amorio tener."

4: 17–19. Rey, *Sumas,* p. 328: "E pues que a los mançebos pueda la guerra bien pareçer los que en la hedat son conplyda despues de tantos afanes debria ser que con seguridat de paz gozasen de graçia [*MS. 9256:* Greçia] de libertad...."

4: 21. Rey, *Sumas,* p. 328: "que le pidades."

4: 21–31. Rey, *Sumas,* pp. 328–29: "'Mas ¿commo non pensades que Pandraso jamas non vos pueda bien querer?; e que el vos bien quisiese e guardase lo que con vos otros posiese, ¿pensades que vos querrian bien nin vos guardarian postura que con vos otros posiesen aquellos a quien vos otros matastes los padres o fijos o hermanos? Non podria ser, ca quando el matador pareçe rezientase la llaga. E ¿commo podra ser fecho de enemigo leal amigo sy de omne a quien non sea fecha calunia alguna a duro puede ser leal fallado? Por que sy a todos pluguiese, a mi pareçeria que lo que al rey Pandraso auiades a pedyr para afyncar en la su tierra que le sea pedido para yr fuera della; e Dios que con este noble caudillo vos quiso ayuntar el vos dara a do quier que vayades consejo onrroso.'"

5: 1–2. Rey, *Sumas,* p. 329: "Titulo ccxxvj. —Del adobo e de la fabla que ouo Bruto con el rey Pandraso."

5: 3–5. Rey, *Sumas,* p. 329: "A todos plugo con este dicho e acordaron en el. E pues asy fue, Bruto enbio por el rey Pandraso e fizole traer ally ante todos e dixole asy: 'Rey Pandraso, bien sabedes commo en pos de tantas premias fuertes....'"

5: 8. Rey, *Sumas,* p. 329: "e de tu grado les quisieses en el tu sennorio e tierra otorgar."

5: 10–12. Salazar abridges. Cf. Rey, *Sumas,* p. 329: "los dioses vsando de su oficio fezieron justicia, e auiendo piadat dellos posie-ronte en el su sennorio e poderio. Mas agora ellos reconoçiendo a los dioses la muy grand merçed que les fizo e non vsando de tu crueza teniendote en su poder non te quieren dar las penas que tu les tyenes mereçidas."

5: 13–16. Rey, *Sumas,* p. 329: "de la tu tierra e que les des nauios e bastymentos con que della en paz salgan e que te dexaran tu tierra en saluo e soltaran a ty. E sy esto por tu voluntad non quieres que por sy lo entienden cobrar, e a donde...."

5: 17. Salazar condenses. Cf. Rey, *Sumas,* pp. 329–30: "Pandraso quando esto oyo fue muy pagado de la razon de Bruto, ca el non cuydaua avn que en esto lo tenia e dixo asy...."

5: 17–22. Rey, *Sumas*, p. 330: "'Fazer deuen los omnes por saluar la vida todas las cosas, avn que sean de aquellas en que verguença puede caber, quanto mas las que razonables son falladas. E por ende, pues los dioses asy lo fezieron [*MS. 9256:* quisieron], yo de mi buena voluntad so plazentero e otorgo todo lo que por ellos fuere demandado, e avn ellos non tanto podrian demandar commo en lo que contra mi muestran mereçer.'"

5: 22–24. Rey, *Sumas*, p. 330: "E asy entonçe quedaron pagados el rey Pandraso de los troyanos e ellos del, e tornaronle entonçe a poder de los caualleros que lo tenian fasta que se tratase lo que menester auian para su viaje, asy de nauios commo de bastimentos."

5: 25–32. Salazar abridges. Cf. Rey, *Sumas*, pp. 330–31: "Los troyanos trataron [*MS. 9256:* tratando] que seria lo que menester auian para sus conpannas. Dixo Asaraco: 'Bruto, yo auia pensado vna cosa que a mi semejaua muy conueniente sy a vos ploguiese; que pues esta guerra e otrosy esta salyda de los troyanos de la sugebçion por plazimiento del rey Pandraso se ha de fazer, e commo en razon de paz, parecer me ya a mi que por que mas fyrme esta cosa fuese a do quier que fuesemos, o por otra vez la ventura echarnos por aqui, que seria bien que fuese pedida la fija Ynojenis del rey Pandraso para vos por muger, la qual yo conozco por muy apuesta donzella e en condiçiones la mas noble, con la qual tu serias bien casado e nos yriamos mas seguros.' Mucho plugo desta razon a Bruto e a todos los suyos; e acordaron todos de la pedyr con todas las otras cosas que acordado auian. E enbiaron al rey Pandraso en el castillo do estaua con otros muchos prisioneros de los mas altos del su regno que con el estauan presos con esta mensajeria al obispo Eleno e a Menprudo."

6: 1–3. Rey, *Sumas*, p. 331: "Titulo ccxxviij. —De las cosas que los troyanos enbiaron demandar al rey Pandraso que les diese." Salazar's titles tend to be longer than those of the *Sumas* MSS.

6: 4–7. These lines correspond to the end of "Titulo ccxxvij" in Rey, *Sumas*, p. 331: "E quando fueron delante del Eleno començo la razon, ca el era muy cuerdo e sabio, e avn entre los griegos syenpre le fuera guardada grand onrra, e dixo asy delante de todos aquellos que ally estauan presos."

6: 7–15. Salazar abbreviates. Cf. Rey, *Sumas*, "Titulo ccxxviij," p. 331: "'Rey Pandraso, los troyanos te pyden que les des çincuenta naos de las que tienes en los tus puertos, e bastimento de viandas para ellas para vn anno; e pidente mas, que les des todos aquellos catiuos que en las tus cibdades estan que a ellos non podieron venir; e otrosy te piden mas, que des a Asaraco por los tres castillos que el te quiere dexar por tuyos diez quintales de oro; e otrosy te piden mas, por que la tu amistad e la suya ayamos [*MS. 9256*: aya mas] fyrmeza que les des la tu fija Ynogenis por muger a su caudillo Bruto, con el qual tu deues tener por bien casada; e otrosy con ella a tu sobryna Ynoxia para Asaraco, e con estas veynte donzellas otras, las quales a tu escogencia casen con caualleros troyanos. E do esto quisieres soltaran a ty e a todos los tuyos, e dar te an los castillos dEspartyno e de Ruparon e de Tironpyno, e otrosy el de Masteleo que tomaron tuyo, e auer an contigo leal e verdadera amistança. Todo esto entienden por sy cobrar e llauar [*MS. 9256:* lleuar] a ty e a los de la tu tierra en la su prision. E por quanto yo en ty sienpre falle mucha onrra querria yo que ouieses buen consejo e que lo que non puedes por mejor acarrear nin escusar que lo fezieses syn prouar mas las fuerças de la ventura, quanto mas que aqui non te cae sy non onrra.'"

6: 16–18. Salazar condenses: Cf. Rey, *Sumas,* "Titulo ccxxjx," p. 332: "Visto e oydo Pandraso e los suyos que en la prision estauan todo lo que el obispo Eleno dixo, auiendo su acuerdo entre sy, Pandraso respondio e dixo asy...."

6: 17–18. Rey, *Sumas,* p. 332: "los menesteres no dexan de los omnes." MS. 6419: "non dexan de cobrar."

6: 19. Rey, *Sumas,* p. 332: "pides."

6: 19–21. Salazar deletes part of Pandraso's statement. Cf. Rey, *Sumas,* p. 332: "quanto mas que avn yo non entyendo que del todo los dioses me ayan seydo contrarios, mas que en pos del mi grand quebranto que me quisieron guardar algunt conforte en yo dar la mi fija a tan alto e a tan noble cauallero commo Bruto, que syento oy non aver mejoria entre todos los byuos."

6: 22. Rey, *Sumas,* p. 332: "cometer."

6: 22–24. Salazar condenses. Cf. Rey, *Sumas,* p. 332: "¿omne desterrado con tan poca gente por fuerça e seso sacar los catiuos de tan luengo tienpo del poderio de Greçia? E por ende yo otorgo la mi fija Ynogenis, e asy faze mi hermano Antigano la suya Ynoxia a Asaraco; e despues todas las otras cosas que por vos son pedidas."

6: 25. Salazar summarizes. Cf. the first lines of Rey, *Sumas,* "Titulo ccxxx," p. 332: "Luego fueron puestos los fyncamientos e posturas de todas estas cosas por rehenes e juramentos, e fue suelto el rey Pandraso e los suyos. E las donzellas fueron todas entregadas en poder de los troyanos, e fueron fechas las bodas de todas ellas muy rica mente, e fueron traydos los nauios e todo lo que fue puesto. E Bruto con toda la otra gente entraron en sus nauios e syglaron por la mar."

6: 25–32. Salazar abridges. Cf. Rey, *Sumas*, pp. 332–33: "Mas quando se ouieron de espedyr los vnos de los otros la ynfanta Ynogenis veyendose partyr de su padre e de su tierra, e non sabia çierta mente para do, las manzillas que fazia e dezia non ha omne que contar las podiese; e dezia asy: '¡Ay de mi, triste, commo los dioses touieron para mi guardados tantos males sy non estaua yo en los çelestiales en el grand Sagitario o en las rodillas del que se manda el cuerno amenazador, en el qual todas las cosas son mouibles; o sy fuy yo engendrada en [*MS. 9256:* de] las muy fieras Amazonas que se deleytauan [*MS. 9256:* deleytan] en las pasadas de las mares e en escudrynnar las tierras! E tan synple donzella commo yo ¿commo se porna a los tan grandes trabajos? En muy grand preçio e cuenta so yo puesta, pues fuy fecha redemidora de la mi tierra e gente.' Muy fuerte se amanzellaua Ynogenis, e a las vezes se amorteçia." For other references to the Amazons in medieval Spanish texts, see my article "Evidence of a Fifteenth-Century *Libro del Infante don Pedro de Portugal*...," *JHP* 1 (1976–77): 94–97.

6: 32. Rey, *Sumas*, p. 333: "Mas Bruto la tomaua en los braços e la besaua e confortauala muy dulçe mente deziendole muy dulçes palabras e conortando a ella e a las otras."

6. 32–35. Salazar condenses. Cf. Rey, *Sumas*, p. 333: "E mandaua toda via a los mareantes que guiasen las naos para el viaje de Troya, ca toda via su entencion era de yr en Troya. E quando de Ytalia partiera con aquella entençion partiera de yr en Troya o en Cartago, que eran tierras de su naturaleza, por que sopiera despues commo reynaua en Cartago Pago. E era aquel entonçe el mas nonbrado e el mas noble que ouiese en Africa, e era de su lynaje e a quien de razon perteneçia la silla de Cartago. E non pensaua de yr alla, mas de yr a Troya e poner toda su dyligençia en la cobrar e restaurar, e que se recobrase en el nonbre troyano."

7: 1–12. Salazar abridges. Cf. Rey, *Sumas*, "Titulo ccxxj," pp. 333–34.

7: 4–5. Rey, *Sumas*, p. 333: "Non tardo mucho que Bruto entro en la mar que tormenta le fue en contrario e por fuerças de vientos echolos en las partes de Asia, e en tierra de Damasco ouieron tomar puerto."

7: 5–7. Rey, *Sumas*, pp. 333–34: "E salyeron en tierra; e andando por ella robando de aquello que mas menester les era pasaron por los lagos de Sodoma e Gomorra, e de que toda aquella tierra ouieron despojado tornaron a la mar por contynuar su viaje."

7: 7–10. Rey, *Sumas*, p. 334: "E en la mar toparon con muy gran conpanna de cosarios que eran allegados sabiendo su fazienda de Bruto; e estos auian robado muchas tierras e muchas gentes, asy por mar commo por tierra. E ouo Bruto grand fazienda con ellos, tanto que vna ora le tenian conquistada toda la mas parte de la su flota. Mas la su nao aferrando con la del capytan de los cosarios salto Bruto en la de los cosarios a muy grand peligro, e abraçose con el capytan e lançolo en la mar."

7: 10-12. Rey, *Sumas*, p. 334: "E tan grand fue el esfuerço que los suyos ally tomaron que se recobro toda la pelea e fueron vençidos todos los cosarios, commo quier que muy mucha gente ally perdio Bruto. Mas las riquezas que ally ganaron fueron tantas que de ally adelante jamas non podieron aver mengua. E fezieron de los catiuos e con los sus nauios vna grant flota, que auia ya en la flota de Bruto çiento e quarenta velas e todas guarnidas."

7: 13–24. This portion of Ch. 7 corresponds to Rey, *Sumas*, "Titulo ccxxxij," pp. 334–35.

7: 13–17. Rey, *Sumas*, pp. 334–35: "E al cabo por fuerça de tormenta ouieron de arribar en tierra de Africa en la prouinçia de Manirtania; e ally salyeron en tierra e el rey della reçebiolos luego con guerra defendiendoles los puertos. E por esto Bruto ouo de aver su guerra con el; e muchos dias estouieron en grandes afruentas. Mas al cabo ouieron de aver batalla, e vençio Bruto e tomo preso al rey e a toda su gente, e rendiolo en tal manera que todo el algo de la tierra fue suyo."

7: 18. Rey, *Sumas*, p. 335: "E entro otra vez en las naos e començo a seguir su camino, e non podiendo aver tienpo el que ellos querian aportaron aquella tierra que en la parte de Europa se llama Germania."

7: 18–24. Rey, *Sumas*, p. 335: "E ally fallaron a Curineo de la muy grant fuerça. E era de los de la gente de Anteneor el de Troya que ally poblara; e tanto le fizo e le prometio que le ouo de lleuar consigo. E non estouieron ally mucho, que luego partieron de ally con la grande codicia que auia de seguir aquel viaje que tenia començado. Mas al punto que en la mar entro luego ouieron contrariedat de tienpo, e tanto [*MS. 9256:* atanto] que porfiando [*MS. 9256:* profiando*] los maryneros contra el tienpo en punto fue de ser todos en perdiçion. E echolos la tormenta en la ysla de Legoçia, que auia un tienpo seydo bien poblada, mas por la guerra de los cosarios estaua entonce yerma, que en ella non auia ningund poblador [*MS. 9256:* morador], mas auia pueblas desiertas."

7: 24–28. Salazar summarizes, leaving out the reference to Brutus' hunt. Cf. the beginning of "Titulo ccxxxiij," in Rey, *Sumas*, p. 335: "Commo dicho es, aporto ally con tormenta Bruto con sus gentes e salyo en tierra. E commo auia en aquella ysla muchos buenos montes e estaua yerma auia muchos venados e tomole voluntad a Bruto de correr ally monte; e mato ally muchos venados, entre los quales dize la estoria que mato una çierua blanca, la qual ouieron por muy grant marauilla. E [*MS. 9256:* e que] fallaron otrosy en aquellos montes, çerca de [*MS. 9256:* contra] vna grand ribera, vn tenplo muy marauilloso que era consagrado a la deesa Diana. E quando aquello ally fallaron ouieron por consejo de fazer ally sacrefiçio a la deesa Diana."

8: 1–7. In Rey *Sumas*, "Titulo ccxxxiij" (p. 336), it is Brutus and not Eleno who calls upon Diana to give them guidance: "E fue el [Brutus] con aquello [the blood of the white stag] antel altar en aquellas vasijas de oro e derramo la sangre por el altar e puso fuego a las otras cosas e tornose a sentar en el cuero e fizo su oraçion en esta manera: 'Sennora Diana, que eres espanto de los montes, tormento de los vencidos, deesa de castidat, dynos a aquellas tierras que nos mandas yr poblar a donde yo te consagre tenplos de vyrgines que te sienpre alaben con cantos e estormentos de muy grand melodia.'"

8: 8–21. These lines correspond to Rey, *Sumas*, "Titulo ccxxxiij" (p. 336), but represent an expanded version of Diana's reply: "Asy estando Bruto en su oraçion adormeçiose e vynole en suennos commo en vision Diana e dixole: 'Bruto, en el mar oçeano a la sententrional parte es vna ysla que antigua mente fue otorgada a los gigantes, mas agora vazia e menguada dellos e de otras algunas gentes esta yerma. Ally es aparejada a ti la silla a donde muchos reys de tu lynaje reynaran e pornan a muchos en angostura e a otros muchos reys [*MS. 9256 adds:* e tu seras ally honrrado e creçeras en muchas gentes], e entonçe faras a mi tenplo de castidat por que yo sea en guarda de la tu generaçion e que se acaben los tus dias en

grand onrra en aquella tierra que te esta aparejada.'" The refer-
ence to Albion is not found at this point in the story of Brutus and
Diana as told in the *General estoria* of Alfonso X, el Sabio (ed. A. G.
Solalinde et al., *Segunda Parte* [Madrid, 1957–61], 2: 272*b*), nor in
Geoffrey of Monmouth's *Historia Regum Britanniae*, Bk. 1, ch. 11.

8: 22–28. Rey, *Sumas,* "Titulo ccxxxiiij" (pp. 336–37), begins
with similar lines but lacks the idea of preferring to go to Troy and
the reference to the "estrecho de Marruecos": "Pues que Bruto desperto del suenno fue muy alegre e conto a los suyos la vision, e ellos
ouieron grand alegria e tomaron grande esperança por que por los
dioses les era sennalado çierto lugar do ouiesen de auer asosiego de
sus grandes afanes. E entraron en sus nauios luego e tomaron su
viaje para las mares de España, e ouieron buen viento e venieron a
aportar a Equitania, aquella que agora llaman Cataluenna."

8: 29. Rey, *Sumas* (p. 337) gives a more explicit reason for land-
ing: "e ouieron de tomar tierra por se reparar de algunas cosas que
menester auian commo omnes de mar."

9: 4–9. Salazar abbreviates. Cf. Rey, *Sumas,* p. 337, lines 4–20.

9: 10–13. Salazar abbreviates. Cf. Rey, *Sumas,* "Titulo ccxxxv,"
pp. 337–38. According to *Sumas,* Cataluenna and Guiana were two
provinces of Equitania (p. 337).

9: 13–16. Rey, *Sumas,* p. 338: "E ally cobro Curyneo muy grand
fama de la su fuerça, ca fallauan en las peleas los golpes que el fazia
que non lo podrian creer los omnes, ca fallauan el omne cortado
çerçe por la çinta, e muchas vezes cortado por el onbro fasta en la
çinta, e otras vezes pasado de la lança a manteniente todo el cuerpo
con las armas."

9: 17. Salazar summarizes. Cf. Rey, *Sumas,* p. 338, lines 10–21.

9: 17–19. These lines correspond to the end of Rey, *Sumas,* "Titulo ccxxxv" (p. 338), and the beginning of "Titulo ccxxxvj" (pp.
338–39). In the *Sumas,* however, the battle occurs in Guiana: "E
entraron en su flota e ouieron buenos tienpos e pasaron el estrecho
e todos los mares de Espanna, que non fezieron salyda fasta que
llegaron do agora se llama el ducado de Guiana; e ally sabiendo que
era aquella tierra de aquellos que auian fecho ayuda al rey Gafario
salyeron en tierra e començaron a fazer guerra" (p. 338).

9: 19–22. Rey, *Sumas,* p. 339: "murio vn primo de Bruto, muy
buen cauallero, que los bretones ouieron por muy grant perdida. E

auia nonbre Tireno; e fue dellos muy llanteado, e fezieronle muy rica e muy onrrada sepoltura. E poblaron ally donde el fue enterrado vna çibdat e llamaronla del su nonbre, Turona, que es aquella que agora se llama Torres."

9: 23–30. Corresponds to Rey, *Sumas*, p. 339, lines 8–23.

10: 1–2. Cf. Rey, *Sumas*, p. 339: "Titulo ccxxxvij. —Commo Bruto paso en la ysla de Albion e commo la partio en tres [*MS. 9256 adds:* partes], e commo de su nonbre tomaron nonbre los bretones."

10: 3. The Biblical reference is lacking in the *Sumas* version, but cf. a similar reference in Geoffrey of Monmouth, *Historia Regum Britanniae*, Bk. 1, ch. 18, and Wace, *Le Roman de Brut* (ed. I. Arnold, SATF [Paris, 1938–40], vv. 1248–50). The Brutus passage with the Biblical reference is also found in three Hispanic universal chronicles that follow Wace: Martín de Larraya's version of the *Libro de las generaciones*, the *Livro de linhagens* or *Nobiliário* of D. Pedro, Conde de Barcelos, and the *Crónica de 1404*. See the collation of these texts by Diego Catalán and María Soledad de Andrés, in *Edición crítica del texto español de la Crónica de 1344 que ordenó el Conde de Barcelos don Pedro Alfonso* (Madrid, 1971–), 1: 247–48.

10: 3–13. These lines correspond to the end of the story of Brutus as found in Rey, *Sumas*, "Titulo ccxxxvij," pp. 339–40: "Asy entro Bruto en la ysla de Albion; e de que en paz fueron asosegados partieronla. E tomo Bruto aquella parte mayor que agora llaman Ynglatierra; e dieron a Curineo aquella de Magot, que agora llaman Cornualla de su nonbre de Curineo. E dieron otrosy a Asaraco aquella prouinçia que agora se llama Escoçia. E ouo este nonbre de un su fijo que fue muy buen cauallero que llamaron Escot. E destos caualleros Bruto e Corineo e Asaraco salyeron los que despues syenpre fueron reys de Ynglatierra. E deste nonbre Bruto tomaron nonbre los bretones. Mas agora dexa la estoria de contar desto e cuenta de otras cosas."

10: 14–27. The Salazar comments concerning the ecclesiastical, economic, judicial, and warfaring customs of England are not found in the *Sumas* nor in the presumed source for the Brutus portion of this text, Alfonso X's *General estoria* (on Leomarte's sources, see Rey, *Sumas*, pp. 35–50). They are also lacking in the *Historia Regum Britanniae* (Bk. 4, ch. 19, Bk. 5, ch. 1), but Geoffrey of Monmouth does carry the genealogy of Lucius back to Brutus and the Trojans and names Lucius first Christian ruler of Britain (concerning Geoffrey's treatment of Lucius, see E. Faral, *La Legénde arthurienne* [Paris, 1929], 2: 162–75; Lucius as a historical personage is described by R. Rees, *An Essay on the Welsh Saints* [London, 1836], pp. 83–86). Wace calls Lucius (Luce) the second king of Great Britain (vv. 5210, 5211, 5257); and his conversion to Christianity is retold in the *Estoire del Saint Graal* (Sommer, *Vulgate*, 1: 272, 278–79) and again with no significant change in the Post-Vulgate *Estoire del Saint Graal* (cf. the Ptg. *Josep*, pp. 353, 359–61). It is not possible to say whether Salazar's allusion to Lucius was found in a now lost Spanish version of Geoffrey or was taken from the Vulgate or Post-Vulgate *Estoire*.

11: 1 ff. Chs. 11–12 represent a compact synthesis of material presumed to have been part of the Post-Vulgate *Roman du Graal* (dated between 1230 and 1240 by Bogdanow, *Romance*, pp. 13, 222–27). It has been theorized that the Post-Vulgate *Roman du Graal* began with a modified version of the early history of the Grail as contained in the Vulgate *Estoire del Saint Graal* (Bogdanow, *Romance*, p. 11). Some fifty MSS of the French Vulgate version of the *Estoire* survive (for a comprehensive list, including fragments, see B. Woledge, *Bibliographie des romans et nouvelles en prose française antérieurs à 1500* [Geneva, 1954], pp. 71–76). These MSS have been divided into two groups, one representing a shorter redaction with less descriptive detail than the other (Bogdanow, *Romance*, p. 157). Three editions of the Vulgate *Estoire* have appeared. Sommer's *Vulgate*, 1, embodies the shorter version. Two MSS of the longer redaction have been published: Le Mans MS. 354, by E. Hucher, *Le Saint Graal ou le Joseph d'Arimathie ...*, 3 vols. (Les Mans, 1874–78); and British Library MS. Royal 14 E. iii, by F. J. Furnival, *Seynt Graal, or the Sank Ryal ...*, 2 vols. (London, 1861–63).

The French text of the Post-Vulgate *Estoire* has not come down to us, but it may be reconstructed from the Castilian and Portuguese versions. Besides the *Bienandanzas* fragments, two other Hispanic adaptations of the *Estoire* have survived. A full text is preserved in a sixteenth-century Ptg. copy, Lisbon, Torre do Tombo, MS. 643, of which a paleographic edition has been published by Henry Hare Carter, *The Portuguese Book of Joseph of Arimathea*, UNCSRLL, 71 (Chapel Hill, 1967). A fragmentary version of a Cast. *Libro de Josep Abarimatia*, copied or adapted in 1469 or 1470 by Petrus Ortiz, forms part of Salamanca, Bibl. Universitaria, MS. 1877 (*olim* Madrid, Bibl. Real de Palacio, II–794; *olim* 2–G–5), and is edited by Pietsch, *Fragments*, 1: 3–53. The Cast. and Ptg. versions would seem to derive from a common original of the early fourteenth-century (see Entwistle, *Legend,* pp. 133–45; Bohigas, *Los textos,* pp. 76–78; Bohigas, 1498 *Baladro,* 3: 192). Bogdanow has corrected Bohigas' early opinion (*Los textos,* pp. 31, 112–17) that the Ptg. *Josep* is closer to the longer redaction of the *Estoire* published by Hucher than to the text edited by Sommer. She finds that the Ptg. *Josep* has a number of readings in common with the shorter version contained in Rennes, MS. 255 (*Romance,* pp. 157–58, and "The Relationship of the Portuguese *Josep Abarimatia* to the Extant French MSS of the *Estoire del Saint Graal,*" ZRPh 76 [1960]: 344).

11: 1–19. As Bohigas points out (*Los textos,* p. 130), the story related in Ch. 11 is a summary of the *Josep Abarimatia.* In the Grail story told by Robert de Boron (*Le Roman de l'Estoire dou Graal,* ed. W. A. Nitze, CFMA, 57 [Paris, 1927]) Joseph does not go to the British Isles, but rather entrusts the Grail to his brother-in-law, Bron, who travels westward with his wife and twelve sons to preach Christianity. The Vulgate *Estoire* places Joseph and his people in Britain, where they propagate the faith by preaching and by acts of violence.

Salazar alters the sequence of events by beginning his summary with the conversion of the pagans, thereby maintaining an illusion of continuity between the previous chapter with its final reference to Luçes Pagano(=Lucius). He then proceeds to relate the origin of the Holy Grail. Several details in the Salazar summary differ from other versions of the *Estoire del Saint Graal.* None of the edited MSS of the Vulgate or Post-Vulgate versions give a specific year for the arrival of the Grail in England, whereas Salazar gives the figure of fifty years after the death of Christ. Joseph's imprisonment of forty years in the *Bienandanzas* is thirty–six years in the Ptg. *Joseph* (p. 88). In British Library Add. MS. 10294, Joseph is told that his prison term is forty-three years (Sommer, *Vulgate,* 1: 17). The figure of forty-two years is found in many of the MSS of the Vulgate (see Hucher ed., 2: 72–78), and the Cast. *Libro de Josep Abarimatia* retains this number (Pietsch, *Fragments,* 1: 7). Salazar's use of forty years and his departure from other Vulgate and Post-Vulgate versions in maintaining the historical father–son relationship between Vespasian and Titus do find parallel, however, in versions of *La Vengeance Nostre Seigneur,* an OFr. poem of the late twelfth or, more likely, early thirteenth century, which was later put into prose and translated into a number of languages, including Spanish and Portuguese (see Entwistle, *Legend,* pp. 130–32). Like the Salazar text, the OFr. poem refers to Titus as the son of Vespasian and has the "vengeance" occur forty years after Christ's crucifixion (W. Suchier, "Ueber das altfranzösische Gedicht von der Zerstörung Jerusalems [*La Venjance nostre seigneur*]," ZRPh 24 [1900]: 169;

Loyal A. T. Gryting, *The Oldest Version of the Twelfth-Century Poem "La Venjance Nostre Seigneur,"* University of Michigan Contributions in Modern Philology, 19 [Ann Arbor, 1952], p. 33; Melitta S. Gahlbeck Buzzard, *"Cest li romanz de la venjance que Vaspasiens et Tytus ses fiz firent de la mort Jhesucrist,* édition manuscrit 5201, Bibliothèque de l'Arsenal, Paris" [Diss., University of Colorado, 1970, pp. 32, 106]. The figure of forty-two years for the "vengeance" is given in the extant Cast. and Ptg. incunabula of the prose version of the *Vengeance,* but, like the Salazar fragment, they refer to Joseph's imprisonment as lasting forty years: *La estoria del noble Vaspasiano enperador de Roma* (Toledo, ca. 1492), sig. D4^r; *La ystoria del noble Uespesiano emperador de Roma* [Seville, 1499], ed. R. Foulché-Delbosc, *"Ystoria del noble Vespesiano,"* RHi 21 (1909): 622; *Estoria de muy nobre Uespesiano emperador de Roma* [Lisbon, 1496], ed. F. M. Esteves Pereira, *Historia de Vespasiano, Imperador de Roma* (Lisbon, 1905), p. 95. The earlier of the two Cast. printed editions has now been edited by David Hook: "A Critical Edition of *La estoria del noble Vaspasiano enperador de Rroma* with a literary and historical study including an account of the transmission of the text" (Thesis, Oxford University, 1977).

Salazar alludes to the Vespasian story as told in the Bible; but as J. Weston points out, the legend concerning Joseph of Arimathea and the Grail is the creation of fictional romance (*From Ritual to Romance* [Cambridge, Eng., 1920], p. 2. What is said in several books of the New Testament is that Joseph of Arimathea was given the body of Christ by Pontius Pilate (Matt. 27: 56–61; John 19: 38–42; Luke 23: 50–53; Mark 15: 43-47).

12: 1–24. Salazar's concise catalogue of those who accompanied Joseph to England and their descendants serves to link the *Josep Abarimatia* branch to the story of King Arthur and his knights and to the Quest of the Grail. Similar genealogies are to be found in the Vulgate *Estoire* and in the Post-Vulgate text embodied in the Ptg. *Josep.* However, several of the proper names are completely different in the Salazar version.

12: 3–6. Bohigas cites the reference to Sador as evidence that Salazar was following a text of the Pseudo-Boron Cycle, now called Post-Vulgate *Roman du Graal* (*Los textos,* p. 131). The Ptg. *Josep* identifies Sador as one of the twelve sons of Bron, son-in-law of Joseph and places him within the genealogy of Tristan (p. 330). Cf. French Tristan texts in which Tristan's father is Meliadus, King of Leonois (see L.-F. Flutre, *Table de noms propres avec toutes leurs variantes figurant dans les romans du Moyen Age écrits en français ou en provençal* ... [Poitiers, 1962], p. 136; G. D. West, *An Index of Proper Names in French Arthurian Prose Romances* [Toronto, 1978], p. 217*a*). In the Ptg. *Josep*, Tristan's father is Metilādeus (*var.* Metilamdes).

12: 7–10. The Vulgate *Estoire* names Pieres (= Salazar's Perron) as a relative of Joseph (Sommer, *Vulgate*, 1: 250), but the Ptg. *Josep* includes Perom among the twelve sons of Bron (p. 330). In the Vulgate *Estoire* Lot's marriage to Arthur's sister (not named) produces four children: Gavain, Agravain, Guerrehes, and Gaheries (Sommer, *Vulgate*, 1: 280). Both the Vulgate *Estoire* (Sommer, *Vulgate*, 1: 281) and the Ptg. *Josep* (p. 362) make it clear that Morderet was not the son of Lot but rather an illegitimate son of Arthur. The story of Morderet's conception is told by Salazar in Bk. XI, ch. 19.

12: 11–15. In the Vulgate *Estoire* Joseph of Arimathea invests his son Galahad (= Salazar's Galaz) with the kingdom of Haucelice (Sommer, *Vulgate*, 1: 282; cf. "Ochelic" in Ptg. *Josep*, p. 363). Haucelice, we are told, was named Gales following the death of Galahad. The Vulgate *Estoire de Merlin* (Sommer, *Vulgate*, 2: 165) names Brimesent as the sister of Arthur who begets Urien's son Yvain. In the Ptg. *Josep* the name of Yvain's mother is not stated (p. 364). However, the Post-Vulgate *Suite du Merlin* (Huth *Merlin*, 1: 201–2) names Yvain as the son of Urien and Arthur's sister Morgain.

12: 16–18. Except for the reference to Sador, both the Vulgate *Estoire* and the Ptg. *Josep* contain this genealogy as part of the story of Corbenic, the Grail Castle (Sommer, *Vulgate*, 1: 286–91; Ptg. *Josep*, pp. 368–73).

12: 19–24. According to the Vulgate *Estoire*, Nascien was called Seraphe before he was baptized (Sommer, *Vulgate*, 1:74), and Nascien's descendants are revealed to him in the form of a scroll (Sommer, *Vulgate*, 1: 203; cf. Ptg. *Josep*, p. 376).

13: 1 ff. Chs. 13–23 contain an adaptation of the Post-Vulgate *Merlin*. This text, like the second branch of the Vulgate Cycle, contains a prose redaction of Robert de Boron's poem *Merlin* followed by a continuation. The first part of the Vulgate and Post-Vulgate versions relates the birth of Merlin and his relationship to Uther Pendragon, the founding of the Round Table, and the birth of Arthur and his coronation as king. The continuation covers the early years's of Arthur's reign, his triumph with the aid of Merlin over a group of rebel barons, and the defeat of the Saxons in Britain and

the Romans in Gaul. The Post-Vulgate *Merlin* sequel to this continuation places new emphasis upon certain episodes such as the conception of Mordred, the revelation of Arthur's true parentage,
Arthur's marriage to Guenevere, and the story of Merlin's love for
Niviene. These and other incidents are used by the Post-Vulgate
adaptor to foreshadow and prepare the reader for later events (see
Bogdanow, *Romance*, p. 11).

The Post-Vulgate *Merlin* survives in various MSS and printed editions. In French there exist a number of MSS: Cambridge, University Library, Add. MS. 7071, partially edited by Patrick Coogan
Smith, *"Les Enchantemenz de Bretaigne"*: *An extract from a
thirteenth century prose romance "La Suite du Merlin,"* UNCSRLL,
146 (Chapel Hill, 1977); the Huth *Merlin* or *Suite du Merlin*, published by Gaston Paris and Jacob Ulrich under the title *Merlin: Roman en prose du XIIIe siècle*, 2 vols. (1886; rpt. ed., New York,
1965); a fragment in Paris, Bibl. Nat., MS. fr. 112, ed. H. O. Sommer, *Die Abenteur Gawains, Ywains und Le Morholts mit den drei
Jungfrauen...*, in *Beihefte zur ZRPh*, 47 (Halle, 1913); and a small
fragment of the *Suite du Merlin* in an unnumbered MS in the State
Archives of Siena, Italy, ed. F. Bogdanow, *Romance*, pp. 228–41.
See Bogdanow, "Essai de classement des manuscrits de la *Suite du
Merlin*," *Romania* 81 (1960): 188–98. An English adaptation of the
Merlin is preserved in Malory's *Tale of King Arthur*, ed. E. Vinaver,
The Works of Sir Thomas Malory, 2nd ed. (Oxford, 1967), 1: 1–180.
As for the Hispanic versions, in addition to the Salazar fragments,
there exists another fragmentary Cast. MS: Salamanca, Biblioteca
Universitaria, 1877 (*olim* Madrid, Biblioteca Real de Palacio,
II–794; *olim* 2–G–5), fols. 282^v–296^v, ed. Pietsch, *Fragments*, 1:
51–81. Two early printed editions of the *Merlin* also survive: *El Baladro del sabio Merlin con sus profecias* [Burgos, 1498], ed. P. Bohigas, 3 vols. (Barcelona, 1957–62); *La demanda del sancto Grial
con los maruillosos fechos de Lançarote y de Galaz su hijo. El primero libro: El baladro del famosissimo profeta y nigromante Merlin
con sus profecias* [Seville, 1535], ed. Adolfo Bonilla y San Martín, in
Libros de caballerías, 1: *Ciclo artúrico–Ciclo carolingio*, NBAE, 6
(Madrid, 1907),pp. 3–162. In comparison with the other known versions of the Vulgate and Post-Vulgate *Merlin*, the *Bienandanzas* adaptation represents a regrouping of incidents with certain changes
in their sequential order.

13: 1–5. Salazar's version of the *Merlin* begins immediately with
the conception of Merlin. The other *Merlin* texts follow the Robert
de Boron poem with an introductory passage on how the devils

plotted to bring about the destruction of mankind by means of a prophet, half human and half devil, known later as Merlin. Salazar defers this passage to Ch. 14 and puts it in the mouth of Merlin himself.

Merlin's birthplace, the Tierra Forana (= Terre Foraine of the French texts, the traditional location of the Grail Castle of Corbenic), is not indicated in other versions of the *Merlin*. The spelling of the name for the incubus varies greatly in the *Merlin* texts: Onquevezes (Bohigas, 1498 *Baladro*, 1: 17), Aquibez (Pietsch, *Fragments*, 1: 76), Enquibedos (Bonilla, 1535 *Baladro*, p. 10*a*), Ekupedes (Huth *Merlin*, 1: 28), Esquibedes (Sommer, *Vulgate*, 2: 17).

13: 5–7. Cf. the advice given to the maiden in Bohigas, 1498 *Baladro*, 1: 31: "e quando de noche en tu cama te acostares, di el credo...e sínate e santíguate...e ten toda la noche la candela encendida, que no ay cosa de que el diablo más huya que de la lumbre do quier que sea." But the advice is not followed: "adormecióse e sin candela e sin hazer ninguna diligencia de las que el hermitaño le havía mostrado." Cf. also Huth *Merlin*, 1: 11–12; and Sommer, *Vulgate*, 2: 8.

13: 9–10. A similar statement appears in other *Merlin* texts at an earlier point in the narration. Cf. Bohigas, 1498 *Baladro*, 1: 23: "En aquel tiempo era costumbre en aquella cibdad que qualquier muger que se le conociese comunicación con algún varón que su marido no fuese, fuese tenida por adúltera e muriese por ello, salvo sino fuese muger publicana." Cf. similar lines in Pietsch, *Fragments*, 1: 60; Bonilla, 1535 *Baladro*, p. 4*b*; Huth *Merlin*, 1: 6; Sommer, *Vulgate*, 2: 5. The custom described here is said to have endured until the time of King Arthur in Garci Rodríguez de Montalvo's reworking of the *Amadís de Gaula* (Bk. I, ch. 1) and in the Prose *Tristan* (Löseth, *Le Roman*, §18).

13: 12. The other Spanish texts of the *Merlin* use the term *juez*. The OSp. form *alcalde* 'judge' is a more general term (see Juan Ruiz, *Libro de buen amor*, ed. J. Corominas [Madrid, 1967], p. 212, n. 509*a*). Salazar also favors the term *alcalde* in the last six books of the *Bienandanzas* (see J. Bilbao, "La cultura tradicional en la obra de Lope García de Salazar," *Eusko-Jakintza* 2 [1948]: 237–38, 244–47).

13: 14. The other Spanish texts use the expression *ombre bueno (honbre bueno)* but not *confesor*. However, the term *confessour (confesseor)* is found in the Huth *Merlin*, 1: 17, and in Sommer, *Vulgate*, 2: 11, together with *preudom*.

13: 18–31. Cf. parallel passages in Bohigas, 1498 *Baladro*, 1: 40–42; Bonilla, 1535 *Baladro*, p. 8; Pietsch, *Fragments*, 1: 71; Huth *Merlin*, 1: 20–22; Sommer, *Vulgate*, 2: 13–14.

14: 1 ff. The scene before the judge parallels the other *Merlin* texts. Cf. Bohigas, 1498 *Baladro*, 1: 43–48; Bonilla, 1535 *Baladro*, pp. 8*b*–10*a*; Pietsch, *Fragments*, 1: 72–77; Huth *Merlin*, 1: 22–29; Sommer, *Vulgate*, 2: 14–18.

14: 21–22. The Salazar text refers to four men, whereas the other texts speak of two. Cf. Bohigas, 1498 *Baladro*, 1: 44: "tomad a vuestra madre e a un amigo de quien fiéys e entrad en una camara apartadamente, e yo tomaré mi madre e mi maestro, e entraremos con vosotros." Cf. Bonilla, 1535 *Baladro*, p. 9*b*; Pietsch, *Fragments*, 1: 74; Huth *Merlin*, 1: 26; Sommer, *Vulgate*, 2: 16.

14: 30–38. Cf. Bohigas, 1498 *Baladro*, 1: 46: "—¿E vós no sabéys bien que la primera vez que con él yazistes, que avíades grand pavor de os enpreñar, e él vos dixo luego que de tal manera era él que nunca muger enpreñaría? E él escrivió quantas vezes yogo conbusco, e en aquella sazón era vuestro marido doliente, e desque esto fué, no duró mucho que vós os sentistes preñada, e dixísteslo al clérigo. ¿Dueña, es verdad esto que yo fablo? E si lo no quisierdes conocer, yo os diré al, por qué lo conoceréys. E verdad es que quando vos sentistes preñada, que lo dexistes al clérigo, e el clérigo dixo en confisión a vuestro marido que yoguiese con vós e le sería provechoso para su enfermedad, e ansí lo fezistes e yogo conbusco, e ansí le fezistes entender que el fijo era suyo, e desde entonces acá vivíades con él encubiertamente, e aún esta noche durmió con vós."

14: 41–42. Cf. Pietsch, *Fragments*, 1: 76: "E el fijo catola e dixol: Madre, quienquier que mi padre sea, dezitmelo; que yo vuestro fijo so e commo fijo vos fare; dezid si es verdad esto."

14: 42–44. Cf. Bohigas, 1498 *Baladro*, 1: 47: "Ella dixo: —Ay fijo, por Dios, merced, que yo no te lo puedo encubrir, mas todo es así como el dixo."

14: 44–49. Cf. Pietsch, *Fragments*, 1: 76: "E quando el juez esto oyo, dixo: Verdad dixo este moço que mejor conoscia el su padre que yo el mio, e non es derecho que yo de su madre faga justicia pues la non fezier de la mia. Mas por Dios e por salvar tu madre ante el pueblo dime quien fue tu padre."

14: 50–61. At this point Salazar has Merlin recount the circumstances of his birth, utilizing material found at the beginning of the other *Merlin* texts. Cf. Bonilla, 1535 *Baladro,* p. 3*a*: "En esta presente historia se cuenta como los diablos fueron muy sañudos quando nuestro señor Jesu Christo fue a los infiernos e saco dende a Adan e a Eua, y de los otros quantos le plugo." In the other *Merlin* texts Merlin gives the judge a brief account of his origins and his gift of prophecy. Cf. Pietsch, *Fragments,* 1: 76: "yo quiero que tu sepas e creas que so yo fijo de un diablo que enganno a mi madre e ha nonbre Aquibez que es de una companna que son suso en el ayre. E Dios quyso yo su saber e su memoria de elas cosas que son dichas e pasadas e fechas. Por esto se yo la fazienda de tu madre. E Nuestro Sennor quiso que sopiese esto de parte de mi padre. E quiso por la buena vida que bivio mi madre e por la verdadera penitençia que este omne bueno le dio que aqui see, e por los encomendamientos de santa yglesia que ella bien tovo e creyo, quiso el Nuestro Sennor que yo oviese tal virtud que yo sopiese todas las cosas que avyan de venir. E esto puedes tu bien provar por una cosa que te yo dire."

14: 62–66. According to the other *Merlin* texts, the judge's father drowns in a river. Cf. Bohigas, 1498 *Baladro,* 1: 47: "—Un secreto te diré en poridad. Tu madre yrse ha agora de aquí a contar al clérigo quanto le yo dixe, e quando el clérigo supiere que lo tú sabes, fuyrá con miedo de ti, e el diablo cuyas obras él siempre fizo, llevarlo ha a una agua e matarle ha, e por esto puedes provar si sé las cosas que han de venir."

14: 67. Salazar suppresses Merlin's conversation with his master Blaise, to whom the other texts have him dictate the story of the Holy Grail. Cf. Bohigas, 1498 *Baladro,* 1: 48–51; Bonilla, 1535 *Baladro,* pp. 10*b*–11*a*; Pietsch, *Fragments,* 1: 77–80; Huth *Merlin,* 1: 30–33; Sommer, *Vulgate,* 2: 18–20.

15: 1–10. In the other *Merlin* texts King Constans of England is said to have had three sons: Maine, Pandragon, and Uter. Upon Constans' death, Maine assumes the throne, but a group of powerful barons kill young Maine and proclaim Constans' seneschal Vertiger as their king. Uter and Pandragon are then ushered out of the country by two guardians. Their exact place of exile is left vague in the French texts: cf. Sommer, *Vulgate,* 2: 22, "en estraigne terre vers orient"; Huth *Merlin,* 1: 36, "en estranges terres viers orient." But the Spanish texts are more specific: cf. Bohigas, 1498 *Baladro,* 1: 53, "contra Oriente...a una cibdad que ha nonbre Borges"; Bonilla, 1535 *Baladro,* p. 12*a*, "a una cibdad que ha nombre Burgos." Salazar's Gaula is closer, at least geographically, to the Brittany or

Little Britain of Geoffrey of Monmouth's *Historia Regum Brit-anniae*, Bk. 6, ch. 9.

15: 11–19. The other *Merlin* texts refer to only one tower without mentioning its location and state that seven astrologers among Vertiger's wise clerks seek the cause of the tower's collapse. Salazar condenses the episode. Cf. Bohigas, 1498 *Baladro*, 1: 54–57; Bonilla, 1535 *Baladro*, pp. 12*b*–13*b*; Huth *Merlin*, 1: 38–42; Sommer, *Vulgate*, 2: 23–25.

15: 20–24. According to the other *Merlin* texts, Vertiger sends out twelve messengers, and four of them come across Merlin playing with other children in a field. Merlin's companion does not speak directly in the Spanish *Baladro* texts, but does do so when interrogated by one of the messengers in the Huth *Merlin*, 1: 42: "C'est [li] fieus d'une feme que onques ne seult qui l'engendra ne onques n'ot pere." Cf. Sommer, *Vulgate*, 2: 25.

15: 25–27. Salazar condenses. Cf. Bohigas, 1498 *Baladro*, 1: 58: "—Yo so aquel niño que vós buscáys e el por qué jurastes que me mataríades e avéys de levar mi sangre al rey Averenguer."

15: 28–37. Salazar summarizes. Cf. Bohigas, 1498 *Baladro*, 1: 66–68; Bonilla, 1535 *Baladro*, p. 16; Huth *Merlin*, 1: 52–54; Sommer, *Vulgate*, 2: 30–31.

15: 37–39. Cf. Bohigas, 1498 *Baladro*, 1: 68–69: "Sabe que so esta torre ha una grand agua, e debaxo dos dragones que no veen nada, e el uno es bermejo e el otro es blanco, e yazen so sendas piedras cerca el uno del otro. E quando sienten el agua pesada que se carga sobre ellos, rebuélvense e el agua represa, e quando se suelta ha grand fuerça, e lo que es sobre el agua fecho cae todo, e así cae la torre...."

15: 39–40. Salazar suppresses the description of the fight between the two dragons, one white and one red. The white dragon kills its adversary, but dies soon after. Cf. Bohigas, 1498 *Baladro*, 1: 69–71; Bonilla, 1535 *Baladro*, pp. 17*a*–18*a*; Huth *Merlin*, 1: 55–57; Sommer, *Vulgate*, 2: 32–33.

15: 41–49. No specific reference to the role of Lucifer is made in the other *Merlin* texts. Cf. Bohigas, 1498 *Baladro*, 1: 71–72; Bonilla, 1535 *Baladro*, p. 18*a*; Huth Merlin, 1: 57–58; Sommer, *Vulgate*, 2: 33–34.

15: 50. Cf. Vertiger's request of Merlin in Bohigas, 1498 *Baladro*, 1: 89: "—Yo veo bien e sé que tú eres el más sabido del mundo e ruégote que me des consejo, e que me digas, si te pluguiere, de qual muerte he de morir."

15: 50–53. Salazar condenses, omitting in the process the symbolism of the dragon episode. The white dragon is said to represent the son of Constans and the red one Vertiger. Merlin explains to Vertiger that his tower will not save him from death. Cf. Bohigas, 1498 *Baladro*, 1: 89–90; Bonilla, 1535 *Baladro*, pp. 22*b*–23*a*; Huth *Merlin*, 1: 60; Sommer, *Vulgate*, 2: 34–35. Salazar's reference to "cuatro pribados" is not found in the other texts.

16: 1–5. In the other *Merlin* texts Vertiger is deserted by his people, who observe the strength of the approaching forces led by Uter and Pandragon. Vertiger retreats to his castle, but Pandragon sets it ablaze, and Vertiger is consumed in the flames as Merlin had predicted. Cf. Bohigas, 1498 *Baladro*, 1: 92; Bonilla, 1535 *Baladro*, p. 23*b*; Huth *Merlin*, 1: 61–62; Sommer, *Vulgate*, 2: 35–36.

16: 5–6. After assuming the throne Vertiger had allied himself with the Saxons and married the daughter of Anguis. Cf. Bohigas, 1498 *Baladro*, 1: 54; Bonilla, 1535 *Baladro*, p. 12*b*; Huth *Merlin*, 1: 38; Sommer, *Vulgate*, 2: 23.

16: 6–20. Salazar summarizes. Cf. Bohigas, 1498 *Baladro*, 1: 93–121; Bonilla, 1535 *Baladro*, pp. 24*a*–32*b*; Huth *Merlin*, 1: 63–89; Sommer, *Vulgate*, 2: 36–50.

16: 8. Cf. Bonilla, 1535 *Baladro*, p. 24*a*: "mas no lo fallaredes si el no quisiere."

16: 18–20. Cf. Bonilla, 1535 *Baladro*, p. 32*b*: "e Merlin le dixo en poridad: 'Sed mucho ardid, ca tu no ayas miedo de morir en esta batalla.'"

16: 21–28. Salazar combines the deaths of Vertiger and Anguis with the final defeat of the Saxons. Vertiger, according to the other *Merlin* texts, had died in the fire set by Pandragon (see commentary above, Bk. XI, ch. 16: 1–5), and later Anguis faces a similar fate at the hands of Uter. Cf. Bohigas, 1498 *Baladro*, 1: 98, 122–24; Bonilla, 1535 *Baladro*, pp. 23*b*–24*a*; Huth *Merlin*, 1: 62, 89–92; Sommer, *Vulgate*, 2: 37, 50–52.

17: 1–6. Salazar summarizes the narrative of Uther Pendragon's initial attempts to win the favor of Igerne. Cf. Bohigas, 1498 *Baladro*, 1: 134–44; Bonilla, 1535 *Baladro*, pp. 36*b*–40*a*; Huth *Merlin*, 98–106; Sommer, *Vulgate*, 2: 58–64.

17: 4–6. Cf. Bohigas, 1498 *Baladro*, 1: 143: "E así fué el duque cercado en un castillo, e ovieron aí algunas escaramuças, e el duque se defendía del rey. E el rey estuvo grand tiempo sobre el castillo, que lo no pudo tomar, e ovo grand pesar e gran cuyta por Yguerna, que no podía él haver, que tanto la amava que se no sabía dar remedio."

17: 6–23. Salazar summarizes. Cf. Bohigas, 1498 *Baladro*, 1: 144–51; Bonilla, 1535 *Baladro*, pp. 42*a*–43*a*; Huth *Merlin*, 1: 107–13; Sommer, *Vulgate*, 2: 64–68.

17: 12. In the French texts the Duke of Tintagel is named Hoel; in Geoffrey of Monmouth he is Gorlois, Duke of Cornwall.

17: 24–27. Cf. Bohigas, 1498 *Baladro*, 1: 152: "el rey dixo que le pesava mucho de la muerte del duque, e que le mostrasen cómo lo emendaría, ca no desamava al duque porque muerte le quisiese dar." The advice given to Uther Pendragon is suppressed in the Salazar text. Cf. Bohigas, 1498 *Baladro*, 1: 152–59; Bonilla, 1535 *Baladro*, pp. 43*b*–45*a*; Huth *Merlin*, 1: 113–20; Sommer, *Vulgate*, 2: 68–73.

Salazar refers to Igerne's two small children. In Sommer, *Vulgate*, 2: 73, only one daughter is alluded to, and she is espoused to King Lot. The Huth *Merlin*, 1: 120, mentions three daughters: the one who marries Lot; a bastard daughter Morgans, who marries King Nantres; and another named Morgue (= Morgain), who later becomes the wife of Urien (1: 263). Bohigas, 1498 *Baladro*, 1: 158–59, speaks of Morgayna (= Morgain) and the daughter married to Lot; Bonilla, 1535 *Baladro*, p. 44*b*, speaks of Morgayna la fada and Elena, wife of the King of Organia. Salazar names Elena as the wife of Lot dOrtania in Bk. XI, ch. 27. See M. Blaess, "Arthur's Sisters," *Bulletin Bibliographique de la Société Internationale Arthurienne* 8 (1956): 69–77.

17: 27–35. Salazar condenses. Cf. Bohigas, 1498 *Baladro*, 1: 159–65; Bonilla, 1535 *Baladro*, pp. 45*a*–46*b*; Huth *Merlin*, 1: 120–27; Sommer, *Vulgate*, 2: 73–77. In these texts, as Bohigas remarks (*Los textos*, p. 132), Antor's son is not named at this point, nor is his age given; but in subsequent passages he is called Kex (Queas, Quia, or Queja in the Spanish texts). Salazar combines several characters in the person of Grifet (see commentary below, Bk. XI, ch. 18: 34–39, Bk. XI, ch. 25: 38–46). Traditionally Grifet (= Girflet), Arthur's cupbearer, is the son of Do de Carduel (see Flutre, *Table des noms propres*, p. 90; West, *An Index of Proper Names...Prose Romances*, p. 138*a*).

17: 35–36. Cf. description of Merlin in Bonilla, 1535 *Baladro*, p. 46a: "vn honbre muy flaco e muy viejo a maravilla."

17: 37–39. In the other *Merlin* texts Uther Pendragon forms the Round Table before his marriage to Igerne. The Spanish texts give no membership figure for the Round Table at this point in the narrative, but the French texts say that it has place for fifty knights. Cf. Bohigas, 1498 *Baladro*, 1: 127–29; Bonilla, 1535 *Baladro*, pp. 34a–35b; Huth *Merlin*, 1: 94–98; Sommer, *Vulgate*, 2: 54–56. On Uther Pendragon's ailment (gout in some texts) and death, cf. Bohigas, 1498 *Baladro*, 1: 164–67; Bonilla, 1535 *Baladro*, pp. 46a–47b; Huth *Merlin*, 1: 127–31; Sommer, *Vulgate*, 2: 77–79.

17: 39–41. Cf. Bohigas, 1498 *Baladro*, 1: 166: "Ya tres días ha que no fabla"; and 1: 167: "Estonces se llegó a su oreja e dixole: —Tú has fecho muy fermosa fin, e yo te digo que tu fijo Artur será rey después de ti por la merced de Dios, e él dará cima a la Tabla Redonda que tú començaste."

18: 1–8. Salazar summarizes. Cf. Bohigas, 1498 *Baladro*, 1: 168–70; Bonilla, 1535 *Baladro*, p. 47; Huth *Merlin*, 1: 131–33; Sommer, *Vulgate*, 2: 79–81.

18: 8–16. Cf. Bohigas, 1498 *Baladro*, 1: 170–71: "avía una plaça grande e llana, en la qual vieron un padrón quadrado, mas nunca pudieron saber de que piedra era, pero algunos dixeron que era de mármol, e sobre aquel padrón avía una yunque, en que estaba metida una espada fasta el ariaz, e quando la vieron, maravilláronse e fuéronlo dezir al arçobispo. E el arçobispo, quando lo oyó, tomó del agua bendicta e las reliquias de la yglesia, e con todos los clérigos e con todo el pueblo salió fuera. E quando vieron el padrón e la espada rezaron salmos e oraciones, e echaron agua bendita, e cató el arçobispo el espada, e fallóle letras de oro que dezían: 'Quien fuere tal que esta espada pudiere sacar, será rey desta tierra por elección de Jesuchristo.'" Cf. Bonilla, 1535 *Baladro*, p. 48; Huth *Merlin*, 1: 134–37; Sommer, *Vulgate*, 2: 81–83. Apparently unique to the Salazar version is the reference to the "rio de Artamisa" (=Thames) and the statement that in twenty successive days no one was found who could draw the sward.

18: 17–29. In the other *Merlin* texts Arthur is not sent to London on an errand by Antor; rather it is Antor's son Kex, in London to be armed a knight, who requests that Arthur fetch his sword from the inn. Arthur, unable to locate it, returns by way of the main square, where he withdraws the sword that Merlin had embedded in the stone. Cf. Bohigas, 1498 *Baladro*, 1: 172–80; Bonilla, 1535 *Baladro*, pp. 48*b*–51*a*; Huth *Merlin*, 1: 137–45; Sommer, *Vulgate*, 2: 83–87.

18: 30-34. As Bogdanow points out (*Romance*, p. 224), Arthur's raiment is not described in the Vulgate text, but references are made to his ceremonial robes and crown in the Cast. *Demanda* and in a reworking of the Prose *Tristan*. Cf. also Bonilla, 1535 *Baladro*, p. 51*a*: "e tomaron a Artur en los braços e leuaronlo al altar, y la corona e la vestimenta estaua ay con que lo auian de sagrar. E vestieronselo, e pues fue vestido, el arçobispo se adereço para cantar la missa." Arthur's coronation is described in similar terms in Bohigas, 1498 *Baladro*, 1: 181. The Salazar text provides additional details concerning coronation festivities.

18: 34-39. Antor's request is made prior to Arthur's coronation in the other *Merlin* texts. Salazar supplants Antor's son Kex with Grifet (see commentary, Bk. XI, ch. 17: 27-36, Bk. XI, ch. 25: 38-46).

19: 1 ff. The continuation of the *Merlin* begins at this point (see commentary, Bk. XI, ch. 13: 1 ff.).

19: 3-16. This passage finds no parallel in the other surviving texts of the Post-Vulgate *Merlin*. As Bohigas points out (*Los textos*, pp. 101–2, 132), the episodes of the mountain cat and the war with the Romans are found in the Vulgate version.

19: 7-9. Salazar's summary of the early Grail story (Bk. XI, chs. 11–12) contains merely an allusion to this information. See Bk. XI, ch. 12: 16-17.

19: 10-13. In Sommer, *Vulgate*, 2: 441–44, Arthur has a fight with a monster cat of the Lake of Lausanne. This episode follows the engagement between Arthur's army and the Romans, which ends in the slaying of the emperor, Lucius. Concerning Arthur's combat with the cat, see E. Freymond, "Artus' Kampf mit dem Katzenungestüm," in *Festgabe für Gustav Gröber* (Halle, 1899), pp. 311–96; J. D. Bruce, *Evolution of the Arthurian Romance*, 2nd ed. (1928; rpt. ed., Gloucester, Mass., 1958), 1: 41, n. 9; A. Micha, "Les Sources de la Vulgate du *Merlin*," *Moyen Age* 58 (1952): 320–22.

19: 13-14. The Vulgate *Merlin* does not include this confused reference to Arthur's coat of arms. However, the Vulgate text does state that the monster cat had dug its claws so deeply into Arthur's shield that they could not be withdrawn, and that Arthur kept the shield with the cat's forelegs (Sommer, *Vulgate*, 2: 443–44). In

French and English traditions, coats of arms attributed to Arthur commonly show leopards, a dragon, or the Virgin. See Gerard J. Brault, *Early Blazon Heraldic Terminology in the Twelfth and Thirteenth Centuries* (Oxford, 1972), pp. 22–24, 44; also E. Sandoz, "Tourneys in the Arthurian Tradition," *Speculum* 19 (1944): 389–420; and C. W. Scott-Giles, "Some Arthurian Coats of Arms," *The Coat of Arms* (Heraldry Society Quarterly) 8 (1965): 332–39, and 9 (1966): 30–35. For the cat as a heraldic symbol, see Julian Franklyn, "A Musion (or Catte)," *Coat of Arms* 1 (1950–51): 45–46, "The Cat in Heraldry," *Coat of Arms* 1 (1950–51): 265–68, and 2 (1952): 117; and Brault, p. 141*a*.

19: 14-16. Bohigas points out (*Los textos*, p. 132) that in the Vulgate *Merlin* the name of the Roman leader is Lucius. However, in the Vulgate text Arthur crosses the sea to help defend the kingdom of Ban of Benoic, which has been invaded by Claudas de la Deserte and Frolle d'Alemaigne, among others (Sommer, *Vulgate*, 2: 257–77). In the *Lancelot* branch of the Vulgate Cycle, Frolle (designated "duc d'Allemagne") is slain by Arthur (Sommer, *Vulgate*, 5: 373–74). In the fifteenth-century Spanish text *El Victorial* or *La Crónica de don Pero Niño* by Gutierre Díaz de Games, Arthur is said to have killed "Frolle, rey de Françia, que tenía el reyno por los emperadores de Roma" (ed. J. de Mata Carriazo [Madrid, 1940], p. 177). Concerning the figure of Frolle, see A. Micha, "La Guerre contre les Romains dans la Vulgate du *Merlin*," *Romania* 72 (1951): 320; E. Place, "Amadis of Gaul, Wales, or What?," *HR* 23 (1955): 104–5. In Bk. IX of the *Bienandanzas* Salazar refers to several historical personages as Duque Flores (*A*, fol. 160b–c, 162b; Herrero, *Las bienandanzas*, 2: 81, 85).

19: 17-22. Salazar resumes the narrative as it survives in other Post-Vulgate texts. Cf. Bohigas, 1498 *Baladro*, 1: 187; Bonilla, 1535 *Baladro*, p. 53. Because Lot's wife remains anonymous in Sommer, *Vulgate*, 2: 128–29, and in Huth *Merlin*, 1: 147, Diego Catalán posed the question whether the Spanish adaptor invented the name Elena (*De Alfonso X al Conde de Barcelos* [Madrid, 1962], p. 399). However, the fact that there must have been another OFr. text of the *Merlin* containing this name was pointed out earlier by R. H. Wilson, who compared Malory's use of "Elayne" and the "Elena" of the Spanish texts (see "Addenda on Malory's Minor Characters," *Journal of English and Germanic Philology* 55 [1956]: 565). On the literary importance of Arthur's sin of incest and its consequences in the Post-Vulgate *Merlin* continuation and the *Mort Artu*, see Bogdanow, *Romance*, pp. 144–46.

19: 22-28. Salazar summarizes. Cf. Bohigas, 1498 *Baladro*, 1: 202–14; Bonilla, 1535 *Baladro*, pp. 58*b*–61*b*; Huth *Merlin*, 1: 155–73. In these texts Arthur learns of his true parentage following the episode of the Questing Beast (see commentary below, Bk. XI, ch. 19: 29-34, Bk. XI, ch. 20: 22-31).

19: 29-34. In Bonilla, 1535 *Baladro*, p. 121*a*, Ginebra (= Guenevere) is the daughter of King Leodogan of Tremileda. The episode of Arthur's marriage to Guenevere is lacking in the 1498 *Baladro* (see Bohigas' note, 3: 110–12). In the 1535 *Baladro* the future occupant of the *silla peligrosa* (= Siege Perilous) remains anonymous at this point (Bonilla ed., p. 123*a*).

20: 1 ff. In the other Post-Vulgate *Merlin* texts the events narrated by Salazar in Chs. 20–23 precede Arthur's marriage to Guenevere. Salazar combines the time and place of both Arthur's dream and the Questing Beast episode.

20: 3-9. Cf. Bonilla, 1535 *Baladro*, p. 53*b*: "quando la dueña se torno para su tierra, la primera noche despues el rey soño vn sueño, que le semejaua que estaua en vna catedra la más rica del mundo, e auia ante el atan gran pueblo de todas edades, que se marauillaua donde tan gran pueblo viniera. E teniendolos todos en derredor de si, vio que salia del vna gran sierpe, y tan fuerte semejança que nunca oyo fablar de tal, que siempre andaua bolando sobre el reyno de Londres a cada parte, e por todos los lugares que yua quemaua todo, assi que no quedaua ciudad, ni castillo, ni villa, que todo no quemasse y destruyesse. E assi quemaua todo el reyno de Londres; y despues que esto fazia, venia a los que estauan con el rey, e cometialos, e mataualos todos; e despues iua al rey, e combatiase con el fieramente, mas a la cima matara el rey a la sierpe, y el quedaua llagado mortalmente."

20: 10-21. Cf. Bohigas, 1498 *Baladro*, 1: 189–90; Bonilla, 1535 *Baladro*, pp. 53*b*–54*a*; Huth *Merlin*, 1: 149–50. The popular motif of the *Beste glatissant* or the Questing Beast appears in a number of late Arthurian texts, among them the Prose *Tristan* and Malory's *Morte d'Arthur*. Concerning this beast and its origins, see W. A. Nitze, "The Beste Glatissant in Arthurian Romance," *ZRPh* 56 (1936): 409–18; L. R. Muir, "The Questing Beast, Its Origins and Development," *Orpheus* 4 (1957): 24–32; Bohigas, *Los textos*, pp. 22–23, 100; Entwistle, *Legend*, pp. 14, 49, 124, 150, 152, 155–56; C. E. Pickford, *L'Evolution du roman arthurien en prose vers la fin du moyen âge d' après le ms. 112 du fonds français de la B.N.* (Paris, 1959), p. 15 et passim.

20: 22-31. Salazar condenses. Cf. Bohigas, 1498 *Baladro*, 1: 190–99; Bonilla, 1535 *Baladro*, p. 56.

21: 1-17. Salazar summarizes. Cf. Bohigas, 1498 *Baladro*, 1: 198–99; Bonilla, 1535 *Baladro*, p. 56; Huth *Merlin*, 1: 158–60. In these texts Merlin explains Arthur's dream in the guise of an old man. Salazar's specific reference to the fatal combat between Arthur and his incestuous son Modred is lacking at this point in the other texts.

22: 1-35. Cf. Bohigas, 1498 *Baladro*, 1: 199–201; Bonilla, 1535 *Baladro*, p. 57. The Salazar text agrees in several details with the Cast. *Demanda* version of this episode (cf. 1515 *Demanda*, Chs. 363–367; Bonilla, 1535 *Demanda*, pp. 301a–303a). In the two *Baladro* texts the name Ypomenes is spelled "Ydomenes" and "Idomenes." As Bohigas points out (1498 *Baladro*, 3: 101), in the Cast. *Demanda* (Ch. 358; Bonilla, 1515 *Demanda*, pp. 296b–297a) the Questing Beast is killed by Palomades, whereas the *Baladro* texts state that Galaz (= Galahad) killed it. Palomades is converted to Christianity before he kills the Beast (see Cast. 1515 *Demanda*, Ch. 344; Bonilla, 1535 *Demanda* pp. 290b–291a). Ypomenes' daughter remains anonymous in the *Demanda* and *Baladro* texts.

23: 1-16. In the *Baladro* texts Merlin's vision is related directly after Arthur's coronation. Apparently unique to the Salazar version is the reference to "las animalias del mundo." Cf. Bohigas, 1498 *Baladro*, 1: 183: "vió Merlín una visión, que estava en un prado fermoso, e en él un roble, e cerca de aquel roble una pertiga pequeña e de poca pro, e no tenía ninguna cosa de fructo. E cabe aquel roble crescía la pertiga, e tomóle la corteza e las fojas, e de sí fízola caer e meter so tierra el roble a la pertiga." Also cf. Bonilla, 1535 *Baladro*, p. 51b.

23: 16-34. As Bohigas points out (*Los textos*, p. 137), in the *Baladro* texts Merlin's vision is explained by Blaise, a figure not found in Salazar's version. Cf. Bohigas, 1498 *Baladro*, 1: 183–84; Bonilla, 1535 *Baladro*, pp. 51b–52a. Also lacking in the Salazar version is the important detail that Merlin's cruel death is punishment for his role in causing Arthur's mother, Igerne, to sin (see Bk. XI, ch. 17: 3-23).

23: 29-34. Salazar suppresses a long series of episodes. Merlin's death is related at the end of the *Baladro* texts. Cf. Bohigas, 1498 *Baladro*, 3: 63–85; Bonilla, 1535 *Baladro*, pp. 149b–154a. On the Post-Vulgate version of Merlin's entombment by the Lady of the Lake

(Niviene or Viviene in some texts), see Bogdanow, *Romance,* pp. 180–83; Roger Sherman Loomis, *The Development of Arthurian Romance* (New York, 1963), pp. 129–30; Bohigas, *Los textos,* pp. 46–52.

23: 33-34. Following the explanation of his vision to Blaise, Merlin tells in the *Baladro* texts of the birth of Lancelot of the Lake. See Bohigas, 1498 *Baladro,* 1: 185–86; Bonilla, 1535 *Baladro,* p. 52*b*. In the Prose *Lancelot* the Lady of the Lake raises Lancelot (Sommer, *Vulgate,* 3: 19 ff.).

24: 1 ff. Ch. 24 contains a brief fragment of the Post-Vulgate *Queste del Saint Graal,* part of the third branch of the *Roman du Graal* together with a *Mort Artu.* No French text of the whole Post-Vulgate *Queste* survives, although fragments are found in Paris, Bibl. Nat., MSS. fr. 112 (Bk. 4) and 343. The second redaction of the Prose *Tristan* also incorporates large sections of the *Queste.* An adaptation is preserved in several Spanish and Portuguese texts: Vienna, Oesterreichische Nationalbibliothek, MS. 2594, fols. 1a–187a, ed. Augusto Magne, S.J., *A Demanda do Santo Graal: Reprodução fac-similar e transcrição crítica do códice 2594 da Biblioteca Nacional de Viena,* 2 vols. (Rio de Janeiro, 1955–70), §§1–626; *La demanda del sancto Grial con los marauillosos fechos de Lançarote y de Galaz su fijo* [*El segundo y postrero libro*] (Toledo, 1515), to Ch. 391; *La Demanda del Sancto Grial con los marauillosos fechos de Lançarote y de Galaz su hijo* [Seville, 1535], ed. Adolfo Bonilla y San Martín in *Libros de caballerías,* 1: *Ciclo artúrico–Ciclo carolingio,* NBAE, 6 (Madrid, 1907), pp. 163–313*a*. On the relationship of the various versions of the Post-Vulgate *Queste,* see Bogdanow, *Romance,* pp. 88-137. The Vulgate *Queste del Saint Graal* has received several editions: Sommer, *Vulgate,* 6: 3–199; F. J. Furnivall, *La Queste del Saint Graal* (London, 1864); and A. Pauphilet, *La Queste del Saint Graal,* CFMA, 33 (1923; rpt. ed., Paris, 1949).

24: 1-2. The combat between Arthur and his incestuous son is related by Salazar in Bk. XI, ch. 25.

24: 3-5. Cf. Cast. 1515 *Demanda,* Ch. 6: "quando llegaron a la silla peligrosa, fallaron y letras nueuamente fechas que dezian 'a quatrocientos e cincuenta e quatro años complidos de la muerte de Jesuchristo en dia de Pentecoste, deue auer esta silla señor'" (cf. Bonilla, 1535 *Demanda,* p. 165*b*). In the Ptg. version the date is given as "CCCCLIII anos" (Magne, Ptg. *Demanda,* 1, §8). Cf. Pauphilet, *Queste,* p. 4: ".CCCC. ANZ ET .LIIII."

24: 5-7. Cf. Cast. 1515 *Demanda*, Ch. 15; Bonilla, 1535 *Demanda*, p. 168*b*; Magne, Ptg. *Demanda*, 1, §16; Pauphilet, *Queste*, p. 8. In none of these texts does Galahad utter the words contained in the Salazar version.

24: 8-17. Cf. Cast. 1515 *Demanda*, Ch. 23; Bonilla, 1535 *Demanda*, p. 171; Magne, Ptg. *Demanda*, 1, §25; Pauphilet, *Queste*, p. 15. These texts do not mention how many times the Grail passed around the Table, nor do they contain the words spoken by the mysterious voice.

24: 9-11. Cf. Cast. 1515 *Demanda*, Ch. 14: "vieron que todas las puertas e finiestras del palacio se cerraron, pero no escurescio por ende, ca entro vn tal rayo del sol por toda la casa, que se encendio; e vino estonce vna gran marauilla, ca no auia cauallero en el palacio que no perdiesse la fabla." Cf. Bonilla, 1535 *Demanda*, p. 168*a*; Magne, Ptg. *Demanda*, 1, §26; Pauphilet, *Queste*, p. 16.

24: 21-23. Cf. parallel passages in Cast. 1515 *Demanda*, Ch. 25; Bonilla, 1535 *Demanda*, p. 171*b*; Magne, Ptg. *Demanda*, 1, §27; Pauphilet, *Queste*, p. 16. However, unlike the Salazar version, these texts do not mention specific knights.

24: 23-24. At this point in the narrative neither the Vulgate *Queste* nor the Spanish and Portuguese versions make reference to the sorrow also felt by the queen. Moreover, Arthur's sorrow is not based upon the thought that he will remain alone, but that many of his knights will die as a result of the Grail quest. Cf. Cast. 1515 *Demanda*, Ch. 26; Bonilla, 1535 *Demanda*, pp. 171*b*–172*a*; Magne, Ptg. *Demanda*, 1, §28; Pauphilet, *Queste*, pp. 16–17.

24: 25-26. Salazar condenses. Cf. Cast. 1515 *Demanda*, Chs. 27–29; Bonilla, 1535 *Demanda*, pp. 172*a*–173*a*; Magne, Ptg. *Demanda*, 1, §§29–31. The bleeding sword episode is not included in the Vulgate *Queste* but is found in a later reworking of the Prose *Tristan* (see Bogdanow, *Romance*, pp. 92–93). In the other Hispanic texts the *donzella* or damsel appears on the eve of the knights' departure. Salazar's reference to the Donzella del Lago (= Lady of the Lake) is lacking in these texts as is the statement that Galván (= Gawain) left the court on his horse ("cabalgando en su caballo").

24: 41-42. At one point in the *Demanda* texts twenty-one knights are said to have died in the Grail adventures, and of these Gawain and Mordred killed three. See Cast. 1515 *Demanda*, Ch. 194; Bonilla, 1535 *Demanda*, p. 235*a*; Magne, Ptg. *Demanda*, 2, §362.

24: 43-47. The culmination of the Grail quest and the deaths of

Galahad and Perceval are narrated in Cast. 1515 *Demanda*, Chs. 375–389; Bonilla, 1535 *Demanda*, pp. 306a–312b; Magne, Ptg. *Demanda*, 2, §§614–24; Pauphilet, *Queste*, pp. 262–80.

24: 47-52. In the *Mort Artu* section of the *Demanda* texts Arthur replaces the dead members of the Round Table upon the advice of Gawain. See Cast. 1515 *Demanda*, Ch. 414; Bonilla, 1535 *Demanda*, p. 332; Magne, Ptg. *Demanda*, 2, §§650–51.

25: 1 ff. Chs. 25–26 contain the climactic episodes of the Post-Vulgate *Mort Artu*. Only two small fragments of the French version, containing the episodes of Guenevere's death and Mark's second invasion of Logres, have survived, in Paris, Bibl. Nat., MS. fr. 340 (transcribed by Bogdanow, *Romance*, pp. 261–70). The remainder of the text must be reconstructed from the Hispanic adaptations, which, in addition to the fragments at hand, include Vienna, Oesterreichische Nationalbibliothek, MS. 2594, fols. 187a–199d, ed. Magne, Ptg. *Demanda*, 2, §§627–706; a short fragment concerning Arthur's discovery of Guenevere's love for Lancelot and the latter's claim of innocence, in Salamanca MS. 1877, fols. 298^v–300^v, ed. Pietsch, *Fragments*, 1: 85–89; Cast. 1515 *Demanda*, Chs. 390–455; Bonilla, 1535 *Demanda*, pp. 312b–338b. On the relationship of the Post-Vulgate *Mort Artu* to the other branches of the cycle, see Bogdanow, *Romance*, pp. 138–55. The Vulgate *Mort Artu* has been edited by Sommer, *Vulgate*, 6: 201–391; J. D. Bruce (Halle, 1910); and twice by J. Frappier (Paris, 1936; Geneva–Paris, 1954).

25: 4-22. Salazar summarizes. Cf. Cast. 1515 *Demanda*, Chs. 421–423; Bonilla, 1535 *Demanda*, pp. 324b–325b; Magne, Ptg. *Demanda*, 2, §§660–62; Frappier, *Mort Artu*, §§176–91.

25: 33-37. Before the publication of the Ptg. *Demanda*, Bohigas (*Los textos*, p. 141) expressed the opinion that the death of Yban (=Yvain) and the detail of the ray of sun ("rayo de sol") were details derived from the Vulgate version of the *Mort Artu*. However, they are found in the Ptg. *Demanda*. Cf. Magne, Ptg. *Demanda*, 2, § 665: "E naquela batalha foram mortos VII reis da parte de rei Artur, e o conto do Braado diz quaes foram. Ali morreu Ivam, filho do rei Uriam..."; and §666: "E diz a estória que, pois tirou a lança dêle, que passou por meo da chaga uũ raio de sol, tam craramente, que bem no viu Giflet; onde os da terra, pois ende ouviom falar, disserom que era miragre de Nosso Senhor e sinal de pesar." It is possible, of cource, that other details in the Salazar fragments thought to derive from the Vulgate may have actually appeared in his primary source.

25: 37. In the *Demanda* texts Mordred's head is hung from a chain on top of a tower. Cf. Cast. 1515 *Demanda*, Ch. 425; Bonilla, 1535 *Demanda*, p. 326; Ptg. *Demanda*, 2, §§669–70. Although the motif of impaled or hung heads is common and not restricted to Arthurian romance, its appearance in this literature has been related to Celtic tradition. See references in Stith Thompson, *Motif-Index of Folk-Literature*, 2nd ed. (1955–58; rpt. ed., Bloomington, Ind., 1975), 5: 225 (Q421.1); and G. Schoepperle, *Tristan and Isolt* (1913; rpt. ed., New York, 1959), pp. 318–19. Concerning the use of the enemy's head as a trophy in early European society, see citations and secondary sources listed in José Blázquez Martínez, *Religiones primitivas de Hispania*, 1: *Fuentes literarias y epigráficas* (Rome, 1962), pp. 21–22.

25: 38-46. Cf. Cast. 1515 *Demanda*, Chs. 426–427; Bonilla, 1535 *Demanda*, pp. 326b–327a; Magne, Ptg. *Demanda*, 2, §§671–72; Frappier, *Mort Artu*, §§191–92. Salazar, having combined several figures in the person of Grifet (see commentary, Bk. XI, ch. 17: 27-36, Bk. XI, ch. 18: 34-39) fails to resolve satisfactorily the episode of Lucan's accidental death. In the other *Mort Artu* texts no mention is made of Lucan's burial nor of a town being named after him.

25: 47-68. Cf. Cast. 1515 *Demanda*, Chs. 432–433; Bonilla, 1535 *Demanda*, pp. 328b–329b; Magne, Ptg. *Demanda*, 2, §§677–79; Frappier, *Mort Artu*, §§192–93. In the Vulgate *Merlin* the sword Arthur withdrew from the stone is called "Escalibor" (Sommer, *Vulgate*, 2: 94). However, in the Post-Vulgate text another sword bears this name, a sword given to Arthur from a hand in a lake. Through a long series of episodes concerning Excalibor and the treachery of Arthur's half-sister Morgain, the reader of the Post-Vulgate *Roman du Graal* knows that the sword which Grifet throws into the lake is not the same sword that gained Arthur the throne and that could have protected him in combat with Mordred. Salazar suppresses the intervening episodes, but does make allusion to Merlin's role in Arthur's acquisition of Excalibor. Concerning the literary use of the Excalibor theme in the Post-Vulgate text, see E. Vinaver, "La genèse de la *Suite du Merlin*," in *Mélanges de Philologie romane...offerts à Ernest Hoepffner* (Paris, 1949), pp. 297–98, and "King Arthur's Sword or the Making of a Medieval Romance," *Bulletin of the John Rylands Library* 40 (1958): 513–26; Bohigas, 1498 *Baladro*, 3: 160; Bogdanow, *Romance*, pp. 174–76.

26: 3-4. Magne, Ptg. *Demanda*, 2, §679: "E foi-se Giflet contra uũ outeiro quanto mais pôde, ca pensou que no outeiro soubesse que veeria pera u rei Artur iria." Cf. Cast. 1515 *Demanda*, Ch. 433; Bonilla, 1535 *Demanda*, p. 329*b*; Frappier, *Mort Artu,* §193.

26: 4-7. Magne, Ptg. *Demanda*, 2, §680: "E nom estêve i muito, que viu viĩr per meo do mar ũa barqueta em que viĩam muitas donas. A barca aportou ante rei Artur e as donas sairom fora e foram a el-rei. E andava antre elas Morgai[m] a encantador, irmaã de rei Artur, que foi a el-rei com tôdas aquelas donas que tragia, e rogou-o entom muito, que per seu rôgo houve el-rei de entrar na barca. E, pois foi dentro, fêz meter i seu cavalo e tôdas sas armas ...." Cf. Cast. 1515 *Demanda*, Ch. 434; Bonilla, 1535 *Demanda*, p. 330*a*; Frappier, *Mort Artu,* §250.

26: 7-9. Text garbled.

26: 10-23. Salazar condenses. Cf. Cast. 1515 *Demanda*, Chs. 435-437; Bonilla, 1535 *Demanda*, p. 330; Magne, Ptg. *Demanda*, 2, §§681-83; Frappier, *Mort Artu,* §§194-95.

26: 24-39. The episode recounted by Salazar is not contained in any known Arthurian text. The other surviving texts of the Post-Vulgate *Roman du Graal* fail to indicate Arthur's final resting place. Bohigas (*Los textos*, p. 143) points out that Arthur was taken not to the Island of Brasil but to Avalon. For explanation of the substitution see, in addition to the commentary below, my article "The Passing of King Arthur to the Island of Brasil in a Fifteenth-Century Spanish Version of the Post-Vulgate *Roman du Graal*," *Romania* 92 (1971): 65-74.

26: 25-26. In his *Suma de geografía* (ed. J. Ibáñez Cerda [Madrid, 1948], p. 86) the early sixteenth-century Spanish geographer Martín Fernández de Encisco places the Island of Brasil at 51° to the west of Ireland. Another sixteenth-century Spanish geographer, Alonso de Santa Cruz, puts the island at seventy leagues from a group of Irish islands called Brasquey al Poniente (*Islario general de todas las islas del mundo*, ed. A. Blásquez [Madrid, 1918-20], 1: 75).

26: 26-29. In his version of the Post-Vulgate *Merlin* Salazar suppresses the story of Merlin's unrequited love for Morgain (see Bohigas, 1498 *Baladro*, 2: 49-50; Bonilla, 1535 *Baladro*, pp. 88*b*-89*a*; Huth *Merlin*, 1: 266). On the figure of Morgain, see F. Bogdanow, "Morgain's Role in the Thirteenth-Century French Prose Romance of the Arthurian Cycle," *Medium Aevum* 38 (1969): 123-33.

26: 30–32. Salazar is aware of the cartographic tradition surrounding the Island of Brasil. On this tradition, see E. T. Hamy, "Les Origines de la cartographie de l'Europe septentrionale," *Bulletin de géographie historique et descriptive*, année 1888, pp. 360–61, rpt. in *Etudes historiques et géographiques* (Paris, 1896), pp. 35–36; K. Kretschemer, *Die Entdeckung Amerika's in ihre Bedeutung für die Geschichte des Weltbildes* (Berlin, 1892), pp. 214–20; W. B. Scarfe, "Brazil as a Geographical Appellation," *Modern Language Notes* 5 (1896): 209; N. A. E. Nordenskiöld, *Periplus: An Essay on the Early History of Charts and Sailing Directions* (Stockholm, 1897), pp. 58–59, 79–80, 113–14; F. Nansen, *In Northern Mists: Arctic Exploration in Early Times* (London, 1911), 2: 228–30, 279–80, 294, 318; T. J. Westropp, "Brasil and the Legendary Islands of the North Atlantic," *Proceedings of the Royal Irish Academy* 30 (1912): 240–47; H. Babcock, *Legendary Islands of the Atlantic* (New York, 1922), pp. 50–67; A. Cortesão, *The Nautical Chart of 1424* (Coimbra, 1954), pp. 73–74; C. O. Sauer, *Northern Mists* (Berkeley–Los Angeles, 1968), pp. 167–68; Samuel Eliot Morison, *The European Discovery of America*, 1: *The Northern Voyages* (New York, 1971), pp. 102–3, 104–5.

26: 32–39. Just when this mysterious voyage occurred is not certain. However, it had to have taken place before Salazar's death in 1476 (on his death, see D. de Areitio, "De la prisión y muerte de Lope García de Salazar," *Revue Internationale des Etudes Basques* 17 [1926]: 9–16; J. de Ibarra y Bergé and E. Calle Iturrino, *La tumba de Lope García de Salazar en San Martín de Muñatones* [Bilbao, 1956], p. 34). The date of the earliest known voyage out of Bristol in search of the Island of Brasil has been cited as 1480 (see J. A. Williamson, *The Cabot Voyages and Bristol Discovery under Henry VII* [Cambridge, Eng., 1962], pp. 19–23). A certain John Lloyd commanded a ship which sailed from Bristol on July 15, 1480, to look for the island to the west of Ireland. We can only speculate how García de Salazar came upon his information, but news of such a "find" could have occurred in the course of his contacts with sailors and merchants at northern Spanish seaports. During the fifteenth century, trade between Bristol and the Basque ports increased sharply (see E. M. Carus-Wilson, *Medieval Merchant Venturers*, 2nd ed. [London, 1967], pp. 49–58; J. W. Sherborne, *The Port of Bristol in the Middle Ages* [Bristol, 1965], pp. 8–9, 11, 15, 23–28; Morison, *The European Discovery*, 1: 103–4; I have not yet seen the recent study by Wendy Childs, *Anglo–Castilian Trade in the Later Middle Ages* [Manchester,

1978]). Salazar alludes to such trade in the last book of the *Bienandanzas* (A, fol. 445b; Herrero, *Las bienandanzas*, 4: 189).

Salazar's reference to the wood on the Island of Brasil raises anew the origin of the word "brasil." Several lines of derivation have been postulated, but a specific etymology has never been established. Some scholars point to an Irish origin. On maps and in manuscripts the word is spelled in various ways, one of them being "Breasail," which may be the Gaelic term for 'fortunate' or 'blessed' (Nansen, *In Northern Mists*, 2: 228; Babcock, *Legendary Islands*, pp. 50–52; R. A. Skelton, *The Vinland Map* [New Haven, 1965], p. 138; Sauer, *Northern Mists*, p. 167; Morison, *The European Discovery*, 1: 103). Evidence in support is found in an inscription on the Fra Mauro map of 1459, in which Brasil is linked to the Fortunate Islands (see Nansen, *In Northern Mists*, 2: 228; Babcock, *Legendary Islands*, p. 52). Another proposed line of derivation ties the word "brasil" to the legendary voyages of St. Brendan. Although the alleged travels of St. Brendan do not take him to an island of that name, one scholar has suggested that by a process of contraction and copying the expression *Brandani insulae* eventually led to the name "Brasil" (the suggestion by Laurence Witten is given in Skelton, *The Vinland Map*, p. 138). A more frequently suggested derivation is that the name is related to various Romance words pertaining to fire or glowing coal, like the Fr. *braise* or the Sp. *brasero*, and, therefore, since fire is normally red in color, that red dyewood from the Far East came to be called "brasil" (see Du Cange, *Glossarium mediae et infimae latinitatis*, 1: 737c; Meyer-Lübke, *Romanisches Etymologisches Wörterbuch*, § 1276; C. Battisti and G. Alessio, *Dizionario etimologico italiano*, 1: 591; Joan Corominas, *Diccionario crítico etimológico de la lengua castellana*, 1: 510a–512a; P. Pelliot, *Notes on Marco Polo* [Paris, 1959], 1: 103–4; Babcock, *Legendary Islands*, pp. 52–55; L. Weiner, "History of the Word Brazil," in *The Histories of Brazil by Pero de Magalhães*, ed. John B. Stetson, Jr. [New York, 1922], 2: 195–203; J. Caetano da Silva, "Questões americanas," *Revista do Instituto Histórico e Geográfico Brasileiro*, 29, pt. 2 [1886], pp. 5–35; José Pedro Machado, "O nome 'Brasil,'" *Revista de Portugal: Língua Portuguesa* 30 [1965]: 191–202, and "'Ainda o nome 'Brasil,'" *Revista de Portugal*, 31 [1966]: 149–56; Antônio Leite Pessoa, *A origem da palavra Brasil* [Rio de Janeiro, 1974]. Also, because the term was applied to the word from which the valuable red dye was extracted, it is argued that the Atlantic island or islands on which brazilwood was found came to be called Brasil, just like the South American Brazil several centuries later (see J. Fischer, S.J., *The Discoveries of the Norsemen in America with Special Relation to Their Early Car-*

tographical Representation [London, 1930], pp. 94, 99–100, 105; Nansen, *In Northern Mists*, 2: 229, n. 1; Gustavo Barroso, "Origens da palavra Brazil," *Revista da Academia Brasileira de Letras* 36 [1931]: 61–79; Sauer, *Northern Mists*, pp. 168–69). Morison, however, believing in the Gaelic origin of the word, states that the dyewood has no bearing on the origin of the name (*The European Discovery*, 1: 103). But the New World territory, named at first Santa Cruz by the Portuguese, later came to be called Brazil because of the important red dyewood commerce, and García de Salazar's use of the term in connection with a coveted wood as well as an island would seem to demonstrate that the several channels of derivation did meet in the legendary island to the west of Ireland before the discovery of the South American territory. Such a conclusion is misunderstood by Derek W. Lomax (in *The Year's Work in Modern Language Studies*, 33 [1971]: 251), in his capsule review of my earlier study, "The Passing of King Arthur to the Island of Brasil...."

26: 39. The island is given a circular shape on many of the maps. Cf. Fernández de Enciso: "es cuasi redonda" (*Suma de geografía*, p. 86).

27: 2–3. Salazar's source for his history of French kings remains unknown (see commentary above, Bk. IX, ch. 8: 1–9). But that it was in French rather than Spanish seems apparent from the following statement: "e reyno este Guillermo enoto que dize en françes Guillelmo el nonbrado" (*A*, fol. 190c; Herrero, *Las bienandanzas*, 2: 142). Also, other proper names mentioned in this section retain some of their original spelling: e.g., Mosen Jacques de Clison, Duque AnRique, Mosen Gudofre de Charluy.

BOOK XVII

47: 1–4. Salazar alters considerably the wording of his source, the *versión vulgar* or longer redaction of Pero López de Ayala's *Crónica del rey don Pedro I*. Cf. Wilkins, *Corónica*, p. 1195: "su entençion era de venir a acorrer a los de Toledo que estauan çercados, e le auian enbiado dezir por muchas de vezes que no tenian viandas, sennalada mente pan, e que non se pudian tener luengo tienpo."

47: 6–8. Cf. Wilkins, *Corónica*, p. 1196: "vn moro que dizian Benharin, que era grannd sabidor, e filosopho, e priuado del rey de Granada; del qual deximos suso que le auia enbiado otra carta, quando el rey don Pedro torno de Vayona, e vençio la batalla de

Najara; e asi agora este mesmo moro, desque sopo que partio el rey
don Pedro de Seuilla para acorrer a Toledo, *e* penso q*ue* auia de
pelear, enbiole otra carta, de la qual el tenor es este."

48: 1 ff. Salazar's text of the exegesis of the Merlin prophecy is a
verbatim copy, badly reproduced, based on a MS version now presumably lost. The Salazar version contains a number of forms and
expressions in common with the several MSS close to the archtype
of the *vulgar* tradition, which has been established by William Lee
Holman and modified by Roderic Charles Diman (see Wilkins,
Corónica, pp. xxii–iv), particularly Madrid, Real Academia de la
Historia, 9–26–1/4764 (*olim* A–13), Escorial X.I.5 and Z.III.15, and
British Library Add. 17906. To these MSS and their variants cited
in the critical apparatus of Wilkins, *Corónica,* may be added Madison, Univ. of Wisconsin Library, MS. 57 (prophecy at fols.
155c–158b). My emendations of the Salazar text are based on readings found in these MSS. The existence of yet additional MS copies
of the Ayala chronicles has recently been brought to light by
Charles B. Faulhaber, "Some Private and Semi-private Spanish Li-
braries: Travel Notes," *La Corónica* 4, no. 2 (1975–76): 81–90.

48: 1–2. This chapter title as well as the rubrics "Sigue(se) la
carta" which follow in the exegesis of the prophecy would appear
to be Salazar's own addition, since they are not found in any of the
MS versions examined.

48: 8–14. In condensing his source, Salazar produces several incomplete sentences. Cf. Wilkins, *Corónica,* p. 1197: "Las cosas que
lo adebdan, quales *e* quantas son, pues tu eres ya sabidor, non es
menester de repetir enojo. Pedisteme que por industria del mi saber, co*n* gran*n*d diligençia *e* acuçia de gran*n*d estudio, otrossi por
manera de gran*n*d seso que en mi fallauas en tus negoçios, que te
fiziesse saber en qual manera podras palpar por verdadero saber vn
dicho de profeçia."

48: 16–23. On the use of animal imagery and symbolism in the
Merlin prophetic tradition, see Rupert Taylor, *Political Prophecy in
England* (New York, 1911), pp. 28, 45–47 et passim; and Lucy Allen
Paton, "Notes on Manuscripts of the *Prophécies de Merlin,*" *PMLA*
28 (1913): 121–39.

48: 65–67. Concerning the crimes, real and alleged, of Peter the
Cruel, see Ramón d'Abadal i de Vinyals, "El gobierno del rey
Pedro," in *Historia de España,* ed. R. Menéndez Pidal (Madrid,
1935–), 14, pp. xcv–cxcviii, and in the same volume Luis Suárez Fernández, "Castilla (1350–1406)," 1–378, at pp. 3–129.

48: 194–97. On the location of Montiel, see Gonzalo Moya, *Don Pedro el Cruel* (Madrid, 1974), pp. 85–87.

48: 228. The date is apparently Salazar's addition, since it is not to be found in any of the MS versions I have examined (see Wilkins, *Corónica*, p. 1212).

BOOKS XXI, XXII, AND XXV

No comprehensive list of Arthurian names as given to actual persons in medieval Spain and Portugal has even been compiled, but Entwistle points out how the Arthurian romances filtered down from courtly society to the lower classes in the common use of Arthurian characters for given names (see *Legend*, p. 238). For additional names, see the second volume of my *A Critical Bibliography of Hispanic Arthurian Material* (London: Grant & Cutler, forthcoming).

Onomastic Index

The index includes all proper names and anonymous characters, arranged in alphabetical order according to the orthography of the Cristóbal de Mieres codex. The Arthurian names found in the last books of the *Bienandanzas* are omitted (see list at pp. 81–82).

ADAN, Adam, Bk. XI, ch. 14: 51.

ADUARTE, Edward II of England, Bk. XI, ch. 30: 1.

AFRICA, Bk. XI, ch. 1: 2; TIERRA DE AFRICA, Bk. XI, ch. 7: 14. *See* CARTAGO DE AFRICA.

ALBION (ALUION), Bk. XI, ch. 8: 14, ch. 9: 25, ch. 10: 4.

ALCALDE, judge who frees Merlin's mother from her sentence, Bk. XI, ch. 14: 2ff.

ALCALDES, judges who condemn Merlin's mother to death, Bk. XI, ch. 13: 12.

ALCARAZ, a land held by the Moors, Bk. XVII, ch. 48: 192.

ALEMAÑA (ALEMANIA), Germany, Bk. IV, ch. 54: 11; Bk. X, ch. 3: 11; Bk. XI, ch. 7: 18. *See* GERMANIA.

ALMONICAS, pagan people of Chaldea who settled in Flanders, Bk. X, ch. 3: 5.

ALFONSO, Alfonso XI of Castile and León, Bk. XVII, ch. 48: 73.

ALUION *See* ALBION.

AMAZONAS. *See* DUEÑAS AMAZONAS.

ANTENOR, Trojan who settled in Germany after Destruction of Troy, Bk. XI, ch. 7: 20.

ANTOR, rustic who gives up his son Grifet to raise young Arthur, Bk. XI, ch. 17: 31, ch. 18: 27, ch. 19: 24, 25.

ARCHILES, Achiles, Bk. XI, ch. 2: 14–15.

ARTAMISA, the river Thames, Bk. XI, ch. 18: 9.

ARTUR DE YNGUELATIERRA, Arthur, king of England, Bk. I, ch. 1: 3; Bk. V, 67: 19; Bk. X, ch. 3: 21, ch. 15: 2, ch. 22: 13; Bk. XI, ch. 12: 8–9, 13, ch. 13: 2, ch. 15: 2, ch. 16: 13, ch. 17: 2–3, 16, 34–35, 40, ch. 18: 1, 17, 30, ch. 19: 1, 4, ch. 20: 1, 3, ch. 21: 1, ch. 22: 1, ch. 23: 1–2, ch. 24: 8, 48, ch. 25: 1, 4, 25, ch. 26: 1, 14, 24, ch. 27: 2, ch. 30: 4, ch. 36: 3.

ASARACO (ASARATO), grandson of Achilles, Bk. X, ch. 22: 7–8; Bk. XI, ch. 2: 14, 17, 19, ch. 5: 26, ch. 6: 10, 12, ch. 10: 8.

AVARIMATIA. See JOSEP AVARIMATIA.

AVE NEGRA, symbolic bird of prey in prophecy of Merlin to Peter the Cruel, Bk. XVII, ch. 48: 16–17ff.

AVENAMATIN, philosopher of the King of Granada who explains prophecy of Merlin to Peter the Cruel, Bk. XVII, ch. 47: 6–7, ch. 48: 2, 4.

AVFERION, DUQUE. See TINTOYL.

BENEÇIA, city of Venice, Bk. IV, ch. 54: 9.

BESTIA LADRADORA. See VESTIA LADRADORA.

BRASIL, YSLA DE, Island of Brasil, Bk. XI, ch. 26: 2, 25.

BRETAÑA, EL DUCADO DE, Dukedom of Brittany, Bk. X, ch. 15: 2–3, 6. See PEQUEÑA BRETAÑA.

BRETAÑA, LA GRAND. See GRAND BRETAÑA.

BRIBIA, the Bible, Bk. XI, ch. 11: 19.

BRISTOL, Bristol, England, Bk. XI, ch. 26: 34.

BRUTO, Brutus, grandson of Aeneas and founder of Britain, Bk. IV, ch. 54: 4; Bk. X, ch. 22: 7; Bk. XI, ch. 1: 14, 17, ch. 2: 1, 4, 17, 20, ch. 3: 1ff., ch. 4: 1, ch. 5: 1ff., ch. 6: 11ff., ch. 7: 1ff., ch. 8: 3ff., ch. 9: 2ff., ch. 10: 1ff.

BURGOS, Burgos, Spain, Bk. XVII, ch. 48: 56.

CABALLEROS, one hundred pagan knights of the Ysla de Gajola, Bk. X, ch. 3: 18, 25; CABALLEROS DE LA TABLA REDONDA, knights of the Round Table, Bk. X, ch. 3: 22–23, 26; Bk. XI, ch. 17: 38, ch. 19: 31, 32–33, ch. 24: 5, 42, ch. 25: 28–29.

CALDEA, Chaldea, Bk. X, ch. 3: 6.

CALEZ, ESTRECHO DE, Strait of Calais (= English Channel), Bk. XI, ch. 15: 13.

CAN, town named after Lucan, Bk. XI, ch. 25: 44.

CAPITAN, captain of corsairs killed by Brutus, Bk. XI, ch. 7: 9; Roman captain killed by Arthur, Bk. XI, ch. 25: 11.

CARDOYN, companion of Tristan and knight of the Round Table, Bk. X, ch. 15: 10.

CARLOS, Charlemagne, Bk. I, 1: 4; Bk. XI, ch. 36: 3.

CARTAGO DE AFRICA, Carthage, Bk. IV, ch. 54: 10; Bk. XI, ch. 1: 2.

CASTILLA, Castile, Bk. XVII, ch. 48: 94, 190.

CABO. See LONGANEAS.

CATALANES, the Catalans, Bk. XI, ch. 9: 2–3, 10.

CATIBOS, Trojan prisoners, Bk. XI, ch. 2: 10, 17, ch. 6: 8.

CHIPRE, Cyprus, Bk. XI, ch. 7: 23. See LOCAÇIA.

ENEAS, Aeneas, Bk. XI, ch. 1: 1, 9.

ENPERADOR DE ROMA, Lucius, emperor of Rome, Bk. XI, ch. 25: 5.

EQUITANIA, Dukedom in France, Bk. XI, ch. 8: 28. *See* GUIANA.

ERLANDA, Ireland, Bk. I, ch. 1: 2; Bk. X, ch. 22: 5; Bk. XI, ch. 26: 26, ch. 27: 2, ch. 30: 3.

ERTON, nephew of Joseph of Arimathea, Bk. XI, ch. 12: 3.

ESCALIBOR, Excalibor, Arthur's sword, Bk. XI, ch. 25: 47.

ESCANIO, uncle of Brutus, Bk. XI, ch. 1: 7, ch. 2: 4.

ESCOÇESES, the Scots, Bk. XI, ch. 10: 23.

ESCOÇIA (SCOÇIA), Scotland, Bk. I, ch. 1: 2; Bk. IV, ch. 54: 12; Bk. X, ch. 22: 4–5; Bk. XI, ch. 10: 2, 8, ch. 27: 1, ch. 30: 3.

ESPAÑA, LA MAR DE, Spanish Sea (Mod. Span. *Mar Cantábrico*), Bk. XI, ch. 8: 27.

ESTROLAGOS, astrologers of Brutus' father Julio, Bk. XI, ch. 1: 11; astrologers of Vertiger (also called *.xij. sabios* and *.xij. clerigos*), Bk. XI, ch. 15: 14, 32, 42.

EVA, Eve, Bk. XI, ch. 14: 52.

FARAMONT, Pharamont, king of France, Bk. IX, ch. 8: 1, 3, 7.

FLAMENQUES, the Flemings, Bk. X, ch. 3: 9–10.

FLANDES, Flanders, Bk. X, ch. 3: 2, 4.

FLORES, Duke Flores, Bk. XI, ch. 19: 15.

FRANÇESES, the French, Bk. IX, ch. 8: 6; Bk. XI, ch. 9: 11, 18.

FRANÇIA, France, Bk. I, ch. 1: 4; Bk. IV, ch. 54: 11; Bk. IX, ch. 8: 1, 4; Bk. X, ch. 3: 9, 11, ch. 15: 2; Bk. XI, ch. 15: 10, ch. 27: 3, ch. 30: 3, ch. 36: 3, 4.

GAJOLA, YSLA DE, Isle of Gajola, Bk. X, ch. 3: 18–19. *See* LUENGA YNSOLA.

GAJUSETE, knight of the Round Table, Bk. XI, ch. 12: 9.

GALAZ, Galahad, son of Joseph of Arimathea whose name was give to city of Lisoarta, Bk. XI, ch. 12: 11, 12; EL SANTO GALAZ, Galahad, son of Lancelot, Bk. XI, ch. 12: 18, ch. 19: 34, ch. 22: 32, ch. 24: 5, 22, 34, 44, 46.

GALIOTE, Galehaut, conqueror and lord of the Isle of Gajola, Bk. X, ch. 3: 24.

GALUAN (GALBAN), Gawain, nephew of Arthur and knight of the Round Table, Bk. XI, ch. 12: 10, ch. 24: 19, 35, 52.

GANUZ, kingdom ruled by Nascien, Bk. XI, ch. 12: 20. *See* VORES DE GANUS.

GARAFIO, king of Guiana, Bk. XI, ch. 9: 2, 4, 8, 10.

GARBAYN, knight of the Round Table, Bk. XI, ch. 12: 9.

GARCIA DE SALAZAR, LOPE, Bk. X, ch. 22: 1–2.

GATO, mountain cat killed by Arthur, Bk. XI, ch. 19: 11.

GATOS ARTUXES, "Arthur's Cats," name given to arms of Arthur, Bk. XI, ch. 19: 14.

GAULA (GAVLA), Gaul, Bk. IX, ch. 8: 4; Bk. XI, ch. 15: 10, ch. 20: 4, ch. 25: 1, 6, 10. *See* FRANÇIA.

GAULOS, the Gauls, Bk. XI, ch. 9: 3, 11.

GERMANIA, Germany, Bk. XI, ch. 7: 18. *See* ALEMAÑA.

GERRES, knight of the Round Table, Bk. XI, ch. 12: 9.

GIFED. *See* GRIFET.

GIFLET. *See* GRIFET.

GIGANTE, giant of Albion, Bk. XI, ch. 8: 14. *See also* MAGOT.

GINEBRA, Guenevere, wife of Arthur, queen of England, Bk. XI, ch. 19: 29, ch. 24: 23, 35, ch. 25: 18.

. GLIFED. *See* GRIFET.

GLIFET. *See* GRIFET.

GRANADA, Granada, Spain, Bk. XVII, ch. 48: 191, 228; REY DE GRANADA, king of Granada, Bk. XVII, ch. 47: 4, 7, ch. 48: 4.

GRAND BRETAÑA, Great Britain, Bk. XI, ch. 10: 6–7, ch. 19: 4.

GRAND DUARTE, Edward III of England, Bk. XI, ch. 36: 4.

GREAL. *See* SANTO GREAL.

GREÇIA, Greece, Bk. IV, ch. 54: 4; Bk. X, ch. 22: 7; Bk. XI, ch. 2: 1, 2, 8, ch. 3: 27, ch. 4: 14, ch. 6: 23.

GRIAL. *See* SANTO GREAL.

GRIEGOS, the Greeks, Bk. XI, ch. 2: 13, ch. 3: 22, ch. 6: 4.

GRIFET (GIFED, GIFLET, GLIFED, GLIFET), son of Antor and Arthur's cup-bearer, Bk. XI, ch. 17: 34, ch. 18: 35, ch. 25: 46ff., ch. 26: 3, 9, 10, 18.

GRUAS, cranes which witness murder of Ibycus, Bk. V, ch. 67: 5, 9, 10, 12, 13.

GUIANA, dukedom in France, Bk. XI, ch. 8: 28, ch. 9: 2, 4, ch. 30: 2. *See* EQUITANIA.

HERMANA, Arthur's sister, Bk. XI, ch. 12: 8. *See* ELENA.

HERMANO, brother of Ypomenes, Bk. XI, ch. 22: 9, 14, 15, 20.

HERMITAÑO, hermit who tells Grifet of having seen Arthur buried by Morgain, Bk. XI, ch. 26: 14.

HOEL, king of Brittany, father of Iseut of the White Hands, Bk. X, ch. 15: 8.

IHERUSALEM, Jerusalem, Bk. XI, ch. 11: 13.

IHESU CHRISTO, Jesus Christ, Bk. XI, ch. 11: 4, ch. 14: 53, ch. 19: 3, ch. 24: 3. *See* NUESTRO SEÑOR.

JANTUS, Ibycus, Greek poet, Bk. V, ch. 67: 1, 11.

JOSEFAZ (JOSES), Josephé, son of Joseph of Arimathea, Bk. I, ch. 1: 3; Bk. X, ch. 22: 10; Bk. XI, ch. 11: 2, 5.

JOSEP ABARIMATIA (AVARAMATIA, AVARIMATIA), Joseph of Arimathea, Bk. I, ch. 1: 3; Bk. X, ch. 22: 9; Bk. XI, ch. 11: 1, 5, 14, ch. 12: 2, 3, 7, 11, 16; ch. 19: 7.

JOSES. *See* JOSEFAZ.

JOSUE, Joshua, Bk. XI, ch. 10: 3; nephew of Joseph of Arimathea, Bk. XI, ch. 12: 16.

JUAN, John, king of England, Bk. XI, ch. 30: 1.

JUDIOS, the Jews, Bk. XI, ch. 11: 17.

JULIO, father of Brutus, Bk. XI, ch. 1: 7, 10, 15, 17.

LABRADORA, peasant woman to whom Antor gives his son after accepting plan to raise Arthur, Bk. XI, ch. 17: 34, ch. 18: 38.

LADRONES, thieves who murder Ibycus, Bk. V, ch. 67: 2, 11.

LANÇAROTE, Lancelot, Bk. XI, ch. 12: 20, 23; LANÇAROTE DEL LAGO, grandson of Lancelot, son of the Lady of the Lake, Bk. XI, ch. 12: 22, 24, ch. 23: 34, ch. 24: 22, 34.

LEODANGA DE NORGALES, father of Guenevere, Bk. XI, ch. 19: 29.

LEONEL, son of Lancelot and knight of the Round Table, Bk. XI, ch. 12: 21.

LEONIS, city of Leonois, Bk. XI, ch. 12: 3. See ELEDUS *and* TRISTAN.

LISOARTA, city which was later named Galaz, Bk. XI, ch. 12: 11. See GALAZ.

LOCAÇIA, former name of Cyprus, Bk. XI, ch. 7: 23. See CHIPRE.

LONBARDIA, Lombardy, Bk. IV, ch. 54: 10.

LONDRES, London, Bk. I, ch. 1: 2; Bk. IV, ch. 54: 9; Bk. X, ch. 22: 5; Bk. XI, ch. 10: 2, 6, 27, ch. 18: 7; CASTILLO DE LONDRES, London Castle, Bk. XI, ch. 25: 19.

LONGANEAS, an Irish cape near which is located the Island of Brasil, Bk. XI, ch. 26: 26.

LORMANDIA, Normandy, Bk. XI, ch. 9: 18.

LORMANES, the Normans, Bk. X, ch. 3: 7.

LOT D(E) ORTANIA, husband of Arthur's half-sister Elena, Bk. XI, ch. 12: 8, ch. 19: 17.

LUCAN, Arthur's major-domo, Bk. XI, ch. 25: 40, 44.

LUÇES PAGANO, Lucius, ruler of London, Bk. XI, ch. 10: 27.

LUÇIFER, Bk. XI, ch. 15: 43. See DIABLO.

LUENGA YNSOLA, the Distant Isle, Bk. X, ch. 3: 19. See GAJOLA.

MAÇEDONIA, kingdom of Macedonia, Bk. XI, ch. 2: 9.

MADRE, mother of Asaraco, Bk. XI, ch. 2: 15, 16; mother of Brutus, Bk. XI, ch. 1: 11, 12; mother of the judge who frees Merlin's mother, Bk. XI, ch. 14: 8ff.; Merlin's mother, Bk. XI, ch. 13: 4–5, ch. 14: 2ff.

MAGOT, giant of Cornwall killed by Corineo, Bk. XI, ch. 9: 27. See PEÑA DE MAGOT.

MARCHO MONUERES, father of king Pharamont of France, Bk. IX, ch. 8: 2, 3.

MAREANTES, Brutus' sailors, Bk. XI, ch. 6: 33.

MARGAYNA (MORGAYNA), Morgain, half-sister of Arthur, Bk. XI, ch. 12: 13, ch. 26: 1, 5–6, 16, 25.

MARIA. See SANTA MARIA.

MARRUECOS, EL ESTRECHO DE, the Strait of Morocco (= Strait of Gibraltar), Bk. XI, ch. 8: 27.

MENBRUDO, a wise Trojan, Bk. XI, ch. 4: 6.

MERLIN, Bk. V, 67: 19; Bk. X, ch. 22: 13; Bk. XI, ch. 13: 1, ch. 14: 1ff., ch. 15: 25, ch. 16: 7, 22, 24, 27, ch. 17: 7ff., ch. 18: 2, 5, 30, ch. 19: 22, ch. 20: 2, ch. 21: 1, 2, 4, 8, ch. 22: 1, ch. 23: 1, 17, ch. 25: 21, 48, 60, ch. 26: 28; Bk. XVII, ch. 47: 6, ch. 48: 1, 13, 130; disguised as an old man *(omne viejo)*, Bk. XI, ch. 20, 22.

MILAN, city of Milan, Bk. IV, ch. 54: 9.

MOÇOS, Merlin's playmates, Bk. XI, ch. 15: 22. See COMPAÑEROS.

MONTIEL, castle in land of the Moors, Bk. XVII, ch. 48: 197. See SELUA.

MORGAYNA. See MARGAYNA.

MORDERET, Mordred, bastard son of Arthur, Bk. XI, ch. 12: 10, ch. 19: 21, ch. 21: 11, ch. 24: 2, ch. 25: 2ff.

ROMANOS, the Romans, Bk. X, ch. 3: 6; Bk. XI, ch. 25: 2, 11.

SABIOS, twelve sages. *See* ESTROLAGOS (of Vertiger).
SADOR, nephew of Joseph of Arimathea, Bk. XI, ch. 12: 3, 16.
SALAMON, Solomon, Bk. V, ch. 67: 17.
SAN MARTIN, home of Lope García de Salazar, Bk. X, ch. 22: 3.
SANTA MARIA, St. Mary, Bk. XI, ch. 14: 5.
SANTO GREAL (GRIAL), Holy Grail, Bk. X, ch. 22: 11; Bk. XI, ch. 11: 2, 7, 9, 16,
    ch. 19: 6, ch. 20: 24–25, ch. 22: 4, 33, ch. 24: 1, 11, 17, 19, 20, 43, 45.
SARAVARRE, EL CANPO DE, Salisbury Plain, Bk. XI, ch. 25: 23.
SARRAS, kingdom of Sarras, Bk. XI, ch. 24: 47.
SCOÇIA. *See* ESCOÇIA.
SELUA, castle of Selva, Bk. XVII, ch. 48: 195, 196. *See* MONTIEL.
SEÑOR, EL, The Lord, Bk. IX, ch. 8: 5, Bk. XI, ch. 22: 23. *See* NUESTRO SEÑOR
    and IHESU CHRISTO.
SEÑOR DE LA TIERRA DE AFRICA, African ruler who does battle with
    Brutus, Bk. XI, ch. 7: 15.
SIERPE RABIOSA, rabid serpent in dream of Arthur, Bk. XI, ch. 20: 7, ch. 21: 9.
SILLA PELIGROSA, the Siege Perilous, Bk. XI, ch. 19: 33, ch. 24: 7.
SILVIAS (SILUIAS) POSTINO, son of Aeneas, Bk. XI, ch. 1: 7, ch. 2: 4.

TABLA REDONDA, the Round Table, Bk. X, ch. 3: 22, 23, 26, ch. 15: 10–11; Bk.
    XI, ch. 12: 10, 15, 23, ch. 17: 38, ch. 19: 30–31, ch. 24: 4, 8, 13, 42, 51, ch.
    25: 28–29. *See* CABALLEROS DE LA TABLA REDONDA.
TIERRA FORANA, the Terre Foraine, Bk. XI, ch. 12: 17, ch. 13: 4.
TINTOYL, DUQUE DE, Duke of Tintagel, Bk. XI, ch. 17: 4. Also called Duque
    Avferion, Bk. XI, ch. 17: 12, 17.
TITUS, son of Vespasian, emperor of Rome, Bk. XI, ch. 11: 18.
TOLEDO, Toledo, Spain, Bk. XVII, ch. 47: 2.
TORENA, town in Normandy named after Toreno, cousin of Brutus, Bk. XI, ch. 9:
    22. *See* TORRES EN TORENA.
TORENO, cousin of Brutus, Bk. XI, ch. 9: 20.
TORRE DEL LLORO, the Dolorous Tower, Bk. X, ch. 3: 25.
TORRES EN TORENA, town in Normandy, Bk. XI, ch. 9: 22. *See* TORENA.
TOSCANA, Tuscany, Bk. XI, ch. 1: 10.
TRISTAN DE LEONIS, Tristan de Leonois, Bk. IX, ch. 8: 8; Bk. X, ch. 15: 9, 10;
    Bk. XI, ch. 12: 5, ch. 24: 22, 34.
TROYA, Troy, Bk. IV, ch. 54: 5; Bk. XI, ch. 1: 2, ch. 2: 7, 11, 12, 18, ch. 4: 7, ch. 6:
    5, 33, 34, ch. 7: 14, 21, 27, ch. 8: 6, 10, 25, ch. 10: 24.
TROYANOS, the Trojans, Bk. IV, ch. 54: 1; Bk. X, ch. 22: 7; Bk. XI, ch. 2: 10, 17,
    ch. 3: 1, 3, ch. 4: 1, ch. 5: 1, 3, 6, 25, ch. 6: 1, 7, ch. 7: 1, 4, ch. 9: 2, 5, 12,
    ch. 10: 1, 4.

VASPASIANO, Vespasian, emperor of Rome, Bk. XI, ch. 11: 18.
VELAMARIN, Belamarín (House of), Bk. XVII, ch. 48: 191.
VELLIDA, Belide, daughter of king Pharamont of France, Bk. IX, ch. 8: 8.
VERTIGUER (VERTIGUO), Vertiger, bastard son of Moynes, king of Britain, Bk.
    XI, ch. 15: 7, ch. 16: 4, 5, 13, 23.

VESTIA LADRADORA, the Questing Beast, Bk. XI, ch. 20: 1–2, 12, 30, ch. 21: 6, ch. 22: 2, 3.

VILLANA. *See* LABRADORA.

VLFIN (OLFIN), subordinate of Uther Pendragon, Bk. XI, ch. 17: 9, 22, 28, ch. 19: 25.

VORES, Bors, knight of the Round Table, Bk. XI, ch. 12: 21; VORES DE GANUS, Bors, the elder, Bk. XI, ch. 12: 21.

VRIAN, Brian, married Arthur's half-sister Morgain, Bk. XI, ch. 12: 13.

VTER (PADRAGON), Uther (Pendragon), legitimate son of Moynes, king of Britain, Bk. XI, ch. 15: 6, 31, ch. 16: 1, 3, 18, 22, 23, 24, 27, ch. 17: 3, 12, 17, 37, ch. 18: 3, ch. 19: 31.

YBAN, Ivain, nephew of Arthur, Bk. XI, ch. 12: 14, ch. 25: 29; YBAN DE BENUYT, Ban of Benoic, father of Lancelot of the Lake, Bk. XI, ch. 12: 23.

YBERNIA, Igerne, wife of Duke of Tintagel, mother of Arthur, Bk. XI, ch. 17: 4ff.

YNGLESES, the English, Bk. XI, ch. 10: 22, ch. 18: 12, ch. 26: 24, 32–33.

YNGUELATIERRA, England, Bk. I, ch. 1: 1; Bk. IV, ch. 54: 5; Bk. X, ch. 3: 9, ch. 15: 2, ch. 22: 4, 11; Bk. XI, ch. 2: 3, ch. 9: 25, ch. 10: 1, 5, 14, 18, 27, ch. 11: 1, 5, 13, ch. 12: 1, 8–9, ch. 13: 3, ch. 15: 1, 3, 53, ch. 16: 2, 3–4, 25, ch. 17: 2, ch. 19: 2, 4–5, 8, 14, ch. 20: 8, ch. 21: 11, ch. 25: 7–8, 15, 20, 24, ch. 27: 1, ch. 30: 4, ch. 36: 2.

YNOMENIS (YNOGENIS), daughter of king Pandraso of Macedonia, Bk. XI, ch. 5: 28, ch. 6: 11, 26.

YNQUEVIDES, incubus, father of Merlin, Bk. XI, ch. 13: 4. *See* ENCOBUS.

YPODONIA, daughter of king Ypomenes, Bk. XI, ch. 22: 6ff.

YPOMENES, ancient king of England, Bk. XI, ch. 22: 5ff.

YRLANDESES, the Irish, Bk. XI, ch. 10: 23.

YSCA, son of Asaraco, Bk. XI, ch. 10: 9.

YSEO DE LAS BLANCAS MANOS, Iseut of the White Hands, Bk. X, ch. 15: 8–9.

YSLA. *See* BRASIL *and* GAJOLA.

YSRRAEL, Israel, Bk. XI, ch. 10: 3.

YTALIA, Italy, Bk. IV, ch. 54: 10, 11; Bk. XI, ch. 1: 5, ch. 2: 1.

Glossary

The glossary is selective. It omits most words recognizable from their Modern Spanish equivalents or found in *The Williams Spanish & English Dictionary* (New York, 1955; rpt. ed., 1963). Verbs are listed under the infinitive, whether or not they appear as such in the text. The persons of the verb are numbered 1 to 6. Nouns and adjectives are usually listed under the singular. The alphabetical arrangement follows the orthography of the Cristóbal de Mieres codex. Abbreviations are self-evident.

ACALOÑADO (p.p. used adjectivally) 'be made a crime' Bk. XI, ch. 1: 20.

ACATAR (vb. tr.) 'look upon, attend' Bk. XI, ch. 6: 5.

ACOMENDARSE (vb. refl.) 'put oneself under the protection, in the hands, of another' Bk. XI, ch. 14: 4–5.

AFERES (m. pl.) 'affairs, matters' Bk. XI, ch. 3: 24.

AFERMOSAR (vb. tr.) 'embellish, adorn' Bk. XVII, ch. 48: 157.

AFIRMAMIENTO (m.) 'affirmation' Bk. XI, ch. 15: 20.

AGORA (adv.) 'now' Bk. X, ch. 3: 3; Bk. X, ch. 15: 3, 4; Bk. XI, ch. 7: 23, ch. 15: 10, ch. 23: 3, ch. 25: 59, ch. 26: 24; Bk. XVII, ch. 48: 53, 180.

AGUELO (m) 'grandfather' Bk. XI, ch. 12: 18.

Al (indef. pron.) 'something else, anything else' Bk. XI, ch. 25: 56; *lo al* 'the other, the other thing' Bk. XI, ch. 4: 4; Bk. XVII, ch. 48: 118.

ALARGAR (vb. tr.) 'lengthen, prolong' Bk. XI, ch. 11: 19, ch. 14: 67.

ALCALDE (m.) 'judge' Bk. XI, ch. 13: 12, ch. 14: 2, 6, 7, 11, 19, 25, 30, 41, 44, 62, 66.

ALGO (m.) 'wealth' Bk. V, ch. 67: 2; Bk. XI, ch. 7: 17; *algos* 'possessions' Bk. XVII, ch. 48: 62, 66.

143

AMISTANÇA (f.) 'friendship' Bk. XVII, ch. 48: 28.

AMOS (pron.) 'both' Bk. XI, ch. 26: 29.

ANIMALIAS (f. pl.) 'animals' Bk. XI, ch. 23: 10, 22.

ANOBLEÇER (vb. tr.) 'ennoble' Bk. XVII, ch. 48: 139.

ANTE (adj.) 'previous, preceding' Bk. XI, ch. 26: 15; *ante que* (conj.) 'before' Bk. XI, ch. 4: 14, ch. 26: 34.

ANTIGO (adj.) 'former, ancient, old' Bk. X, ch. 3: 3, ch. 15: 1; Bk. XVII, ch. 48: 191.

AQUESTA (adj. f.) 'this' Bk. V, ch. 67: 9.

AQUESTE (pron.) 'this one' Bk. XVII, ch. 48: 205.

ARDIT (adj.) 'brave' Bk. IX, ch. 8: 6.

AREDEDOR (adv.) 'around' Bk. XI, ch. 24: 13.

AREFEZMENTE (adv.) 'easily' Bk. XI, ch. 18: 26.

ASENTARSE (vb. refl.) 'sit down' Bk. XI, ch. 24: 5.

ATANTO (adj., adv.) 'so, so much' Bk. X, ch. 3: 10, 12; Bk. XI, ch. 18: 16, ch. 22: 9.

AVENIMIENTOS (m. pl.) 'matters of the future' Bk. XI, ch. 15: 50.

AVENIR (vb. intr.) 'happen, occur', pret. 6 *avenieron* Bk. XI, ch. 2: 2.

AVENTURADO (p.p. used adjectivally) 'blessed, happy' Bk. XI, ch. 18: 12.

AVER (vb. tr., perf. aux., impers.) 'have, possess, obtain', pres. indic., 3 *ha* 'there is, there are' Bk. XI, ch. 3: 28; pres. indic. 5 *avedes* Bk. XI, ch. 3: 25; pret. 1 *ove* Bk. XI, ch. 21: 5; pret. 3 *ovo* Bk. IX, ch. 8: 4; Bk. X, ch. 15: 7; Bk. XI, ch. 1: 5, ch. 12: 14, 20, ch. 13: 5, ch. 18: 4, ch. 19: 31, ch. 21: 13, ch. 25: 10, 60; Bk. XVII, ch. 48: 94, 203; pret. 6 *ovieron* Bk. XI, ch. 1: 19, ch. 4: 1, 8, ch. 9: 17, 20, ch. 25: 23; imperf. 5 *aviades* Bk. XI, ch. 4: 29; pres. subj. 5 *ayades* Bk. XI, ch. 13: 23; imperf. subj. 2 *ovieses* Bk. XVII, ch. 48: 31, 180, 219; imperf. subj. 3 *oviese* Bk. XI, ch. 9: 29, ch. 25: 25; Bk. XVII, ch. 48: 33; pres. part. *oviendo* Bk. XI, ch. 7: 15, ch. 16: 4, 21, ch. 21: 4; *aver de* + inf. 'be to, must, have to', pres. indic. 5 *avedes* Bk. XI, ch. 4: 14; pret. 3 *ovo* Bk. XI, ch. 17: 27; pret. 6 *ovieron* Bk. XI, ch. 6: 26, ch. 7: 22; *averse* (vb. refl.) 'hold one's own, fight', pret. 6 *se ovieron* Bk. XI, ch. 3: 16–17.

AVERGOÑADO (p.p. used adjectivally) 'embarrassed' Bk. XI, ch. 18: 26.

AVONDAR (vb. intr.) 'be enough, sufficient' Bk. XVII, ch. 48: 96.

AY (adv.) 'there' Bk. XVII, ch. 48: 94, 182.

AYUNTAR (vb. tr.) 'convoke, assemble' Bk. XI, ch. 14: 12.

BASTEÇERSE (vb. refl.) 'supply oneself' Bk. XI, ch. 2: 19.

BASTEÇIDO (p.p. used adjectivally) 'supplied' Bk. XI, ch. 3: 16.

BRASIL (m.) 'brazilwood' Bk. XI, ch. 26: 36.

BUSCAR (vb. tr.) 'look for', pres. indic. 5 *buscades* Bk. XI, ch. 15: 26.

CA (conj.) 'since, because, for' Bk. IX, ch. 8: 4; Bk. XI, ch. 1: 23, ch. 4: 11, 26, ch. 5: 21, ch. 8: 10, ch. 14: 24, ch. 15: 42, ch. 16: 9, ch. 17: 9, 32, ch. 18: 12, 22, 32, 37, ch. 20: 25, ch. 24: 39, ch. 25: 8, 59, 62, 63, 65, ch. 26: 8, 27, 30, ch. 30: 3; Bk. XVII, ch. 48: 19, 25, 56, 159, 162, 165, 203, 219.

CABE (prep.) 'next to, near' Bk. XI, ch. 20: 6.

CABO (prep.) 'next to, near' Bk. XI, ch. 23: 24.

CALONIA (f.) 'calumny, slander' Bk. XI, ch. 4: 27.

CAPITANA (f.) 'vessel, ship, galley' Bk. XI, ch. 7: 8.

CASTIGADO (p.p. used adjectivally) 'informed, advised' Bk. XI, ch. 18: 29.

CATIBERIO (m.) 'captivity' Bk. XI, ch. 3: 2.

CATIBO (m.) 'captive' Bk. X, ch. 22: 7; Bk. XI, ch. 2: 10, 13, 17, ch. 6: 8, 23.

ÇERTEFICADO (p.p. used adjectivally) 'certified, attested to' Bk. XVII, ch. 48: 27.

ÇIBDAD (f.) 'city, town' Bk. X, ch. 22: 5; Bk. XI, ch. 1: 4, ch. 8: 6, ch. 10: 5–6, 19, 26, ch. 11: 11, ch. 12: 3, 11, 16, ch. 18: 7, 10, 18; Bk. XVII, ch. 47: 1, 5, ch. 48: 56, 180.

ÇIBDADANO (m.) 'city dweller, townsman' Bk. XI, ch. 10: 20.

ÇIBUDAD (f.) 'city, town' Bk. I, ch. 1: 2.

ÇIVDAD. *See* ÇIBDAD.

COBDIÇIA (f.) 'covetousness, cupidity' Bk. XI, ch. 7: 22.

COBDIÇIOSO (adj.) 'anxious, eager' Bk. V, ch. 67: 16.

COBIERTO (p.p. used adjectivally) 'covered' Bk. XI, ch. 26: 5.

COBRIR (vb. tr.) 'incase, box up', pres. indic. 4 *cobremos* Bk. XI, ch. 14: 53.

COCHILLOS (m. pl.) 'principal feathers' Bk. XVII, ch. 48: 166.

COMEDERA (f.) 'eater' Bk. XVII, ch. 48: 61.

COMEDIO (m.) 'interim', *en este comedio* 'in the meantime' Bk. XI, ch. 18: 17.

COM(M)O (adv.) 'when' Bk. XI, ch. 13: 7, 11, 21, 24, 26, 28, ch. 14: 4, 6, 9, 63, ch. 15: 9, 25, 50, ch. 16: 10, ch. 17: 18, ch. 20: 18, 19, 26, ch. 22: 29, ch. 23: 13, ch. 24: 13.

COM(M)OQUIER QUE (indef. relative) 'howsoever, even though' Bk. XI, ch. 1: 20, ch. 7: 12, ch. 13: 13, ch. 14: 41, ch. 22: 19–20; Bk. XVII, ch. 48: 180.

CONBENENÇIA (f.) 'agreement' Bk. XI, ch. 9: 28.

CONORTAR (vb. tr.) 'reassure, console, comfort' Bk. XI, ch. 6: 32, ch. 21: 16, ch. 24: 49.

CONPLIDO (p.p. used adjectivally) 'expired, be up, reached' Bk. XI, ch. 1: 9, ch. 4: 18, ch. 21: 12; 'perfect' Bk. XI, ch. 5: 30; 'lapsed, passed' Bk. XI, ch. 14: 3; 'fulfilled' Bk. XVII, ch. 48: 219.

CONPLIDERO (adj.) 'that which must be executed, fulfilled' Bk. XI, ch. 6: 2, ch. 10: 16.

CONPLIR (vb. tr.) 'execute, discharge, obey, be sufficient' Bk. XI, ch. 14: 3, ch. 17: 7; Bk. XVII, ch. 48: 39; Bk. XVII, ch. 48: 219; *conplirse* (vb. refl.) 'come to be true, be realized', pret. 3 *se conplio* Bk. XI, ch. 23: 29, ch. 24: 4.

CONSENTIR (vb. intr.) 'consent', pret. 3 *consentio* Bk. XI, ch. 14: 56.

CONSEXAR (vb. tr.) 'advise', pret. 3 *consexo* Bk. XI, ch. 22: 14.

CONTEÇER (vb. intr.) 'happen' Bk. XI, ch. 9: 1; Bk. XVII, ch. 48: 120, 199.

CONTINO (adj.) 'continuous' Bk. XI, ch. 4: 10, ch. 18: 15.

CORONICA (f.) 'chronicle' Bk. XI, ch. 27: 3.

CORRER (vb. intr.) 'run', *correr monte* 'hunt' Bk. XI, ch. 1: 15, ch. 20: 4.

COSA (pron.) 'nothing' Bk. XI, ch. 13: 30, ch. 14: 43, ch. 19: 6, ch. 23: 15, ch. 24: 10.

COSARIOS (m. pl.) 'corsairs, pirates' Bk. XI, ch. 7: 6, 9, 11.

CREAR (vb. tr.) 'raise', pret. 3 *creyo* Bk. IX, ch. 8: 7.

CRUEÇA (f.) 'cruelty' Bk. XI, ch. 5: 11.

CURARSE (vb. refl.) 'believe, give credit to, depend upon' Bk. XI, ch. 14: 27.

CUYDAR (vb. tr.) 'plan, think, try' Bk. XI, ch. 7: 14, ch. 14: 57, ch. 15: 9, 46, ch. 17: 17, 29, ch. 20: 29, ch. 25: 2, 40, ch. 26: 28.

CUYTADO (adj.) 'worried, grieved' Bk. XI, ch. 21: 8.

DANBAS (adj. f.) 'both' Bk. XI, ch. 25: 25.

DAR (vb. tr.) 'give', pres. indic. 1 *do* Bk. XI, ch. 14: 46; *dar de las alas* 'flap wings' Bk. V, ch. 67: 18.

DARDANIA (adj. f.) 'Dardanian, Trojan' Bk. XI, ch. 3: 7.

DEBISO. *See* DEUISAR.

DEESA (f.) 'goddess' Bk. XI, ch. 7: 25, ch. 8: 5, 23.

DELEYTARSE (vb. refl.) 'delectate, delight oneself' Bk. XI, ch. 6: 28.

DEMANDA (f.) 'quest, search' Bk. XI, ch. 24: 2, 20, 38, 43.

DEMANDAR (vb. tr.) 'ask for, seek' Bk. XI, ch. 5: 1, 22, 32, ch. 6: 2, ch. 9: 10, ch. 14: 31, ch. 18: 5, ch. 24: 47.

DENDE (adv.) 'in it, of it, with it' Bk. XVII, ch. 48: 53, 109.

DESCOBIERTO (p.p. used adjectivally) 'exposed, uncovered' Bk. XVII, ch. 48: 95.

DESCOBRIR (vb. tr., vb. refl.) 'discover, reveal, make known' Bk. XI, ch. 17: 6–7, 10, ch. 19: 24.

DESMANO (m.) 'disorder' Bk. XVII, ch. 48: 149.

DESONRRADO (adj.) 'dishonored' Bk. XI, ch. 23: 4.

DESPEDIRSE (vb. refl.) 'bid farewell, say good-bye', pres. part. *despediendose* Bk. XI, ch. 15: 26.

DESPLANAR (vb. tr.) 'explain' Bk. XVII, ch. 48: 184.

DESTORBAR (vb. tr.) 'obstruct' Bk. XI, ch. 15: 32.

DESTRUYÇION (f.) 'destruction' Bk. XI, ch. 1: 2, ch. 2: 11, 13.

DEUDO (m.) 'debt, obligation' Bk. XI, ch. 4: 16.

DEUISAR (vb. tr.) 'inform, give notice of' Bk. XI, ch. 21: 1, ch. 22: 1, ch. 23: 1, 3, 4.

DEXAR (vb. tr.) 'leave', pluperf. 3 *dexara* Bk. XI, ch. 16: 26.

DEZEÑIR (vb. tr.) 'loosen, take off, ungird', pret. 3 *dezeñio* Bk. XI, ch. 25: 47.

DEZIR (vb. tr.) 'say, tell', pres. indic. 3 *diz* Bk. XVII, ch. 48: 65, 130; pret. 5 *degistes* Bk. XI, ch. 14: 36; pret. 6 *dixieron* Bk. V, ch. 67: 13; Bk. XI, ch. 1: 21, ch. 14: 25, 52, ch. 15: 17, 36; pluperf. 3 *dixiera* Bk. XI, ch. 8: 23–24; imperf. subj. 3 *dixiese* Bk. XI, ch. 17: 32, ch. 22: 14; imperf. subj. 6 *dixiesen* Bk. XI, ch. 15: 15; pres. part. *deziendo* Bk. XVII, ch. 48: 160.

DINO (adj.) 'meritorious, worthy' Bk. XI, ch. 3: 6.

DO (adv.) 'where' Bk. XI, ch. 3: 9, ch. 5: 15, ch. 25: 62.

DONDE (adv.) 'whence, from where' Bk. XI, ch. 2: 8, ch. 8: 25.

DOQUIER (adv.) 'wherever' Bk. XVII, ch. 48: 66.

DORMIR (vb. intr.) 'sleep', pret. 3 *dormio* Bk. XI, ch. 13: 4, ch. 17: 15, ch. 19: 20, ch. 22: 13; imperf. subj. 3 *dormiese* Bk. XI, ch. 14: 36; pres. part. *dormiendo* Bk. XI, ch. 8: 9, ch. 13: 7, ch. 23: 6, 31.

ECHAR (vb. tr.) 'throw', fut. subj. 2 *echares* Bk. XI, ch. 25: 56; pluperf. 3 *echara* Bk. XI, ch. 25: 58.

EMENDAR (vb. tr.) 'indemnify, make restitution' Bk. XI, ch. 17: 25.

ENÇELADO (p.p. used adjectivally) 'concealed, covered up' Bk. V, ch. 67: 11.

ENCOBRIR (vb. tr.) 'hide, conceal' Bk. XI, ch. 14: 44; Bk. XVII, ch. 48: 161; pret. 3 *encobrio* Bk. XI, ch. 24: 51; pres. part. *encobriendo* Bk. XI, ch. 17: 24.

ENDE (adv.) 'in it' Bk. XVII, ch. 48: 22, 28; *por ende* 'therefore, for this reason' Bk. XI, ch. 3: 6, ch. 5: 19–20, ch. 6: 18, 23, ch. 14: 8, 21, 42, ch. 21: 15–16.

ENFORCARSE (vb. refl.) 'hang oneself', Bk. XI, ch. 14: 65.

ENPLEADA (p.p. used adjectivally) 'given as a wife' Bk. XI, ch. 6: 20.

ENPOS (prep.) 'after' Bk. XI, ch. 1: 16, ch. 15: 53, ch. 18: 4.

ENPREÑAR (vb. tr.) 'impregnate' Bk. XI, ch. 22: 13, 14.

ENREQUEÇER (vb. intr.) 'become rich' Bk. XI, ch. 26: 36–37.

ENSEÑAR (vb. tr.) 'teach, show', fut. subj. 3 *enseñare* Bk. XI, ch. 15: 48–49.

ENTENDER (vb. tr.) 'understand', pres. subj. 5 *entendades* Bk. XI, ch. 3: 35, ch. 14: 23.

ENTENDIDO (p.p. used adjectivally) 'exposed, made known' Bk. XI, ch. 18: 30.

ENTREPETRAÇION (f.) 'interpretation' Bk. XVII, ch. 48: 189.

ENVARGANTE (prep.) 'despite, notwithstanding' Bk. XI, ch. 19: 23.

EREGIA (f.) 'heresy' Bk. X, ch. 3: 10.

ESCAEÇER (vb. tr.) 'forget' Bk. V, ch. 67: 8.

ESCOGIENÇIA (f.) 'selection, choice, choosing' Bk. XI, ch. 6: 12.

ESPAUOREÇERSE (vb. refl.) 'become terrified' Bk. XI, ch. 13: 24.

ESTADOS (m. pl.) 'steps, measures' Bk. V, ch. 67: 21–22.

ESTAR (vb. intr.) 'be', imperf. subj. 3 *estobiese* Bk. XI, ch. 3: 7; 'stand' Bk. XI, ch. 15: 18.

ESTONÇES (adv.) 'then' Bk. XI, ch. 5: 23, ch. 8: 19, ch. 9: 4.

ESTROLAGO (m.) 'astrologer' Bk. XI, ch. 1: 11, ch. 15: 32.

ESTROLOGIA (f.) 'astrology' Bk. XI, ch. 15: 33.

FAMA (f.) 'fame', *fazer fama* 'make something known' Bk. XI, ch. 25: 15.

FAZER (vb. tr.) 'do, make', pret. *fezistes* Bk. XI, ch. 14: 37; pret. 6 *fezieron* Bk. X, ch. 22: 11; Bk. XI, ch. 9: 21, 23; fut. 5 *fariades* Bk. XI, ch. 14: 32; imperf. subj. 3 *feziese* Bk. XI, ch. 13: 10, ch. 15: 17; imperf. subj. 6 *feziesen* Bk. XI, ch. 4: 8; fut. subj. 3 *feziere* Bk. XI, ch. 18: 37.

FINIESTRA (f.) 'window' Bk. XI, ch. 24: 15.

FIUZA (f.) 'confidence, trust' Bk. XVII, ch. 48: 32.

FORÇOSO (adj.) 'strong, heavy' Bk. XI, ch. 7: 13.

FORNEÇER (vb. tr.) 'fill, furnish' Bk. XI, ch. 24: 50.

FRIURA (f.) 'cold, coldness' Bk. XI, ch. 23: 11.

FUENDO. *See* SER *and* YR.

GELO, GELA (pron.) 'it to him, her (etc.)' Bk. XI, ch. 14: 35, ch. 15: 49, ch. 17: 20, ch. 18: 37, ch. 20: 2, ch. 25: 33.

GRUA (f.) 'crane' Bk. V, ch. 67: 5, 9, 10, 13.

GUERRAR (vt. intr.) 'wage war, fight' Bk. X, ch. 3: 12–13.

GUISAMIENTO (m.) 'armament' Bk. XI, ch. 2: 6.

GUISAR (vb. tr.) 'order, arrange' Bk. V, ch. 67: 8, 12; Bk. XVII, ch. 48: 214.

HA. *See* AVER.

HI (adv.) 'there' Bk. XVII, ch. 48: 186.

(H)ONRRA (f.) 'honor' Bk. XI, ch. 1: 10, ch. 6: 6, 14, ch. 8: 21, ch. 9: 21; Bk. XVII, ch. 48: 6, 115.

(H)ONRRADAMENTE (adv.) 'honorably' Bk. XI, ch. 2: 6, ch. 11: 15.

(H)ONRRADO (p.p. used adjectivally) 'honored' Bk. XI, ch. 6: 4, ch. 21: 12, 16–17, ch. 23: 3, ch. 25: 5, 13.

LAZDRAR (vb. intr.) 'suffer' Bk. XI, ch. 22: 25.

LEUAR (vb. tr.) 'carry, take, lead' Bk. IV, ch. 54: 3; Bk. V, ch. 67: 18; Bk. XI, ch. 5: 16, ch. 6: 33, ch. 17: 8, ch. 18: 19, ch. 26: 1, 25; Bk. XVII, ch. 48: 113.

LOGAR (m.) 'place' Bk. XI, ch. 18: 22; Bk. XVII, ch. 48: 102, 201, 203, 215.

LUENGAMENTE (adv.) 'for a long time' Bk. XI, ch. 16: 17, 25–26.

LLEGAR (vb. intr.) 'arrive, reach', fut. subj. 3 *llegare* Bk. XI, ch. 14: 63.

MAGUER (conj.) 'although' Bk. XVII, ch. 48: 33, 89, 216.

MAREANTE (m.) 'navigator' Bk. XI, ch. 6: 33, ch. 26: 30.

MANTENER (vb. tr.) 'maintain', imperf. subj. 3 *mantoviese* Bk. XI, ch. 19: 32.

MEATAD (f.) 'half' Bk. XI, ch. 24: 48.

MENTIR (vb. intr.) 'lie, deceive', pret. 6 *mentieron* Bk. XI, ch. 15: 30; fut. subj. 3 *mentiere* Bk. XI, ch. 15: 29.

MESMO (adj.) 'same, very' Bk. XI, ch. 9: 22, ch. 17: 16, ch. 23: 1, ch. 26: 8, 19; Bk. XVII, ch. 48: 127, 139–40, 195; *el mesmo* 'he himself' Bk. XI, ch. 25: 10, 37.

MESTURAR (vb. tr.) 'reveal, denounce' Bk. V, ch. 67: 10.

MIRAGLOS (m. pl.) 'miracles' Bk. XI, ch. 11: 8.

MONTAR (vb. tr.) 'amount, gain' Bk. V, ch. 67: 4.

MONUMENTO (m.) 'tomb' Bk. XI, ch. 23: 31–32.

MORIR (vb. intr.) 'die', pret. 3 *morio* Bk. XI, ch. 1: 9, 18, ch. 2: 16, ch. 9: 19, ch. 16: 22, ch. 17: 37, ch. 23: 32; pret. 6 *morieron* Bk. XI, ch. 24: 47, ch. 25: 3, 12, 24; fut. 3 *morra* Bk. XVII, ch. 48: 186; fut. 5 *moriredes* Bk. XI, ch. 13: 23, ch. 15: 42; cond. 3 *moreria* Bk. XI, ch. 16: 17; imperf. subj. 3 *moriese* Bk. XI, ch. 13: 15, ch. 17: 38; pres. part. *moriendo* Bk. XI, ch. 1: 13.

MOSTRAR (vb. tr.) 'show', pres. indic. 5 *mostrades* Bk. XI, ch. 24: 30.

MUCHO (adv.) 'very' Bk. X, ch. 3: 4, 7, 19; Bk. XI, ch. 7: 25, ch. 17: 4, ch. 18: 17, ch. 19: 18, ch. 20: 10, ch. 22: 7, 12, ch. 26: 27, Bk. XVII, ch. 47: 3.

MUNDARIA PUBLICA (f.) 'prostitute' Bk. XI, ch. 13: 10.

NOBLEÇER (vb. tr.) 'ennoble' Bk. XVII, ch. 48: 144.

OME. *See* OMNE.

OMILDOSAMENTE (adv.) 'humbly, meekly' Bk. XI, ch. 5: 6.

OM(N)E (m.) 'man' Bk. V, ch. 67: 15; Bk. XI, ch. 1: 22, ch. 2: 20, ch. 4: 10, 27, ch. 6: 22, ch. 9: 15, ch. 11: 7, ch. 13: 8, ch. 14: 28, 38, 52, ch. 15: 19, 20, 25, ch. 16: 10, ch. 17: 36, ch. 18: 11, 16, 33, ch. 20: 22, ch. 22: 12, 19; Bk. XVII, ch. 48: 121, 176, 226.

ONDE (adv.) 'where' Bk. XVII, ch. 48: 180.

ONRAR (vb. tr.) 'honor' Bk. XVII, ch. 48: 3.

ONRRA. *See* HONRRA.

ONRRADA. *See* HONRRADO.

ONRRADAMENTE. *See* HONRRADAMENTE.

OSAR (vb. tr.) 'dare', pluperf. 3 *osara* Bk. XI, ch. 17: 10.

OTROSI (adv.) 'also, likewise, furthermore' Bk. I, ch. 1: 1; Bk. XI, ch. 2: 14, ch. 4: 19, ch. 6: 10, ch. 10: 18, ch. 19: 14–15, ch. 22: 7; Bk. XVII, ch. 48: 10, 71, 88, 113, 118, 135, 174, 186.

OVIENDO. *See* AVER.

PAGADO (p.p. used adjectivally) 'pleased, happy' Bk. XI, ch. 5: 17; Bk. XVII, ch. 48: 148.

PANAR (m.) 'honeycomb' Bk. XVII, ch. 48: 17, 71, 79.

PARESÇER (vb. intr.) 'appear' Bk. XI, ch. 4: 26.

PARTIDA (f.) 'region' Bk. X, ch. 3: 11; 'part' Bk. XI, ch. 7: 8.

PASADA (f.) 'passage' Bk. XI, ch. 6: 28.

PEDIR (vb. tr.) 'ask for, request', fut. subj. 5 *pedierdes* Bk. XI, ch. 3: 32, ch. 4: 21.

PEDRICAÇION (f.) 'preaching, sermon' Bk. XI, ch. 11: 10.

PEÑOLAS (f. pl.) 'feathers' Bk. XVII, ch. 48: 20.

PERO QUE (conj.) 'although' Bk. XI, ch. 1: 22, ch. 16: 16.

PESANTE (adj.) 'afflicted, sad' Bk. XI, ch. 8: 24.

PLAZER (vb. tr.) 'please, suit', pret. 3 *plogo* Bk. XI, ch. 5: 3, 31, ch. 14: 52, imperf. subj. 3 *ploguiese* Bk. XI, ch. 4: 28.

PODER (vb. tr., vb. intr.) 'be able, can', pres. indic. 5 *podedes* Bk. XI, ch. 15: 48; pret. *podieron* Bk. XI, ch. 6: 9, ch. 24: 11, ch. 26: 37, 38; imperf. subj. 2 *podieses* Bk. XVII, ch. 48: 105; imperf. subj. 3 *podiese* Bk. XI, ch. 18: 16; Bk. XVII, ch. 48: 30, 114, 226; imperf. subj. 6 *podiesen* Bk. XI, ch. 16: 8; Bk. XVII, ch. 48: 178; pres. part. *podiendo* Bk. IV, ch. 54: 6; Bk. XI, ch. 17: 5, ch. 22: 10.

PONER (vb. tr.) 'put, place', pret. 6 *posieron* Bk. XI, ch. 5: 10, ch. 9: 21–22; imperf. subj. *posiese* Bk. XI, ch. 4: 23.

POR QUE (conj.) 'in order that, so that' Bk. XI, ch. 5: 28, ch. 6: 34–35, ch. 8: 20, ch. 14: 60, 66, ch. 15: 44; Bk. XVII, ch. 48: 182.

PORIDAD (f.) 'secret, confidence' Bk. XI, ch. 14: 62.

PREMIA (f.) 'coercion, force' Bk. XI, ch. 5: 5.

PRESION (f.) 'imprisonment' Bk. X, ch. 3: 26; Bk. XI, ch. 5: 23, ch. 6: 17.

PROFIAR (vb. tr.) 'profess' Bk. X, ch. 3: 10.

PROFIÇIA (f.) 'prophecy' Bk. XVII, ch. 48: 133, 172, 207.

PROFIDIAR (vb. tr.) 'profess' Bk. XI, ch. 8: 26.

PROSPUESTO (m.) 'proposition, scheme' Bk. XI, ch. 4: 12.

PUEBLA (f.) 'town' Bk. IV, ch. 54: 9, 10; Bk. X, ch. 22: 6.

QUERER (vb. tr.) 'want, wish', pret. 2 *quesiste* Bk. XVII, ch. 48: 179; pluperf. 6 *quisieran* Bk. XI, ch. 8: 25; imperf. subj. 2 *quisieses* Bk. XI, ch. 5: 7, 8; imperf. subj. 3 *quisiese* Bk. XI, ch. 1: 22; imperf. subj. 6 *quisiesen* Bk. V, ch. 67: 3; fut. subj. 2 *quisieres* Bk. XI, ch. 5: 15; pres. part. *quisiendo* Bk. XI, ch. 24: 25, ch. 25: 17.

QUISIENDO. *See* QUERER.

QUISTION (f.) 'question' Bk. XI, ch. 4: 3, Bk. XVII, ch. 48: 138.

QUITO (adj.) 'free' Bk. XI, ch. 14: 46.

RABIDO (adj.) 'kidnapped' Bk. XI, ch. 6: 31.

RAZENTARSE (vb. refl.) 'renew oneself' revive' Bk. XI, ch. 4: 26.

RAZON (f.) 'speech, words' Bk. XI, ch. 5: 31, ch. 6: 7.

REÇEUIR (vb. tr.) 'receive', pret. 1 *reçeui* Bk. XVII, ch. 48: 14.

REYNAMIENTO (m.) 'reign' Bk. XI, ch. 18: 1.

ROBADERA (f.) 'robber, thief' Bk. XVII, ch. 48: 62.

ROBRE (m.) 'oak' Bk. XI, ch. 23: 8.

SABER (vb. tr.) 'know', pres. indic. 5 *sabedes* Bk. XI, ch. 14: 30, ch. 23: 17; pret. 3 *sopo* Bk. XI, ch. 13: 8, 11, ch. 16: 10, ch. 25: 5; imperf. subj. 3 *sopiese* Bk. XI, ch. 15: 51, ch. 17: 22, 32, ch. 22: 28, ch. 23: 6, ch. 24: 40; imperf. subj. 6 *sopiesen* Bk. XI, ch. 16: 16; pres. part. *sopiendo* Bk. XI, ch. 9: 4; ch. 15: 22, ch. 17: 8, 35, ch. 18: 4–5, 19, 21, ch. 19: 5, 19, 23, ch. 26: 35.

SABIEZA (f.) 'learning, knowledge, wisdom' Bk. XI, ch. 23: 30.

SABOR (m.) 'pleasure, desire' Bk. XI, ch. 17: 15.

SABROSO (adj.) 'pleasing, delightful' Bk. XI, ch. 23: 9, 21.

SACAR (vb. tr.) 'draw, take out', fut. subj. 3 *sacare* Bk. XI, ch. 18: 11, ch. 24: 33.

SACREFIÇIO (m.) 'sacrifice' Bk. XI, ch. 7: 26, ch. 8: 2, 8.

SALIR (vb. intr.) 'leave', fut. 3 *salira* Bk. XI, ch. 14: 65.

SALUD (f.) 'greetings' Bk. XI, ch. 3: 4.

SEGUIR (vb. tr.) 'follow', cond. 3 *siguiria* Bk. XI, ch. 17: 33.

SEGURANÇA (f.) 'certainty' Bk. XI, ch. 4: 18–19.

SENIFICAR (vb. tr.) 'signify, mean' Bk. XI, ch. 23: 20, 21; pres. indic. 3 *senefica* Bk. XI, ch. 23: 23.

SENTENTRION (m.) 'north' Bk. XI, ch. 8: 12.

SENTIR (vb. tr.) 'feel', pret. 6 *sentieron* Bk. XI, ch. 5: 6; pres. part. *sentiendo* Bk. XI, ch. 25: 38.

SEPOLTURA (f.) 'sepulchre, tomb' Bk. XI, ch. 9: 21, ch. 25: 66, ch. 26: 13, 18.

SER (vb. intr.) 'be', pres. indic. 1 *so* Bk. XI, ch. 15: 26, ch. 23: 23, ch. 25: 31; pres. indic. 5 *sodes* Bk. XI, ch. 14: 20, 41; pret. 1 *fue* Bk. XI, ch. 25: 63; pret. 2 *fueste* Bk. XI, ch. 25: 54, 67; pluperf. 3 *fuera* Bk. XI, ch. 15: 52; imperf. subj. 3 *fuese* Bk. V, ch. 67: 21; Bk. XI, ch. 1: 3, 20; imperf. subj. 6 *fuesen* Bk. XI, ch. 2: 18; imper. 2 *sey* Bk. XI, ch. 16: 18; p.p. *seydo* Bk. XI, ch. 2: 13; pres. part. *seyendo* Bk. V, ch. 67: 11; Bk. X, ch. 3: 21; Bk. XI, ch. 1: 14, ch. 7: 7, ch. 10: 27, ch. 16: 1, 17, ch. 19: 5, 17, ch. 21: 2, 12, ch. 25: 42; Bk. XVII, ch. 48: 37, 138; pres. part. *fuendo* Bk. XI, ch. 1: 11.

SERVIR (vb. tr.) 'serve', imperf. subj. 6 *serbiesen* Bk. XI, ch. 13: 17.

SIMIENTE (f.) 'semen' Bk. XI, ch. 15: 19.

SO (prep.) 'under' Bk. XI, ch. 3: 7, ch. 5: 5, ch. 15: 37, ch. 23: 15, 22, 27; Bk. XVII, ch. 48: 160.

SOBEJO (adj.) 'abundant, profuse' Bk. XI, ch. 21: 4.

SOBIR (vb. intr.) 'rise' Bk. XI, ch. 24: 45; *sobirse* 'go up, climb', pret. 3 *sobiose* Bk. XI, ch. 26: 3.

SOFRIR (vb. tr., vb. intr.) 'suffer, endure' Bk. XVII, ch. 48: 8, 32, 123, 217.

SOLTAR (vb. tr.) 'explain', pres. subj. 5 *soltasedes* Bk. XI, ch. 23: 16.

SOMIR (vb. intr.) 'sink' Bk. XI, ch. 23: 15; pret. 3 *somio* Bk. XI, ch. 23: 26.

SOÑAR (vb. tr.) 'dream', pluperf. 3 *soñara* Bk. XI, ch. 20: 30.

SOPIENDO. See SABER.

SUJEÇION (f.) 'subjection' Bk. XI, ch. 5: 7–8.

SUDITOS (m. pl.) 'subjects' Bk. XVII, ch. 48: 81.

SUPERFLUYDAD (f.) 'superfluity' Bk. XVII, ch. 48: 129.

SUSO (adv.) 'above', *de suso* 'above' Bk. XI, ch. 15: 38; Bk. XVII, ch. 47: 8.

TALLA (f.) 'tax' Bk. XI, ch. 10: 17.

TENER (vb. tr.) 'have, possess', pres. indic. 5 *tenedes* Bk. XI, ch. 4: 20, ch. 13: 23; fut. 1 *terne* Bk. XVII, ch. 48: 227; fut. 3 *tenera* Bk. XI, ch. 4: 15; pret. 6 *tobieron* Bk. XI, ch. 6: 27; pres. part. *tobiendo* Bk. V, ch. 67: 6–7; Bk. XI, ch. 17: 6, ch. 18: 26–27; *tobiendose por pecador* 'considering himself a sinner' Bk. XI, ch. 26: 11; *tener de* + inf. 'have to' Bk. XI, ch. 13: 21.

TOBIENDO. *See* TENER.

TRABESAR (vb. tr.) 'cross' Bk. XI, ch. 8: 27.

TRAER (vb. tr.) 'bring', pres. indic. 3 *traye* Bk. XVII, ch. 48: 124; pret. 6 *traxieron* Bk. XI, ch. 18: 24; pluperf. 6 *traxieran* Bk. XI, ch. 26: 16; imperf. subj. 6 *troxiesen* Bk. XI, ch. 24: 9.

TRASFIGURADO (p.p. used adjectivally) 'transfigured, transformed' Bk. XI, ch. 17: 13.

TRANSFIGURARSE (vb. refl.) 'be transfigured, transformed' Bk. XI, ch. 16: 9.

TREBEXAR (vb. intr.) 'play' Bk. XI, ch. 15: 21.

VASTEÇIMIENTO (m.) 'supplies, provisions' Bk. XI, ch. 5: 13, ch. 6: 8.

VASTIÇIMIENTO. *See* VASTEÇIMIENTO.

VENIR (vb. intr.) 'come', pret. 6 *venieron* Bk. X, ch. 3: 5–6; fut. 3 *verna* Bk. XVII, ch. 48: 130; fut. 6 *vernan* Bk. XI, ch. 23: 23; imperf. subj. 6 *veniesen* Bk. XI, ch. 15: 12; pres. part. *veniendo* Bk. XI, ch. 18: 14, 28.

VER (vb. tr., vb. intr.) 'see', pret. 5 *vistes* Bk. XI, ch. 22: 30; pluperf. *viera* Bk. XI, ch. 20: 31, ch. 26: 15, 20; pres. part. *veyendo* Bk. XI, ch. 1: 16, ch. 7: 8, ch. 13: 25, ch. 17: 8, ch. 22: 11, ch. 25: 44.

VERGUEÑA (f.) 'embarrassment, shame' Bk. XI, ch. 5: 19.

VERTUD (f.) 'virtue' Bk. XI, ch. 25: 48.

VESION (f.) 'vision' Bk. XI, ch. 23: 16.

VEZAR (vb. tr.) 'teach' Bk. XI, ch. 23: 30.

VIRGINES (f.) 'virgins' Bk. XI, ch. 24: 46.

YAÇER (vb. intr.) 'lie, lie down', pres. part. *yoguiendo* Bk. XI, ch. 17: 39.

YMAGINANÇA (f.) 'imagination' Bk. XVII, ch. 48: 204.

YNIGROMANÇIA (f.) 'necromancy' Bk. XI, ch. 15: 48.

YNSOLA (f.) 'island, isle' Bk. X, ch. 3: 20; Bk. XI, ch. 8: 13.

YOGUIENDO. *See* YAÇER.

YR (vb. intr.) 'go', pres. part. *fuendo* Bk. XI, ch. 18: 23, ch. 20: 4; *irse* 'go away', pres. part. *fuendose* Bk. XI, ch. 25: 50.